# Differentiatio Teaching and Learning

## Principles and Practice

Tim O'Brien and Dennis Guiney

CONTINUUM
London and New York

**Continuum**
The Tower Building
11 York Road
London SE1 7NX

370 Lexington Avenue
New York
NY 10017–6503

www.continuumbooks.com

© 2001 Tim O'Brien and Dennis Guiney

First published 2001

**British Library Cataloguing-in-Publication Data**
A catalogue record for this book is available from the British Library.

ISBN   0-8264-5126-8 (hardback)
       0-8264-5125-X (paperback)

Typeset by Kenneth Burnley, Wirral, Cheshire
Printed and bound in Great Britain by Cromwell Press, Trowbridge, Wiltshire

# Contents

Acknowledgements     vii

Introduction: Unpacking differentiation     ix

1    Teaching and learning in the real world     1

2    Beliefs and stereotypes     19

3    I teach . . . and you learn?     36

4    Dynamic teaching, dynamic learning     52

5    Personal constructs and differentiation     71

6    Applying fluid thinking     90

7    Models of learning     108

8    Self-esteems and emotional differentiation     132

9    Teaching and learning: a real world analysis     156

Bibliography     172

Index     175

# Acknowledgements

We would like to thank Bryony, Mairídgh, Pauline, Tom, Max and Alex for their support while we were writing the book. We would also like to thank Anthony Haynes of Continuum for his encouragement when we were conceptualizing the book.

# Introduction:
# Unpacking differentiation

As a consumer you may have had the recent experience of making a new purchase, perhaps of an essential household item. After unpacking it you may well have looked for the handbook of instructions on how to use the new purchase. Such instructions aim to help us with our learning but they often unintentionally create a learning difficulty. So, manufacturers usually differentiate instructions by the inclusion of a simple section on how to deal with problems when they arise: this is often called a 'troubleshooting' menu. These 'user guides' are interesting in how they engage the reader in learning. They often begin in this way:

> Congratulations on your new purchase, we are certain you will get many hours trouble-free use from what you have bought, *but* to ensure that you receive maximum performance we enclose a useful guide for your convenience. We hope that there will not be any difficulties, but if there are, please consult the guide.

The expectation here is one of success for all and the differentiation is provided for when things go wrong for some. As far as we know it is not possible to make a single purchase which guarantees to deliver hours of trouble-free teaching and learning. No book can serve such a vast and complex purpose. However, unlike the user guides, *Differentiation in Teaching and Learning: Principles and Practice* proposes that differentiation should be seen as integral to learning, not an add-on for those situations when things do not go as well as planned and problems occur. Differentiation is not about troubleshooting. It is a concept that has to be seen in an inclusive way, applying to everyone. We hope that this book will provide you with many new insights, perspectives, models, frameworks and questions, debating points and, most importantly, practical applications to help you in whatever teaching and learning system you work. We also hope that it will provide you with a smile or two along the way. At times we have used humour to illustrate some very serious points, as respectful humour is yet another important strategy for differentiation.

Applying the principles and practice of differentiation is vital because successful, high-value teaching and learning is fundamentally a human process that is based upon building, developing and sustaining positive relationships. This book aims to help you enjoy and explore the unpredictability of such relationships by providing you with the tools necessary to improve practice at each and every level within teaching and learning systems.

## Differentiation is not a 'buzzword'

This book confronts and addresses differentiation. This term has been around in teaching learning systems for many years, so much so that it has taken on the label of being a 'buzzword'. As a consequence it is not seen as integral to every teacher and learner interaction. Whilst teachers are exhorted to differentiate learning to enable curriculum access, the concept can be rejected and devalued because of the 'buzzword' culture. At worst, it may be completely dismissed, as teachers wait for the next 'buzzword' and the initiatives associated with it to come along.

What seems to have happened with differentiation is that, whilst definitions can be found for the term, there is a lack of clarity and detail available about what lies behind the definitions. For example, is curriculum differentiation the same as a differentiated curriculum? There is also a lack of clarity on how to achieve differentiation in practice. The word is casually applied to the processes and intention as well as the tools and practice. In this book we have sought to provide systematic, grounded, practical, applicable and useful advice on *how* to differentiate in the real world as teachers and learners experience it. This world includes an increasingly wider range of needs that teachers and learners present with: needs that result from very complex interactions.

This book sets out to encapsulate the principles and practices of differentiation in action. It does this by describing in detail the various ways in which you may wish to think about, and practise, differentiated approaches. We have not presented a complex definition of the term 'differentiation', as this book seeks to set out the fields within which *your* definition of this term will operate. We present the thinking and practice that are necessary to enable you to provide your own active definition of this term, as it will be applied within your own work place. For some teachers, this may well be the first time that they have engaged in such a comprehensive and valuable task.

The contents of this book are intended to be challenging, to cause you to question, to delve deep into what is taking place inside and outside your head, the heads of colleagues and of the learners that you teach. In doing this we have aimed to provide examples and anecdotes throughout this book in order that you may be able to identify with examples that are taken from the real world. This should enable you to ground the thinking in everyday practice. The book presents a principled basis upon which to develop what is referred to as 'grounded teaching and learning'.

We have designed this book so that it provides differentiated learning. It is a *differentiated book on differentiation*. As it is differentiated, we hope that you will use and experience it differently from other books. With this in mind, we have designed it to be read sequentially, chapter by chapter, building up a picture of the field of differentiation and grounded learning in action. This is why it begins by analysing principles and closes with two case studies. However, in relation to individual learning styles, we are conscious that this may not be the preferred way for all readers, it may not serve everybody's learning needs to take a sequential approach. For this reason you will find that it is possible to read the chapters in an order that works for you and we aim to help you in this process by cross-referencing throughout. For example, if you begin by reading Chapter 6 it will guide you to other relevant chapters as you work through it. This book is cross-referenced and indexed in an unusual manner, both continuously through the text and more commonly at the end. You will also notice that a decision has been made not to overload it with academic references. Obviously some references are given but additional material that might be useful to you is included in the bibliography.

# Chapter content

The book constantly moves from the macro level (the broad areas of differentiation) to the micro level (the more individualized areas) and back again. It looks at differentiation from a wide perspective as well as from the focused precision of individual interactions. Chapter 1 begins with a consideration of the issues involved in understanding differentiation and the principles that apply to it in the real world. In this chapter we emphasize that all teachers are learners and all learners are teachers. We then invite you, in Chapter 2, to consider the powerful nature of beliefs and stereotypes and how they can limit the process of differentiation. Chapter 3 tackles the assumption that when a teacher teaches a learner learns. For this chapter we have developed a framework for teacher and learner outcomes to help you to analyse the success of differentiation in your own work place and practice. Chapter 4 explores the areas that affect our ability to learn, considering four main factors, teaching, emotional, social and cognitive. Of course a key component of teaching and learning is that everyone involved is an individual. How teachers see themselves, how learners see themselves, and how they see each other is central to developing relationships. Chapter 5 looks at how understanding 'personal constructs' can help us to improve our ability to differentiate.

Often in teaching we find ourselves in challenging situations of varying degrees, situations where we seem to have to 'think on our feet'. Chapter 6 looks at how effective teachers deal with this. Here we present a framework for fluid thinking as opposed to fixed thinking and demonstrate how it relates to practice. It may seem reasonable to assume that a teacher will have a model inside their own head of how learners learn. Chapter 7 presents the 'tourist' approach to differentiation in order to show that this is not always the case. Therefore this chapter explores in detail two process models of learning: one that is social and one that is cognitive. This ties in closely with Chapter 8, which considers emotional differentiation. If you glance at the title of this chapter, please do not think that the term 'self-esteems' is a typographical error – it is not! You will need to read the chapter to find out why. Finally, Chapter 9 draws together all of the differentiated thinking and practice that appears throughout the book. Two case studies are presented and you are invited to create the third one. The purpose of the two case studies is to encourage you to continue to develop your analytical skills. The third case study allows for you to ground the analysis in your own practice. The book closes with some words of wisdom from learners.

## Differentiating the text

You will notice that the chapters are punctuated by a series of sections that ask you to respond in a variety of ways to the text that you will have just read. These encourage you to use the book in a 'self-help' manner. There are four types of task that you are invited to respond to. These being:

- *Reflection points.* These ask you to make time and space to consider the arguments, issues and questions raised in the text. This is a time of personal reflection designed to acquaint you further with the thinking and practice that is being dealt with. Reflection points often invite you to consider a situation or scenario and then relate this to your own practice and experience. There are no right or wrong answers. We may provide our analysis and then ask you to provide your own thinking.
- *Dialogue points.* These are similar to reflection points but ask you to work with someone you know in your current work place – supporting the notion of developing a series of critical friends. Sometimes you will be asked to work with someone you do not know so well in order to seek new points of view, new insights, new questions and new opportunities. Dialogue points are for you to share opinions that have been built and developed by reading the text and to explore the assumptions, values and beliefs that exist in a teaching and learning system.
- *Case points.* These use examples of real teaching and learning experiences and scenarios to reinforce and illuminate the principles and practice of differentiation. They are offered so that you can see how thinking and practice have or have not been applied. They offer insights into how teachers and learners structure and construct their world. As a sense of humour is vital in the professional lives of teachers, inevitably some of these are humorous.

- *Action points.* As implied in the title, these invite you to do something – to take action – to apply new learning in your work place, usually in order to illuminate further a particular point or piece of thinking. These build on your reflections, dialogues, analysis of case points and represent differentiation in action.

If you look at the combination of these types of tasks, allied to a thorough reading of *Differentiation in Teaching and Learning: Principles and Practice*, you will see that it has been designed to provide a structured and analytical progression and grounding in differentiation. This can also be used as the basis for individual or whole system continuing professional development and in-service training.

We hope that you enjoy reading this book as much as we have enjoyed writing it. Moreover, we hope that teachers and learners benefit from it.

TIM O'BRIEN
DENNIS GUINEY
*September 2000*

# 1 Teaching and learning in the real world

## All teachers are learners

The intention of this book is to remain practical and focused upon improving a teacher's ability to think about the breadth of factors that influence teaching and learning. The ultimate aim is to improve a teacher's ability to teach and a learner's ability to learn. Throughout this book we refer to all people involved in 'giving' learning as 'teachers' and all those involved in 'receiving' learning as learners. In a learning system – such as a classroom, a professional team or a school – this would most usually imply that the adults are viewed as 'teachers' and the pupils are 'learners'. We would wish to explore this belief further by suggesting that everyone has the potential, and should be given the opportunity at certain points in daily interactions, to be both a teacher and a learner. We are aware that such a naming of the role 'teacher' (deliberately using a lower case 't') calls into question issues amongst the adults involved, in terms of their professionalism, training, responsibility and status for example. However, using the lower case form of teacher denotes our intention of emphasizing the *relationship* that exists between teacher and learner. Of course, issues of exercised power and status cannot be ignored, but the key point here is to stress that the basics of teaching and learning begin with a relationship.

Improving our ability to teach can be achieved through the process of thinking about teaching and learning as well as engaging in the process of teaching and learning. We have chosen to write about the area of differentiation because in our work with teachers we have found that the concept of 'differentiation' is regularly raised as an issue. It is raised in the context of 'we are told that we have to differentiate but we want or need support in how to do it well'. Those responsible for managing learning find that, in many schools, the days have gone where a teacher could stand in front of a classroom of learners, teach a lesson without interruption, and assume that everybody has learned what has been taught. This type of practice belongs to an 'I teach, you learn' model.

We cannot assume that just because a teacher teaches a learner learns what was intended. The process is far more complex than one of received input and intended outcome. This is because teachers, when engaging with learners, are not involved in programming machines; the learning process involves humans who are diverse in their needs, development, attitudes, values and beliefs. They also operate within systems that are founded upon specific philosophies and ideologies. As a consequence, many teachers will be pleased about the passing of such didactic practice.

This traditional model of non-interactive teaching also carries inherent assumptions about everybody being the same as a learner, with the same capacity, ability and potential to learn. It also fundamentally assumes that all learners learn at the same pace – a pace that is defined by the type of teaching that they receive. Learning theory, and personal experience, informs us that this is not so. With much talk of learners adopting different learning styles and strategies, and entering the classroom with diverse learning needs, the notion that the teacher simply has to impart knowledge by transmission teaching is undermined. Firstly, because in this model the teacher is only 'giving' information. This information becomes knowledge when learners can process it and apply it – for example to procedures and to propositions. Secondly, because the model of a teacher as a person who communicates information without the requirement of developing a dynamic relationship with learners – or the learners developing relationships with each other – does not match a learning system where the increasingly more complex needs of learners have to be addressed. As a consequence of the diversity of learners, the teacher is called upon to move beyond the accommodation of pupils into the areas of adaptation – or 'differentiation'. In this respect the teacher can be seen actively to mediate learning. We are not referring to a teacher as a 'facilitator' (often a passive role) but as a 'mediator' – an active, exciting, creative, energetic and responsive role. There is a substantial difference between mediation and facilitation – as there is between accommodation and differentiation. Accommodation involves the pupils 'being there' and decisions about this are often taken at a policy level. This includes decisions about which type of school a learner will attend (mainstream or special, for example) as well as what type of groups they will learn in within their school (setting and streaming). Differentiation involves the pupils *learning there*. That encapsulates the difference.

We have acknowledged that, in our work with teachers, the concept of differentiation is a regular source of debate. Even in the most prescriptive of climates, where teachers are given a syllabus to teach, or a curriculum programme to follow, they still wish to engage in discussion about the *how* rather than the *what* of teaching. We shall be addressing both of these questions in this book. The process and tools of differentiation are complex. They require a focus upon the teaching plan, the teaching and learning interaction and then an evaluation of what took place. Evaluating teaching and assessing learning outcomes are valuable because they enable the teacher to ensure that continuity and progression in learning can take place. Through the process of differentiation they can be consistently and confidently matched to learning needs and this allows the pace of progression to increase.

### Why differentiation?

We use the word differentiation throughout this book as it is used in education legislation in the United Kingdom (UK). Legislation states that all children are entitled to a curriculum that is 'broad, balanced, relevant and *differentiated*' (our italics). First, it is important to see differentiation as a natural human process that is evident in the first year of our life. From a very early age we make sense of the world by showing more of an interest in people than we do in inanimate objects – we differentiate between the two. As babies who are only a few months old, we begin to differentiate socially by selecting some adults that we like to interact with more than others. It is usual that the main caregivers are the most popular for us to interact with. However, for some children there will be a large group of adults from whom they like to receive attention. Many months later we differentiate in a different way – over time it is our main caregivers whom we want to be with mostly and this can result in behaviours such as crying to express anxiety or fear at not being close to them.

We would like to emphasize that we support the principle that, in a teaching and learning system, differentiation should be a process for all. Furthermore, we propose that it is only meaningful if it is a process for all. If we see the concept of differentiation in this way then we must ensure that the tools for differentiation are also available to all members of the learning community. For example, if a teacher has 30 learners in their group and only decides to differentiate the work to extend and enrich learning for the most able, the other learners will miss out. Similarly, if a teacher only decides to differentiate the work for those who are labelled as having learning difficulties, then this group of people receive high value learning and others do not. Another consequence of only differentiating for identified ability groups is that some learners begin to see themselves as average, and at worse anonymous. *All* learners deserve learning enrichment.

It is a child's legal right to have a curriculum that is differentiated to meet their needs. The assumption here about the curriculum is that it is presented as a package that can be delivered and it is the teacher's professional responsibility to adapt it so that each learner can progress. A match has to be made between the material that is being taught and the needs of the learner. We could say that when this match occurs the learning is grounded in who you are and how you learn. For obvious reasons, we refer to this as *grounded learning*. The learning connects with you, it is accessible: it means something to you. It also connects you with your own concept of self: it helps you to understand yourself. It is the type of learning that provides positive answers to the questions: 'What does this piece of learning say about me? What does it tell me about who I am, what I am capable of and where I belong?' Grounded learning is rooted in who you are.

Some would argue that differentiation is a process akin to adapting resources. Others propose that differentiation is more complex and involves adaptation of teaching approaches, strategies and methods. These definitions present differentiation as both a process and tool but they can still limit our ability to think deeper. What has to remain under scrutiny is what exactly is happening *inside* a teacher's head when they think about teaching – what are their beliefs and attitudes about teaching? This has to be inextricably linked to an analysis of what their beliefs and attitudes are about learning and learners.

Although some teachers are comfortable working within the confines of their classroom, they belong to larger systems and subsystems where they may or may not be so comfortable. These systems are part of a wider social and political culture. The point here is that teaching does not take place within a vacuum. In this book we aim to encourage you to ask reflective questions about the learning system that you work within as well as the learning that you provide. You will be challenged to consider how you define teaching and learning. You will be asked to take a journey within your own head as well as that of the learners for whom you are responsible.

## Teaching and learning: intimate or distant?

Teaching and learning can be intimate or distant. The teaching provided through the traditional, non-interactive, model of 'transmission teaching' may remain distant for most learners for most of the time. Simply transmitting information to learners does not mean that it will connect with them – that they will learn it. It may connect with them and their preferred learning styles; but then again it may not. This may be due to a variety of reasons: such as it lying beyond the realms of their experience or culture. If it does not connect, it is *distant learning*.

Teaching can also be intimate or distant. For example, a teacher may well teach a group of what are often called 'disaffected' learners. Such learners could be seen as experiencing distant learning because, for multiple reasons, they might see no connection between what is being taught and their learning. The task for the teacher is to develop a relationship with the learners and their learning so that it becomes meaningful to them. This we refer to as *intimate learning*. When learning is distant, everybody is treated the same and has to learn the same thing in the same way. Individuals seem to be lost somewhere in the equation. In essence, distant learning is based upon equality of treatment. In reality it can create learning difficulties. Intimate learning, however, connects with you as an individual. It helps to develop your understanding of your 'self'. It also connects you with the curriculum that is on offer and ultimately with the learning system and community that you belong to. This type of learning is grounded in who you are as a person and the preferences that you make and techniques that you adopt in terms of your own learning style and strategies. In essence, intimate learning is based upon equality of learning opportunity. Whilst we chose the term 'differentiation' as the broad descriptor for the process of matching teaching to learning need, it may provide clarification if we were to describe the type of learning that occurs when such connections are made as 'grounded learning'. In this way differentiation can be seen to be a constellation of connective strategies designed to bring about grounded or intimate learning.

## What do we mean?

To understand the nature of differentiation, and how it occurs at different levels, we need to begin by considering what we mean, and do not mean, by teaching and learning. The opportunity for teachers to be given time to engage in critical debate about the nature of teaching and learning is vital. Over twenty years of research, studies identify five broad categories of what people assume learning to be:

- Gaining more knowledge.
- Memorizing and reproducing.
- Acquiring and applying procedures.
- Making sense or meaning.
- Personal change.

Research also suggests that teachers categorize teaching as follows:

- Imparting information.
- Transmitting knowledge.
- Facilitating understanding.
- Changing learner's conceptions.
- Supporting students learning.
                (Mortimore, 1999)

Recent research also illustrates that teachers reject definitions and models of teaching that oversimplify the complex tasks they undertake when they teach. As well as rejecting simplistic and crude models of what they do, teachers also comprehensively reject the notion that they only work according to one model (Gipps *et al.,* 1999). In our work with teachers we find that they can be quite precise in defining what they think teaching is and that their definitions fit into the categories mentioned above. These definitions offer an insight into the working model that teachers carry in their heads and put into practice when they are teaching. The model that is inside each teacher's head will combine an individual philosophy about the aims and intended outcomes of education, with a belief about the approach and practice that will best allow this to happen. In most cases the model will be responsive to the experience of being a teacher – it will be affected by your own teaching biography and experience and will develop over time. There may be some teachers who continue to teach with the same style and methods no matter what the needs of their pupils might be, but our experience tells us that many teachers are keen to develop their professional skills and understanding. As a consequence their model of teaching becomes more fluid and effective and learners are the beneficiaries.

In our professional discussions with teachers we have found that they tend to define their concept of teaching by splitting it into two areas: the professional skills that teachers require and the personal qualities that make an effective teacher. The models that they put forward vary greatly in terms of flexibility. The following lists are non-hierarchical and include a selection of definitions that teachers have presented to us:

*Professional skills of a teacher*
- Organizational skills – an organized classroom provides the basis for good teaching.
- Observational skills – accepting that observation involves interpretation and that this could be affected by the teacher's belief systems.
- An ability to understand the pupil's 'informal' communication systems. This is especially important for those working with pupils who experience communication difficulties.
- Creating situations whereby pupils can use intuition and be given responsibility.
- An ability to individualize learning and resources.
- An ability to develop targets and to use objectives-based planning.
- An ability to provide pupils with investigative skills.
- Ensuring that there is always a daily plan that is well communicated to pupils and other staff if necessary.
- Establishing boundaries that are consistent but fair.
- Developing approaches that support the pupils in managing communication with the world around them.

- An ability to know where the pupil is in terms of their learning.
- Continually and consistently mediating information.
- An ability to 'think on your feet'.
- Delivering a comprehensive knowledge of the subject that you are teaching.

*Personal qualities of a teacher*
- Empathy – with both the difficulties and needs of the pupils.
- An enthusiasm for what you are teaching.
- An interest in professional development.
- An interest in up-to-date research.
- A willingness not to take problem behaviour personally.
- A willingness to adapt a plan to meet an individual's needs.
- A sense of humour.
- A sense of proportion.
- A caring nature.
- An inquisitive nature.
- Actually liking to be with children and young people!

---

**DIALOGUE POINT**

You may choose to discuss these definitions of teaching and learning with:

a) a colleague you work with regularly;
b) a colleague in a different part of the system;
c) a colleague from an external support service;
d) as a school team.

- To what extent do you agree with these definitions?
- To what extent do you disagree and why?
- Are there others you would add to the list?

---

Are these skills and qualities something that can be learned through training and professional development and experience or are they mainly intuitive? We still find the view amongst practitioners that a teacher's skills and personal qualities are inherent – as if teaching is based upon a form of genetic intuition. We have all met charismatic and exceptional teachers some of whom will be described by colleagues as being 'a born teacher'. We also find the counter-view that teaching is like being a craftsperson, it is an art involving skills and processes that you can learn through training and develop through apprenticeship and practice. During the theorizing of teaching the importance of being able to reflect upon and evaluate your own practice is always given a high profile by practitioners.

We have found that teachers, in general, find it far more difficult to define learning. When discussing differentiation of learning, we have noticed a tendency for teachers to bring the discussion around to learner difference rather than teaching difference. In unstructured discussion about teachers' theories of learning, the discussion content will change and descriptions about the practicalities and difficulties of teaching will suddenly take over or resurface unbidden. This is why we have structured this book in a particular manner – by using a menu of points within the text that enable your thinking and discussions about learning to remain focused.

Here are some of the definitions that practitioners have offered us, as to what learning is. We present them in their words without any attached analysis.

- Processing information in your brain.
- Acquiring new skills.
- Changing your behaviour.
- Something that takes place within teaching frameworks.
- Something that can be measured by data.
- Something that cannot be measured by data.
- Using your memory.
- Understanding information that you knew nothing about previously.
- Satisfaction and pride in what you have done.
- Slowly making sense of something until you understand it.
- Cognitive stimulation.
- Developing understanding.
- Demonstrating that you have taken on knowledge – by transferring and generalizing learning into other areas of the curriculum.
- Independence – to achieve this may involve repetition and reinforcement.

- Feeling good about achievement.
- To be able to do something yourself – *your* learning.

It is clear that the role of the teacher is multifaceted. It is also clear that different people conceptualize teaching and learning in different ways. We can see that differentiation is already taking place in the way that people view their role as teachers within the learning systems in which they work.

Although this might be presenting the case in a bipolar fashion, it is true to say that one teacher might define what they do in very different terms to another. One example could be a teacher who views their role and responsibility as imparting information so that it can be processed and meaning made from it, thus allowing information to become knowledge. The view here would be that a teacher can continually provide learners with information – for example on how to apply certain skills – but it always remains as information unless skills can be applied in the specified context or generalized into different situations. When a learner can do this, information is transformed into knowledge. So, information about how to make a clay pot, prepare and cook a meal from a culture that is different to your own, or safely participate in a parachute jump, for example, will remain as 'information' unless the learner demonstrates that they understand a task and can participate in it. When approaching the task in future they have knowledge to hand, rather than information.

Another example could be a teacher who sees their role quite differently. Their first concern may be linked to developing creativity and imagination – cultivating a sense of wonder, unfolding a world of new experiences and developing the mind so that it enhances a learner's individuality by encouraging them to extend beyond the norms of given boundaries and concepts. This is very different to the view of teaching offered by the teacher in the first example. Both are teachers but their view of teaching and learning is substantially different.

How teachers perceive their role will have a direct impact upon what they do when involved in the act of teaching. How they perceive learning will have a similar effect. How they define the interface between the two highlights the intellectual complexities of being a teacher. This is why differentiating or adapting the curriculum is an extremely complex process – we all begin from different starting points with the intention of achieving different end points!

Whilst the notion of a shared and common understanding of what differentiation is remains, at one level, a romantic ideal, it is possible to begin by agreeing on the *principles* for differentiation (O'Brien, 1998a). This can enable teachers to work within a shared framework.

## Principles for differentiation

Within any learning system there has to be a focus upon the capacity of both the individuals and the system to learn. Differentiation is not about 'troubleshooting' for some – it is a concept and practice that must apply to all. In an educational setting we propose that the *principles* of differentiation will always be the same whereas the *application* of differentiation has to be different. The following principles apply:

- *All children have a right to high quality education.* The nature of school populations is changing. In 'developed' countries these changes occur owing, for example, to the advances in medicine and technology which enable more children to survive after pregnancy and birth complications. As a consequence there are increasing numbers of children alive who have multiple sensory impairments. These children will attend schools in countries where there has been a legislative and philosophical commitment to all children being educable. In countries where this is not the case they may receive healthcare rather than education. In 'developing' countries, the prevalence of severe malnutrition amongst children (UNICEF, 1996) has educational as well as the more obvious ethical implications. It is not uncommon for malnourished children to develop difficulties in language development, visual-motor processing and in social development. Studies have shown that children who suffer from nutritional deprivation encounter moderate to severe difficulties in the areas of emotional and cognitive development (Aboud and Alemu, 1995).

    Demographic factors can affect a child's ability to learn too. There are children who encounter rural and urban deprivation, where unemployment is rife, housing is officially declared as unacceptable and their family context places them at risk of abuse and neglect. For example, the children in the

United Kingdom who live in families where alcohol abuse is a cause for serious concern – almost one million families (NCH, 2000) – should not have their right to high quality education taken away from them. Some of these children may present with emotional and behavioural difficulties but each of them is unique and should not be penalized by low expectation and an impoverished curriculum. The right to high quality education has an associated right – the right to participate in differentiated learning experiences. This means that the teacher must always consider the process of differentiation. In a recent discussion with one of the authors, a teacher stated 'First of all they want me to teach . . . and now they are telling me that then they want me to differentiate as well.' This was directed at curriculum managers. In the context of the principles of differentiation, such a statement is completely invalid.

- *Every child can learn.* Education and learning is an organic and human process. It is not simply about being able to attend a school. Education for all is a principle that has to be both promoted and evaluated within learning systems. The severity of a child's long- or short-term needs and difficulties should never create a response, either from a teacher or from an institution, that results in a decision that 'this child is incapable of learning'. The moral and ethical implications are evident if this occurs, especially when this label is applied to those pupils with the most severe, profound and multiple difficulties and needs.

- *Every teacher can learn.* The term teacher, as used here, refers to someone who knows what you do not know. This can be a peer, a parent or carer, or any person who is responsible for managing learning within a classroom. The notion that training to become a teacher is completed once initial teacher education at college or university is over has to be challenged. The value and outcomes of the teacher–learner relationship are drastically reduced when the teacher believes that the only person capable of learning is the person with the 'learner' label.

- *Learning is a process that involves mutual relationships.* Learning is a social and active process. Therefore it depends upon activities that take place within social contexts. Through interaction with others we can learn about ourselves – this is part of the process of making meaning of the world to which we contribute. If a learning system can agree to the principle that learning is dynamic and it is through responsive and collaborative relationships that we can change, then the potential for mutual success increases.

- *Progress for all will be expected, recognized and rewarded.* When a learning task is set there has to be an expectation that everyone can achieve and make progress. The task has to be demanding, but it must always be related to the emerging capabilities of learners. Differentiation in action can be seen when a teacher explains a task to a group. It should be explicit that all members of the group are expected to make progress. Once the task is under way the skilful teacher searches out progress. Of course, progress is a relative concept and some learners depend upon the finely tuned eye of an active teacher to find it. Once it is found the teacher can reward it with praise that is sincere, timely, regular and, most importantly, specific. It is good to know exactly what you are being praised for.

- *People and learning systems can change for the better.* As teachers, we have all met pupils who challenge our self-belief and cause us to feel de-skilled. We may also have met pupils who inform us of how difficult they intend to be. One of the authors used to teach exactly this type of pupil. When meeting him for the first time, the pupil said '. . . think of the baddest pupil that you have met . . . well, you ain't seen nothing yet because I'm going to be twenty times as bad as that'. A positive learning environment flourishes upon the principle that a pupil like this can change for the better. Whilst teachers may not be able to change all elements of a child's socio-emotional conditions, they can have a major influence upon them. This is why productive, sensitive and responsive relationships lie at the heart of good teaching, as do grounded learning and differentiation.

> **REFLECTION POINT**
>
> Imagine that you were asked to wear a T-shirt that communicated the principles that inform your practice. This would enable the learners to know what type of relationship they can develop with you. What would you write on your T-shirt? Why?

## Learning needs – what are they?

All human relationships involve an element of differentiation – whether planned or unplanned. Differentiation is based upon principles. Once principles have been agreed and can form the basis for the ethos of a learning system, models need to be developed, applied and then re-developed. If there is an agreement that one element of differentiation involves matching teaching style to learning need then the system must consider how it identifies learning needs. By gaining data from teachers and learners a model can be developed as to how the learning system identifies learning needs – what is done about meeting these needs is another matter. The model should be continually tested against what is happening within the system. If models are not open to critique then the system can become complacent and produce learners that do not exploit their potential to learn.

Norwich (1996) proposes that there are needs that are *common*, *exceptional* and *individual*. Exceptional needs are those that arise from characteristics that are shared by some pupils and not by others – such as hearing impairment or high musical ability. He argues that a model that separates needs in this manner highlights what is both integral about mainstream education and different from it in terms of specialized provision.

A model of *common*, *distinct* and *individual* needs, informed by discussions with Norwich, has been applied to the process of differentiation (O'Brien, 1998b). This model emphasizes that whilst teachers may plan teaching for a whole class group, they cannot assume that if they teach it to the whole class everyone will engage in high quality learning. This is because a whole class group contains a selection of smaller groups and a collection of individuals.

- COMMON NEEDS – Everyone is the same
- DISTINCT NEEDS – Some people are similar
- INDIVIDUAL NEEDS – Everyone is different

Learners in any classroom can be seen in this way – one whole group who have learning needs in common, a collection of smaller groups with similar needs, and individuals whose needs are unique. The commonality of all pupils is the starting point for differentiation. If learners are seen as one whole group first of all, then the tools for differentiation can apply to all of them. A learning system that views learners in this way will, for example, define learning disability as an element of diversity rather than as a deficit within the community. This is an inclusive view of a learning community. The model proposes that all learners have some learning needs that are common. These include being respected as a learner and a communicator and, crucially, feeling a sense of belonging. However, the thinking must not stop there. The teacher has to focus upon the distinct groups within the classroom and their learning needs. Distinct learning needs are those needs identified by the groups that learners belong to such as gender, family, culture, faith community and disability for example. Finally there are individual needs, needs that make someone unique and set them apart from others.

### 'But they are all children to me . . .'
To support you in viewing needs in this way, imagine that you are the only girl in a classroom group. You feel that being female is an important part of making you who you are and therefore it is something of which you are proud. You would not want your teachers to dismiss this and pretend that you were male – exactly the same as everybody else. You would want them to see you as someone who has needs in *common* with everybody else but also as someone with *distinct* needs that relate to your *gender*. However, you would also not want your teacher to think that you were exactly the same as all of the other girls in the school or wider community. This produces the potential for stereotyping and does not allow for your individuality. Therefore, you would also want your *individual* needs understood too. Through this method of progressive focusing your needs can be understood and met. You can be seen as belonging to groups but also as being unique. You can begin to receive learning that is grounded in who you are.

You are part of a whole class group, you belong to a distinct group within the class (you may well belong to other distinct groups too) and you are also an individual.

The same type of thinking would apply if you happened to be somebody who had a specific learning disability. First, you would want to be seen as having needs in common with all of your peers (whether they were educated in the same type of school as you or not). You would also want a teacher to understand needs you have that are similar or typical of people who have a disability like yours. Again, you would not want your teacher to assume that all people with specific learning disabilities are the same. However, if there was any information available about your disability that might typically require certain teaching approaches, for example the benefits that learners with Down syndrome gain from a high level of visual sequencing, you would want your teacher to find out more about it. Obviously, you would also want your teacher to be able to identify and understand your individual needs that make you unique.

There is a dilemma in exactly where a teacher should begin in the process of understanding learning needs. Should they see everyone as individuals first or should they begin by analysing the commonalities of the whole group? Individuality, especially in settings where learners have complex cognitive, social and emotional needs, can become overwhelming. We propose that, in terms of engaging in the process of differentiation, the teacher should begin by exploring what learners have in common – such as developing a sense of belonging and feeling that they are involved in respectful relationships and interactions.

The teacher who asserts that 'they are all children to me' will never move into understanding the distinct and individual needs of learners. They will only see common needs. They will also, intentionally or unintentionally, disengage from a debate about the process of teaching and learning. There are also serious questions to be asked about national and international systems that claim to be designed to enable teachers to plan to provide teaching that will meet the individual needs of pupils when some clearly fail to do so. These become 'they are all children to me' systems. Some of them – such as Individual Education Plans or Individual Learning Programmes – are applied through targets that are, at best, only related to a generic group to which the pupil is labelled as belonging. On occasions, finding the individual within them is almost impossible. Such individual planning must be active, responsive and accountable to the individual (Guiney, 2000).

Targets that are set should demonstrate knowledge of the needs of individuals. For example, targets which make assumptions about the needs of pupils with Autistic Spectrum Disorder in implying that all of them experience all of the components of a triad of impairment at a similar level and intensity. At worst, targets are set that are common to all pupils. In the UK the legal document of a learner's special educational needs and how they can be met, is referred to as a 'statement'. Some of these documents never get beyond common needs. They may state that a specific individual '. . . requires a positive relationship with a teacher, clear and consistent boundaries, a differentiated curriculum and regular links with the family'. These are prerequisites for all pupils. The individual becomes elusive when individualized processes become so vague and meaningless. As well as not supporting the learner they also provide no real guidance for the teacher. The help that vague documentation offers in directing teaching is negligible.

## Learning involves change – so does teaching

Lastly in this chapter we wish to recognize the power and emotional dynamism of teaching and learning. It is important at the outset to make our views on this clear. We believe that emotional aspects of teaching and learning are always relevant. In other chapters, especially Chapter 8, we bring these considerations to the fore. This book will therefore have more to say on this and related matters later, but for now we note that when we learn something new, and when we teach something new, we become involved in a process of change. Learning and teaching are risky, difficult at times, but can also be fun. Learning is competitive and involves raw and basic emotions. Learning also involves success and failure. Sometimes not trying to learn can be emotionally safer than trying and then failing.

Learners and teachers may well present the behaviour that is associated with these emotions but, for various reasons, the emotions themselves cannot be acknowledged or the root of the behaviour may not be recognized. When we learn, how we are able to learn in the future changes forever. This happens because we are not who we were before we learned it. Our state of being has changed, we are different now and as a consequence our perception of the environment has changed too – no matter how small this learning increment may be. When we associate all learning with change it is helpful to consider the emotional responses that occur during change. We would argue that ignoring the causation of such responses reduces the effectiveness of a teacher. Later in the book the nature and processes involved in emotional differentiation will be explored in more detail. For now, the reasons for proposing that teachers need to become involved in such a process are briefly outlined. The responses that are outlined are based upon the work of Bannister and Fransella (1986).

Change, for the teacher and the learner, may involve:

- CREATIVITY – This is the reaction of the learner demonstrating that they have been open to new learning.
- FEAR – This is a reaction that can occur when an awareness of imminent but incidental change takes place.
- THREAT – This is a stronger reaction than fear because the change is seen as imminent but comprehensive. It can challenge your confidence in yourself as a learner.
- ANXIETY – This reaction occurs when you become concerned that the change that is about to take place involves areas that are beyond your control or outside the range of skills that you have to deal with change.
- AGGRESSIVENESS – This response is defensive and may occur when someone's perception of 'self' is under threat.
- HOSTILITY – This represents a continued aggressive response. It may be a reaction that is used to prevent new learning from having to take place.
- IMPULSIVITY – This prevents you from making new choices.

All of us, at certain times and in certain contexts, can be affected by such reactions – singularly or in combination. Differentiation needs to take account of these responses and plan to harness this energy in a positive manner.

# 2 Beliefs and stereotypes

In this chapter we aim to develop your interest in thinking about the relationship between teaching and learning. This, of course, involves reflecting upon the relationship between teacher and learner. The relationship between teachers and learners and how teachers typically come to construe learning and learners is a fascinating area. It is also one of those many apparently simple and uncomplicated areas of life that only reveals its true complexity when we begin to eyeball it – to regard it more directly and regularly. By regarding it in this way and tackling its complexity we can ultimately improve provision for learners.

We have previously stated that learning and differentiation is a human process and is therefore influenced by beliefs and attitudes that are held by teachers and learners who work within learning systems. Learning is not simply about cognitive processes – emotional and social factors are important too. By referring to learning systems we aim to highlight the fact that teaching does not take place within an isolated arena – what a teacher does in a classroom is affected by social, cultural and political factors. We also aim to remind readers that learning systems are organic and are influenced by and responsive to what takes place within and without them. The purpose of this chapter is to encourage you to consider your belief systems about the process you engage in on behalf of the learners with whom you work. This is an important prelude to the succeeding chapters where we will focus in a more detailed way on individual areas of differentiation. In the words of an ancient Taoist saying, 'by knowing from where you begin you are enlightened as to how far you can travel'.

Belief systems form the essential structure of learning and teaching environments. Often, beliefs and attitudes will be strongly held by teachers but at an informal and implicit level. It seems, in our experience, that learning systems often fail to address these issues formally.

Instead this debate can become acted out in many different ways. Sometimes teaching difficulties are manipulated and become identified as learning difficulties. Transference can occur whereby the needs of a particular learner are used against them and teaching questions are left unresolved. In extreme cases learners are blamed for learning difficulties and this dismisses the required debate about teaching. This also reinforces an attitude that the teacher need not discuss or reflect upon their own involvement in the teaching process because the learners hijack and destroy it. It is not the teacher's responsibility but the learner's fault. This produces formulations that we have come across such as: learners choose to display problem behaviour, or it is their fault that they cannot, for example, read and write at the level that the teacher would like them to. We view this as a natural defence system in relation to the need for collegiality. Whilst this may well be perceived as a positive attribute from a teacher standpoint, the learner and the teacher actually lose out.

---

### ACTION POINT

As learning is a multisensory process, we would argue that understanding learning involves the same type of processing. This invites you to become involved in a vital task that takes place at different levels. Take time to look at the teaching and learning system that you work in with new senses. Through analysing your own sensations you can begin to make sense of the learning systems to which you belong.

*Visual checks*
- Look with a new eye.
- Look big and look little.
- Look far and look near.
- Look hard and look easy.
- What do you see?
- Why does it look this way?
- What does this looking tell you about the learning system you work in?

➤

*Aural checks*
- Listen to your learning system.
- How does it speak to itself?
- Who listens to whom?
- When and why?
- Who speaks?
- Who speaks the loudest?
- Who listens?
- Who has a voice?
- When is it loud?
- When is it quiet?
- Is anyone unheard?
- What does this listening tell you about the learning system you work in?

*Tactile checks*
- How does the system feel?
- What is the topography of the whole learning system?
- What is the topography of your immediate learning environment?
- What does it smell like?
- What does this tell you about the learning system you work in?

To understand the systems and how you can differentiate between and within them you will also need to make other checks.

*Personnel checks*
- Who has responsibility for all of these sensations?
- What is their view?
- What is your view?
- When did you last have a dialogue about the system?
- With whom?
- What does the range and style of these interactions tell you about the learning system you work in?
- What does it tell you about your own sense of worth?

➤

*Visitor checks*
- How does the system present to visitors?
- How do you know?
- Do they tell you?
- How do they tell you?
- Do you ask them?
- How and when?
- Why?
- When did you last visit another different type of learning system?
- To what extent could this become included in a plan that relates to your own personal and professional development?
- What do you think visitors make of the learning system you work in?
- What impression is the system seeking to impart?
- Why?

*Learner checks*
- How does the environment match the needs of all of your learners?
- How do they react to this environment?
- What does it tell them about their sense of worth?
- What does it tell them about your sense of worth?
- What does it say to them about learning?
- What does it say about teaching?
- What does it say about your joint task?

This list is not intended to be exhaustive or hierarchical but aims to provide a route to a private or joint dialogue. There are no correct or incorrect responses to these points, only your own personal knowledge and opinions about how your learning system works. These can be further developed through the process of dialogues with your peers and colleagues about their views on these same points.

# Teacher and learner relationships

Having thought about the underlying principles conveyed, at least in part, by the experience of exploring the responses that you gave to the previous action point, we now wish to explore the more personal aspects of the learning system, those that are located within the heads of teachers. Again this is a challenging task and one that is not often confronted. This is a major reason for attempting it.

In training that we have carried out with many teachers, we have found they are always extremely pragmatic about the teaching role and task. They also seem to find it easier to talk about the differences between learners rather than analysing what these differences mean in terms of differentiation. In fact, in some conversations discussions about teaching difference are carried out in a context that claims to be about learning difference. This may well be a necessity of working in such a complex role within complex systems. We would ask here that you reflect beyond the level of pragmatics and consider openly and in some detail, with yourself or with a colleague, what you believe is implied or 'given' in the very next interaction you will have with a learner or learners under your care. A reflection point is provided on the following page to facilitate this debate. This debate is presented as worthwhile because learners and teachers will benefit from the outcomes. Initially, this may not seem to you to be related to differentiation. It may seem unrelated to setting a task that will provide education for all. In fact, it is an integral part of the earlier stages of the process of differentiation in action. This enables you to be better at providing intimate or grounded learning.

We are not suggesting that there are easy answers. We hope that an inclusive learning system will have the foresight and confidence to ask such questions both formally and informally. By engaging in this process you are helping your own learning system to develop.

Having considered these issues, you will become increasingly more aware that teaching and learning is an unpredictable and risky affair. There do not seem to be simple answers to questions that superficially seem to be so obvious. It is this that makes it such a demanding and rewarding challenge. It is also this that makes it enjoyable. We are concerned with your beliefs as teachers but we must remember that learners, with their beliefs, are also constantly trying to make sense of learning systems. The processing of this information will be

**REFLECTION POINT**

What are your views of the relationship you are about to enter between you as teacher and your potential learners? Here are ten questions aimed to illuminate the relationship.

1. In your view how does the teaching-learning process work? (For example, is a learner an empty vessel to be filled up or is learning just 'out there' to be discovered?)
2. If I teach it will they learn it?
3. What happens if they have learned it and know it before I have taught it?
4. How will I know?
5. What happens if they have not learned it after I have finished teaching it?
6. How will I know?
7. What happens if I finish teaching before or after they finish learning?
8. What happens if they finish learning before or after I finish teaching?
9. How can I plan to teach if I multiply these questions by the number of learners in the class?
10. To what degree does this mean that the larger the class size the more difficult the teaching task will be?

influenced by factors associated with their own group dynamics and external social factors. This is why, at times, they may process learning in such a way that teaching intentions do not match learning outcomes. Of course, there are also times when what the teacher intended the learners to learn does take place.

During the course of our everyday work we have visited numerous learning systems and aim to provide some insights into teacher–learner interactions that are taken from the real world. These insights can demonstrate what is taking place in the process of learning that occurs during teacher–learner interactions.

**CASE POINT**

*Having a whale of a time?*

This example occurred during a science lesson in a large high school. The learners were fifteen years old. The teacher had been talking about the cycle of life and the food chain. The lesson, focusing upon life in the oceans, had been interactive and the learners appear to have enjoyed it. It was about to end. A hierarchy of the complexity and interdependence of life in the sea had been outlined, with the teacher carefully and slowly introducing and reinforcing new and more specialized technical language. The teacher moved from describing 'small life forms', also referred to as 'micro-organisms', to whales, the largest creatures on earth. The learners were also informed that whales are actually mammals like humans – they are not fish at all.

The teacher was drawing the lesson to an end and recapping the details and content. At this point we have noted that teachers often move to ask quite close-ended questions. If they wish to ask a particular learner what will be for them a challenging question, they typically, almost unconsciously, add differentiation through structuring or scaffolding the question for that learner. It seems to be an almost intuitive form of differentiation.

The teacher and class had started at the top of the food chain, speaking and receiving answers about whales and sharks. Marcel was sitting on his own at the back of the class and it was his turn to answer a question. The teacher wanted Marcel to provide an example of life at the other end of the scale, where the teacher had talked of 'multiple organisms'. It was clear that the teacher wanted to illuminate for the whole group of learners the size of the whale in comparison to its microscopic food source, plankton. The script went as follows:

Teacher: 'Let me see . . . (looks around the room) . . . yes, Marcel . . . let me ask you a question. What is the name of the tiny, almost microscopic plant life that the whales have to seek, follow and gulp down in vast quantities?'

Marcel (attentively and after some evident thought): 'Are the whales swimming in the oceans in search of multiple orgasms sir?'

## Construing teaching and learning

We have asked you to spend some time considering the relationship you are just about to enter and we then gave an example of how individual learners process information in a manner that the teacher did not intend. Teaching and learning is about being human and consequently there is always room for individualized meanings. This often represents a mismatch between teaching intention and learning outcome and can illuminate where a learning difficulty has occurred – as we have now seen. Although such real life incidents provide teachers with entertaining anecdotes, remaining analytical about what we are doing when teaching will reduce these errors.

There are various models that describe the teacher–learner relationship. Whilst we acknowledge that there may be an inherent simplicity in aiming to apply one singular model to a complex situation, we shall select one model to highlight the process involved in looking at what is your common daily experience from a different perspective. We have deliberately chosen a model that may challenge your response to new learning.

### Taking a different view

Psychoanalytic theory would suggest that the teacher–learner relationship is akin to that of a parent or carer and child. It is not our intention to deal with theoretical issues associated with psychoanalysis in any rigorous manner at all, but rather to present the basics to aid your understanding of how a particular model could be applied. This will also help to provide a counterpoint to your own thinking.

Based on the work of Melanie Klein (1988) and the Educational Therapy movement, teaching and learning are likened to the instinctive necessity of eating and feeding. Thus teaching and learning is a basic human instinct and motivation. The psychoanalytical model asserts that teaching is a nurturing instinct as natural and as necessary for full human development as putting a baby to the breast. At the breast all of the needs of the baby are fulfilled. The baby is totally dependent upon the mother; there is no need to be anxious or to experience any type of fear.

From a psychoanalytic viewpoint this analogy is fundamental to understanding the nature of teaching and learning. The teacher is providing the nourishment for the learner – learning. This is so fundamental that it has become part of our professional language. Much of the language of teaching and learning contains feeding, eating and nourishment imagery. Consider these phrases used by teachers:

- He is not very good at taking in new information and knowledge.
- She needs a lot of time to digest new material.
- This topic is very sensitive and some will find it hard to swallow.
- He bit off more than he could chew when he tried to do that task on his own.
- She is not as clever as people think – all she can do is regurgitate information.
- He has problems because he is not receiving the correct curriculum diet.
- She hungers for new learning.
- That will give them food for thought for the future.

The link highlighted here is the similarity between teaching and learning and food as forms of nutrition. Knowledge is also represented as food for the mind. From our earliest experience of learning there is a match between the degree of dependence and independence that is developmental in nature. Early years education, just like early food, is provided in manageable portions, it is designed to be easily digestible. Young children at nursery or playgroup often get 'messy' in the act of partaking in both. As time moves on expectations change and the food and the learning become harder, more substantial and finally we expect development into self-dependence, independence and ultimately interdependence and lifelong learning.

This also reflects changing patterns of provision of nurturing in a developmental sense. The baby begins by being fed and is entirely dependent on her carer for sustenance. The simile with the teacher–learner relationship is clear. As the child or learner grows she becomes able to tolerate a variety of tastes and can widen her horizons. However, the teacher is still there and highly supportive but not as directly involved. How many children will inadvertently (or otherwise) call their female infant teacher 'mum' by mistake at some time or other? How many will still do the same even if their teacher is a man?

Lastly it has not escaped our notice that in many of the successful schools we have visited which provide specialized education for children with learning difficulties, food and feeding are highly bound up with curriculum design and differentiation. A great deal of thought, planning and energy are given to making mealtimes enjoyable and collegiate times of the day. In some cases, targets are set for mealtimes. Many schools recognize eating as a special time for those learners with the most profound and multiple sensory disabilities. In certain contexts with these learners, the process of eating encapsulates a life and death situation. The professional skills and knowledge of the person involved in supporting the child are vital, as one slight mistake might lead to a chain of events that could be fatal.

By a brief consideration of a psychoanalytic perspective we have sought to illuminate one interpretation amongst many of the relationship that is about to exist when you next interact as a teacher with a learner or group of learners. This interpretation proposes a very close developmental and nurturing link underpinning the relationship between teachers and learners. This link would appear easier to see in 'early years' education and may be less clear in secondary education, for example. In the UK, nurture groups have been set up for learners with social and emotional difficulties and fragmented family situations since the 1960s. The aim of such groups is to counteract negative interactions by providing teaching situations that take into account intrinsic childhood experiences. Interestingly, within these groups food is seen as symbolic of a relationship (Bennathan and Boxall, 2000).

We are not saying that the psychoanalytic interpretation is the only interpretation, but are encouraging you and your learning system to consider how *you* interpret this relationship, as it is an important first step in building up your approach to differentiation. Having been offered one model of how to understand the teacher–learner relationship you may wish to revisit the ten questions and reflect further upon your own model.

## I'm just a stereotype

How belief systems grow and develop would fill a large volume of books about psychology, philosophy, politics, religion and other areas. It is not our purpose here to deal in with such a wide-ranging perspective on these issues, but rather to highlight only a few areas where further attention can aid differentiation. We are aware of the influence of 'Personal Construct Psychology' (Kelly, 1955) and will discuss this in more detail in Chapter 5. Let us now move on to look at the impact of labels and stereotypical thinking in a little more detail. This will be used as a lead-in to asking you to think more clearly about the impact this has in your learning environment and learning system.

### Stereotypical thinking

We all use stereotypes. It could be argued that stereotypes are social constructs in themselves and therefore perform a useful function. For example, a stereotype might enable a person to predict what might occur in a given situation. They may be especially helpful in situations where a person could be in potential danger. However, we would argue that the fact that they are constructs represents their limitations. Stereotypes can often remain untested and this holds inherent difficulties especially within learning systems where labels and status are interrelated and so often applied in a casual or dismissive manner. Constructs should always be tested. It may be argued that they will continually be tested through the process of social interaction. Challenging stereotypes is also important. It ensures that majority groups do not terrorize or humiliate minority groups. By challenging stereotypes teachers are encouraged at all times to move beyond what they currently know, feel, think and do. Although this may seem an obvious point to make, in doing so they are involved in the process of differentiation. It is the essential process that enables intimate or grounded learning to take place.

---

**CASE POINT**

*The physical education teacher and the sociologist*
Two teachers had worked in the same school for many years. They were busy people and although they were colleagues they would not describe each other as friends. In fact, they had never really found time to talk to each other about their jobs, let alone observe each other in the process of teaching.

➤

One was a tall, strong, athletic woman, bronzed by the sun for most of the year. Even in winter months she insisted on cycling to school wearing a running vest and shorts. Her physical prowess was important in how she viewed herself. She regularly organized school skiing trips and adventure holidays. She had a pastoral management role that meant she had overall responsibility for 300 learners aged twelve and thirteen. She was a competitive person and a teacher who was seen to have 'good control' over the learners in her classroom. This control was not oppressive, as she could be relaxed and witty with them.

The other teacher was a small, pale-skinned man. He was bearded and had a quiet demeanour. He was known to have a serious approach to his work. He was very softly spoken, described by colleagues as 'gentle' and he saw himself very much as a subject specialist. He was knowledgeable about his subject and began his career with high expectations of the learners that he worked with. However, over the years his attitude to learning and learners had tended to become characterized by his colleagues as 'some children want to learn, some are not keen, and the worst are not even interested'. As a teacher of several years' standing he had enough experience to deal well with a wide range of children's needs. He was seen as having good mediation skills as a product of both his personality and his subject experience.

The two teachers had always regarded each other's subjects as being easier in many ways to teach than their own. After all, in a one-hour PE lesson you spend at least fifteen minutes with the students getting changed. Then they have to collect equipment, be shown what to do, be sorted into teams and begin a team game. The teacher simply walks around in the sunshine blowing a whistle or shouting instructions. Finally, the last fifteen minutes are taken up with returning equipment, changing out of sports kit and showering. Let's be honest – not much preparation is required for that.

In teaching sociology (a pretend and pretentious version of a

➤

social science), you need a large collection of videotapes so that you can critique the latest films and soap operas. You will also need boxes full of newspapers so that you can engage in cultural analysis by cutting out headlines. If you are not doing that, the learners will be aimlessly debating the rights and wrongs of abortion, drugs and the death penalty. Let's be honest – not much preparation is required for that.

During one freak term, both of our teachers become ill and each have to take a week off. In an amazing set of coincidences, they are ill during term-time, rather than becoming ill in the vacation as teachers often are. Secondly, they are off in following weeks. First one, then the other.

For the purposes of this example another amazing coincidence occurs: our two teachers find themselves being stand-in teachers for a whole week covering lessons for each other. Our PE specialist is left wondering how the sociology teacher manages to keep the learners' interest, and answer their inquisitive and insightful questions in what is potentially a difficult subject area. This is made worse by having to teach within a confined space within the classroom. The sociology teacher is amazed by the amount of thought that has to be given to even the simple basics of PE, such as health and safety, and the difficulty of direct instruction often to large numbers of learners in open spaces. The persistent rain did not help either!

We leave the scene with both teachers now back in their respective departments. The PE teacher is glad to be back as head of department and last week he made a decision to shave off his beard. The sociology teacher, back in her classroom, seeks to reconcile the twin areas of the demand of assessing learning that takes place when learners talk to each other in groups with that of arranging a parents' consultation evening for students in her year group. Still she need not worry, as a relaxing ski trip is only a few months away – for as we all know, school trips are never stressful for teachers, they are holidays!

In reading this story you will have been taken on a journey that will have raised questions about some of your own stereotypical thinking. Reflect upon this thinking. We do not apologize for exposing any inherent stereotypical assumptions that arose. The point is that, in psychological terms, stereotypes illuminate how you bring order and predictability to the world. Where they become less useful is when they become taken for granted; applied automatically as a tool of negative power; become unquestioning and over relied upon and are used as a means of labelling others. You may wish to consider the nature of the stereotypical judgements you made as you read this scenario, where they came from and why you hold them.

## Did we really say that? Did we really think that?

. . . and did we really mean that? We have shown that we all use stereotypes. Which ones are used by the learning system in which you work? What do they say about the value and status of you as a teacher? What do they say about the value and status of learners? Stereotypes promote explicit and concrete images. They do not promote fluidity of thought. They also convey powerful messages. In the day-to-day experience, and sometimes the stresses, of teaching such messages can be transmitted without questioning. The system of transmission does not only involve teachers, it also involves others too. We are including a list of some 'typicals' that we have come across in our time in classrooms. The purpose in providing them is not to explore them now. At later stages in your own thinking and learning you may wish to come back to them and look at them from differing perspectives. All of the situations and comments are real. Respect for confidentiality requires us to alter names. A context is provided where necessary:

> 'In ten years time he will be in prison for rape.' (Jerome is eight years old and is experiencing some emotional difficulties.)

> When one of the authors was taking a group to the cinema, the usher noticed a learner who was a wheelchair user. His response was to contact the manager and announce loudly and publicly: 'I may need help, nobody told me I'd have a wheelchair in this party.'

Children who use wheelchairs seem to be prone to this type of reaction. When another of the authors was taking a group to the cinema, one of the learners in the group was a wheelchair user. On arrival the person who was pushing the chair was stopped by the manager of the cinema (it is too obvious to mention that at no point was the learner spoken to). The adult was informed: '. . . you cannot bring a chair in here, that kid is a fire hazard.' The argument being that other people might not be able to escape quickly enough if a wheelchair was blocking their escape route.

An educational psychologist (EP) enters a classroom for an unobtrusive observation of a learner who has been presenting with challenging behaviour. The teacher stops the whole class from participating in their group activities as the EP enters, and says: 'Will the child with special educational needs stand up so that the psychologist can get a good look at you.'

An EP arrives to meet a group of six learners in a special school. The teacher introduces one of the learners as follows: 'This is Farzan, he has got emotional and behavioural difficulties.'

During a coffee break in a school, a discussion began about recent behaviour difficulties that were believed to be increasing, especially amongst the boys. This comment was made: '. . . girls need counselling, boys need special education.'

A statement written by a teacher on a circulated memo that was due to be discussed with parents and senior managers about the progress of Damien, who presents with challenging behaviour. The request on this memo reads: Please write down what you feel this child needs to continue to make progress. A history teacher responded in this way: 'Forget all of your child-centred ideas, what he really needs is a good slap!'

Teacher interview with EP two days before the end of a busy term. Discussing Tracey who presents with challenging behaviour: 'I've discussed this with my teaching union – I am not having her back in my class again. I am not teaching her.

I absolutely refuse. You are the EP – I want something done now. I want you to put her in the back seat of your car and drive her to that special school down the road. Explain to the head-teacher what she is like, leave her there, they know how to deal with kids who cannot be taught. That is their job. Do not give me any excuses, just do it.'

'He just does not seem to know right from wrong. It is as if he is evil – I swear I have seen a mad look in his eye. One of the parents here works in a hospital – she says he is psychotic. Do you agree that he should see a psychiatrist?' (Séan is four years old. He has been non-compliant in the nursery for the past month.)

Teacher talking about Sabrina, who encounters general learning difficulties. 'I do not want to be judgemental but what can you expect – you should see the home she comes from.'

Teacher: 'Frankie, you promised you would learn your spellings properly this week but you have got virtually all of them wrong. Are you stupid?'
Frankie: 'Don't call me stupid. I am not stupid. I did learn them Miss, but I learnt the letters in a different order to what you marked as right.'

In a meeting that is looking at curriculum planning for Sundeep, who has Down Syndrome. Sundeep has recently become aggressive towards some of his peers.
Teacher: 'I am especially concerned about his behaviour because children with Down Syndrome are always so affectionate and loving.'

In a primary classroom, the teacher had organized an interactive learning activity and explained how the learners needed to get into groups and then find information from each other. Joanna rushed off excitedly to join a group. Teacher: 'Not you Joanna, you are on the special needs table – you have a worksheet to do.'

During a public self-marking of twenty number problems in a junior class:
Teacher: '. . . and put up your hand if you got less than five correct out of twenty. Ah, just you again Jamal . . . you may as well keep your hand up for next week as well.'

---

**REFLECTION POINT**

- What were your reactions to these anecdotes and comments?
- How did they make you feel?
- To what extent can you imagine similar comments being made in the learning system in which you work?

---

As part of the culture of teaching, such anecdotes are often shared. This is another reason for including them. Our intention is not to affirm fixed stereotypes but to present them so that they can be very closely scrutinized for their real meaning and the unspoken negative attributions that underpin them. They provide an insight into how teachers view some learners, and may also provide an insight into how teachers see themselves. Whenever such stereotypes are expressed and transmitted they need to be challenged. If you do not challenge them, then you comply with them.

# 3  I teach . . . and you learn?

In the previous chapter we began to explore teachers' beliefs about the relationship they are to enter with learners. In this chapter we intend to look in greater detail at the intended outcome of this relationship: learning. We wish to consider what learning is and how it takes place in relation to teaching. In this more challenging chapter, we offer a conceptual formulation of teacher–learner outcomes. We also introduce the notion of teacher–learner value.

## Teacher–learner outcomes

We proposed earlier that when a teacher teaches it is not necessarily the case that a learner learns what the teacher intended. The supposition that teaching equals learning suggests an equal and balanced relationship between teacher and learner. The balance is based upon one teaching while the other one learns. However, the thinking you have done already suggests that this is often not the case – the relationship is not always equal. This may be owing to various factors relating to how explicit teaching is, what approaches are being used and within what framework the teaching and learning exist. When the teacher–learner relationship is established, we can posit, in simplistic terms, several teacher–learner outcomes. We identify such outcomes in terms of the notion of *teacher value* and *learner value*. These are easily defined as the worth (both in terms of essence and utility) of the teaching taught and the learning learnt. In theory, at least, this worth or utility would form a perfect match between teaching intention and learning need. For the purpose of explanation and illumination, this 'optimum value' is represented by a notional figure – in this case the number 1.

We can begin by considering a positive example of teacher–learner value, where the relationship works best. This will involve a teacher teaching what was intended, in a successful fashion. It can be described like this because, owing to the value of the teaching, the learner has successfully learned what was intended. This outcome represents an *optimum teaching and learning value.* Everything has gone well. There was a good match between what the teacher had to teach, for example skills or information, and the learners' ability to receive and use this teaching in order to take the next step in their learning. It is the perfect teaching outcome that we all strive for as teachers. It is important here to emphasize that we are not talking about a mechanistic input and output model, from teacher to learner, that does not require social interaction. The teaching and learning system can involve a variety of organizational strategies such as peer tutoring for example. In this optimum scenario, the whole process of teaching has been planned and executed successfully by the teacher and learners have learned what was intended. They may well have learned other things along the way too.

### *Responding to feedback*

It is also important to reinforce that this type of optimum situation is based upon knowledge of learner needs and an acceptance that there are diverse ways of knowing. A previous knowledge of needs adds to the success of the teaching and learning. This knowledge of needs is often detailed in a learning plan. Optimum teaching and learning is not simply a process that occurs when a teacher reacts to learner difficulties. Successful teachers are often those best able to hold their learning plan in mind but who are open to and able to react to the mood, context and needs of the group and individuals within it. They are responsive and sensitive to learner feedback and use it to redefine their plan and subsequently enrich both teaching and learning. The thinking and questioning framework involved in this process is considered in detail later in Chapter 6.

The optimum situation represents success from its initial starting point of conceptualization – it is not the sudden reaction to an emerging learning difficulty. However, this is not intended to imply that the process of teaching should not be open to environmental feedback and intervention. We are proposing that differentiation has to occur before the starting point of teaching a group as well as after it. If it only happened before the starting point, then teaching could not be responsive to learning needs. If it only occurred during teaching then teachers would be reactive rather than responsive to learning difficulty. We are proposing planning and structures that positively allow and encourage creativity and the ability for both teachers and learners to use and be aware of mutual feedback.

It is most important to underline that this optimum value of 1 is a *notional* figure. Let us imagine the scenario where you have a lesson that is well matched to the needs of a particular learner. You teach in a high school and Nicola arrives at your lesson having had a problem in a previous lesson with a different teacher. She is clearly upset. The others in the group are debating loudly the rights and wrongs of who did what, how and why. You have to react to this new information you have received and are receiving. Temporary, short-term difficulties have to be dealt with. A teacher, in this context, will make a new match between teaching value and learning value. It is unlikely that you will achieve all you had hoped for with these learners during this particular interaction. It may take some time for the group and Nicola to settle. You do not lower your expectations but you do have to reformulate the teaching value against learning value. This still has a notional value of 1, even though the learning outcome is now not what was originally in mind. Yet the new and old values for teacher and learner alike cannot, must not, be considered in relation to each other. They are notional values and the new formulation is the optimum that was felt to be achievable in the new circumstances.

### An illustration of teacher–learner outcomes

Let us now return to the point of illustrating the four possible outcomes we have identified by reference to notional teacher–learner values.

1. The best teacher–learner relationship occurs where the teacher teaches value 1 and the learner learns value 1.
   This is represented as TV1 → LV1.
2. Where the teacher has taught value 1 (TV1), but where the learning value has been less than the teacher intended it to be.
   This is represented as TV1 → LV < 1.
3. Where the teacher has taught less than value TV1, but where the learning has been successful and equal to the optimum.
   This is represented as TV<1 → LV1.

4. This is the least successful relationship and we are sure that everyone can recall examples of this. It is hoped that such examples provide negative experiences that can be reflected upon so that the situation can change for the better in future. It takes place where the TV has been less than 1 and the LV has been less than 1.

   This is represented as TV<1 → LV<1.

As far as we are concerned these four simple equations can therefore be used to represent every teaching learning relationship that you will take part in. This is because they are intended to represent a continuum of teacher value and a continuum of learner value (see Figs 3.1 and 3.2). When the teacher and learner interact, the outcome of the relationship can be plotted at a point on each relevant continuum. At their best these relationships are fluid and flexible; at their least successful point they are fixed and often stuck.

**TV <1** ——————————————————— **TV**

(fixed)                                                       (fluid)

**Figure 3.1 The teacher value continuum**

**LV <1** ——————————————————— **LV**

(fixed)                                                       (fluid)

**Figure 3.2 The learner value continuum**

The interaction could also be represented this way:

| | | |
|---|---|---|
| High value teaching | → | High value learning |
| High value teaching | → | Low value learning |
| Low value teaching | → | High value learning |
| Low value teaching | → | Low value learning |

We know that some readers typically gloss over such representations because, as teachers, they find themselves in the same position as younger learners when they are about to be challenged to think in a different way. As a reader, you may prefer textual explanations and therefore you may have already made a decision to ignore the diagrams and rejoin the text at this point. Your own learning history may tell you that you cannot or do not learn by trying to make meaning from such diagrams. However, we would encourage you to return to the diagrams, take time to process the information therein and then to continue by reading this text-based explanation.

To have encapsulated *every* teacher–learner relationship in just four forms is a large claim to make, and so it will be important to consider what each means in more detail. It is important to remember that we are presenting a simplified notion of teacher–learner relationships and not entering into the variables involved in the complexity of every teacher and learner interaction.

Having simplified the teacher and learner relationship in this manner there is no implication that the interactions you are about to be involved in are not inherently complex. We have deliberately chosen to present the broadest forms of relationships in order to exemplify our thinking. In this way, the four forms can be applied to your own practice, as if they were a template for planning for differentiation and assessment. As a teacher, you could then make judgements about the teacher and learner value that was planned for and occurred in a specific lesson or series of lessons. This can be done for individuals and groups. We present this to you as an analytical framework that enables you to think about what you do: to improve your ability to differentiate. It is intended to help you too in dealing with the complexities of the task and the interaction by reference to the four forms.

## The four forms of teacher–learner outcomes

Having described four forms of outcomes it is also important to detail them. This should enable you to map these onto your own teaching and learning experiences to check out the validity of our proposition.

### Outcome 1

Here we have a teaching and learning situation in which the teacher has in mind an intended teaching plan that they equate with the teaching and subsequent learning that they plan to bring about. The teaching is well matched to the learners' needs in order to bring about a positive change or step in their learning. As previously stated we view this as an optimum teaching and learning relationship and have a notional value of 1 to express the worth and utility of that piece of teaching and that particular piece of learning. It is set at 1 as the teacher feels they can teach it and feels that the learners are equipped to learn it. In this scenario the teacher delivers a piece of teaching over a period of time and has in mind clear teaching and learning outcomes that are accurately matched to each other.

This teaching is then 'broadcast' – it is offered to the learner in varying means of communication and with varying intensity, according to their needs, to bring about the next step in their learning. In essence, it makes its way from the inside of the teacher's head to the inside of the learner's. To do this, the teacher will have made decisions about how teaching routines and procedures will be executed, and about what the learner's next step can be. For example, they will have asked questions about the level of instruction, the level of exploration and investigation or the level of collaboration that is required. They will consider the long- and short-term needs of the learners. They will have reflected upon what they learned previously and how they learned it – the level of their skill base. They might also have considered issues relevant to developmental levels – but most importantly in this reflection they must not see developmental levels as being fixed. There will also be questions regarding the need to employ any specialist techniques or resources for groups or individuals. This is a process that all teachers will recognize.

In this scenario, the teaching intentions are explicitly broadcast and are received by the learner – consequently the learning response exactly matches the teacher's intentions. If the teaching had a notional value of 1 then we envisage the learners gaining additional learning value of 1 also. Hence TV1 → LV1. There has been a happy congruence between teaching value and learning value. This also describes the optimum degree of 'fit' or 'match' between the teacher and the learner and we will say more about this in some detail later in the following chapter.

The relationship described here shows that the teacher knew something and has successfully imparted this to the learner. This has been done so that the learner, in relation to this piece of learning, now knows what the teacher knows. We feel that in real life most people would probably judge this to be one description and example of successful teaching and successful learning.

## CASE POINT

Consider this example. A high school teacher is ready to teach about climate in the Amazonian rainforest. She decides that one way of achieving this will be to draw and analyse bar graphs using comparative data that shows annual rainfall in Manaus, Brazil and in London, England. The teacher has a teaching plan to deliver learning that she has judged to have utility and to be of worth for learners. Thus she has derived, perhaps unconsciously (certainly without the notional value of 1 that we assigned for ease of illustration), a teaching value from the skills, values and information that she is about to impart. The teacher must also have made choices and decisions about the opportunity cost in terms of value of teaching this topic, at this time, to this learner or group of learners in terms of its utility and worth. There is such a cost in teaching and learning interactions because teachers are involved in acts of selection about what to teach and when to teach it, and what not to teach and when not to teach it. Even in a learning system that remains very prescriptive about teaching content, teachers still make decisions about which elements of content will be 'broadcast' to the learners and how this can take place to best effect. Therefore something is selected whilst other items are rejected.

So the teacher has made decisions about the teaching value. She must also be involved in the process of making decisions about the learning value, as the two are dynamic and interrelated. These decisions may well be so closely linked that in the teacher's mind the teaching value and learning value are the same thing, to the degree that they can be substituted, the one for the other, at least prior to the actual teaching or 'broadcasting' that will take place. In fact we would question that the one is the same as the other in reality, as it is at this point that learner considerations must be taken into account, through a process of differentiation. In this example the teacher has accurately matched teaching and learning decisions. The learners were able, as a next step in their learning to: read the data; plot it in bar graph form; analyse and compare; reach conclusions and

➤

provide accurate feedback to her. This is the manner in which they confirm the value of their learning in terms of the value of her teaching.

The planning, for teaching and learning, will probably have been done formally. It can also occur informally when, due to learner responses, teachers have to react instantly 'on their feet' in the classroom. We are suggesting that because teaching and learning involve relationships, teaching plans must be matched to learning plans which involves consideration of learning values.

A more extreme example may help set these value and matching processes in context. A nursery teacher is planning a lesson on number work for his learners. He takes into account decisions about what could be taught, what can be taught, what needs to be taught, when and why. In this example, some of his major considerations include the fact that all of the learners are new arrivals in the nursery and that most can count up to three in sequence, with some verbal and visual prompting. He knows this from their learning profiles that he has read in detail and found useful. He also knows that some can recognize number forms up to four, and a few have correspondence when counting up to four. The teacher has to construct a teaching and learning plan. In this case, he considers that teaching long division will have value for these learners (notional TV1) in extending and enriching their learning. The teacher judges that this is well matched to the learners' needs and abilities and that they can receive this teaching as the next step in their number experience (notional LV1). In this unlikely example, it would be reasonable to assume that this will not be an optimum situation.

The issues that have been considered so far involve formulations that are delivered in a single or a series of teacher–learner interactions and which bring about a change in the learners — by way of them now knowing what the teacher intended them to know. Over the period of teaching, something has been 'broadcast' from the teacher, and something has been 'received': learning by the learner.

## REFLECTION POINT

In job interviews, teachers are often asked to describe a piece of teaching that they are proud of – a situation where they set out to teach something and it worked very well for them and for the learners. At times, teachers often select the learning of one particular learner.

Think of the last time that you were involved in an optimal teacher–learner relationship.

- To what extent can you recognize these teacher–learner values that we have described above?
- Why did it go so well?
- What factors contributed to this success and where do you think they were located – in the teaching, learning, or in both?
- If asked why you were proud of this teaching, what would you say?

### Outcome 2

Secondly we describe a teaching situation where the teaching value remains the same, according to the principles we have set out, but for reasons that seem to be unclear, the learning value falls short of the optimum. Teaching seems to have outpaced learning. The teaching has been 'broadcast' but for whatever reason the 'reception' has resulted in learning taking place at a value that is less than was planned and broadcast. In this instance we identify what we term a mismatch between the teaching and learning. It is important to note that we are not proposing that learning has not taken place at all – as we feel that some learning will always take place. Learners will always be making decisions that are informed by learning. What has taken place has not been at the same value as it was intended and taught.

It is not necessary to provide examples of each and every one of these forms but in relation to the example given previously this would be where the teacher is 'broadcasting' about rainfall comparisons between different types of climates, but this learning has not taken place. Yet perhaps learning has taken place up to the level of better understanding how to draw raw data in bar graph form. The teacher had judged that the skills necessary to organize the data had been mastered and the learners were ready to look at comparing and analysing. For some or all of the pupils though, this learning was not achieved *on this occasion.*

---

**REFLECTION POINT**

In general, this reflection point sets the same task as that above but asks you to think of a time when the value of your teaching did not bring about an equal increase in the value of learning. You may want to think about it from the view of yourself as a learner with regard to a particular piece of teaching that did not quite work for you. You may want to think about what you would have suggested to the teacher about changes in teaching methodology that could have helped you to learn.

---

### Outcome 3

This describes a situation whereby for whatever reason the learning value arising from a teacher–learner interaction is greater than the teaching value that was broadcast. Learning seems to have outpaced teaching. In this scenario the learners have been able to add more value to the teaching than was intended or even perceived by the teacher. This might have been because many of them already knew what was being taught and demands were not made beyond that point. Perhaps teacher expectations of the learner or learners were too low? It may have been that the particular item of teaching enabled or facilitated new insights to be made on behalf of the learner. The gaining of new insights we refer to as 'penny dropping' moments and these are discussed in Chapter 7.

Another way of looking at this would be if this piece of learning enabled the coming together in a new or more usable way, the conjoining of other elements of learning, so that learning forges ahead beyond what may have been predicted. We can also look at this form in another way, perhaps a more human way – at the level of recognizing that all teachers have days when the best prepared lessons still do not seem to work as they would want them to. Planning and detail may be right and linked with long experience of subject matter and learners' needs but for some reason the broadcast is not up to the standard that we set for ourselves. In effect this reduces the teaching value, certainly at the point of broadcast, yet it may be possible for learners on this occasion to still extract high value from a below par teacher interaction.

---

**REFLECTION POINT**

Once again the task is as set out above but it may only be possible to reflect on this occasion from the perspective of the teacher. Think of examples when learning has taken place above the level of the teaching value that you felt you had delivered. Then apply the same questions and thinking that has proved useful in previous reflection points.

---

## Outcome 4

Lastly, form four describes a situation where neither the teacher or learner value has been optimized for whatever reason. This describes a negative interaction for teachers and learners. In this instance the value of teaching and learning falls way below the optimum and it will be hard to find a match between the teacher and learner. This results in a poor fit or an intense mismatch. The reasons for this can be manifold. Some could include lack of teacher and learner experience, poor conceptualization, lack of an understanding of the intensity of interactions required, differing views about the value of knowledge, mutual lack of motivation and poor decision making by both groups.

---

**REFLECTION POINT**

The task of this reflection point will now be clear to you. In this example you can consider a piece of teaching or learning that just did not work or deliver value. Just as every teacher will need support during their career, every teacher will also experience interactions where things seem to have gone completely wrong. Think about when this has happened to you:

- Why did the teacher–learner relationship fail and to what extent can you gauge where this stemmed from?
- What could have been done differently? By whom, when and why?
- In the context of your own example, who would need to change what to improve the teaching learning values?

---

## Considerations

These four forms require further examination. After all, the purpose of this book is to think about the process of differentiation that has to take place in order to achieve optimal value. Therefore it is important to take another look. The four forms could be described in the following ways.

1. Teaching value optimized to learning value. Outcome: intentional success.
2. Teaching value above learning value. Outcome: unintentional failure.
3. Teaching value below learning value. Outcome: unintentional success.
4. Low teaching value equal to low learning value. Outcome: intentional failure.

The first list only enables us to view the four forms from the perspective of the teacher. We must also look at these in terms of the learner's point of view:

1. Planned progress through the curriculum: typified by success.
2. Intermittent progress through the curriculum: typified by failure/success.
3. Intermittent progress through the curriculum: typified by success/failure.
4. Lack of progress through the curriculum: typified by failure.

What teachers and learners would always strive for is the optimum scenario, form 1, but in the real world and with the process of teaching and learning being so complex this is hard to achieve all of the time. What teachers and learners would wish to avoid would be the situation typified under form four, with very little progress being made in learning. They would certainly want to avoid form four being a regular occurrence. It could be argued that perhaps forms two and three most accurately describe the everyday reality of outcomes for learners even though teaching is highly planned and aims to be responsive. The task for differentiation is to reduce the incidence of learning outcomes occurring by way of forms two and three, to eliminate form four and to increase those occurring via form one.

Many authors describe differentiation as teaching that intends to meet individual needs. We have recognized the complexity of teaching because we can see the inherent difficulties in viewing learners as one homogeneous group. The task of teaching is made more challenging as the desirable learning outcomes described here must be multiplied by both the number of learners that the teacher is 'broadcasting' to and the complexity of their learning needs. This raises a question about teacher–learner value and class size. We are not aiming to suggest that teaching a group of 30 learners in a mainstream setting is necessarily easier or more difficult than, for example, teaching six learners who have multiple sensory and physical disabilities. Some people may take this standpoint; we would not agree with them.

### Outcome 2 – looking again

$TV1 \rightarrow LV{<}1$

We now want to pay particular attention to this, the second form whereby we posit a teacher–learner outcome scenario of the teacher value being optimal and the learner value being less than optimized. The question posed is whether this is really a credible state of affairs in the classroom. We are not questioning that this form exists but wish to look at more detail as to where the room for change occurs in this particular form of teacher–learner outcome – change that involves analysis of the principles and practice of differentiation. This involves individual and group reflection and discussion. It may also involve debate and disagreement. We invite you to engage in critical dialogue. Your discussion, like the forthcoming dialogue points, may well be lengthy.

---

**DIALOGUE POINT**

- Re-read the four forms and examples above. Teach a colleague what you have understood from the points we have made about the four forms of learner teacher outcomes. This is a good way of understanding and reinforcing your own learning.
- With a colleague, return to the thinking that you did at the point where you had read and then thought about form 2.

➤

---

You may wish to use to use the prompt questions and dialogue points below to aid the discussion and debate you hold with your colleague.

- It is suggested that there are only four possible outcomes from all teaching learning interactions. To what extent can this be true? Surely we must be able to think of lots more? If so, what are they?

- It is suggested that some teacher–learner interactions result in learners learning what the teacher taught. Talk with a colleague: How far do we agree with this? Why do we agree? Can we support our agreement with examples? How far do we disagree? Why? What examples do we base this view upon?

- It is suggested that some teacher–learner outcomes end by the teacher imparting less learning to the learner than was intended. For what reasons might we agree with this? For what reasons might we disagree? What examples do we base these views upon?

- It is suggested that some teacher–learner outcomes result in the learners learning less than it was their potential to learn at that time. How far do we agree? How can we make judgements about the potential of learners? How do we make such judgements?

- It was suggested that some teachers and learners do not begin their interactions trying to optimize the relationship regarding a particular element or item of learning. This could be seen as spoken or unspoken 'negotiated agreement' to hold off learning perhaps in place of some other goal. For example, a quiet classroom along the lines of the teacher implicitly or explicitly broadcasting this message – 'do not bother me and I will not bother you'. This is a classroom where a learning truce exists and the outcome will be 'intentional failure'. Do we agree that this happens? Why or why not? What examples do we base this on?

- Would all of these scenarios, if they do describe the totality of possible teacher–learner outcomes, benefit from differentiation? To what extent do we agree? Why? Why or why not? What reasons and what examples do we base this upon?

In relation to differentiation, we are interested in the form where the potential optimum teacher value results in learning value that is below the optimum. This requires further exploration too. Remember that in such an interaction there is the potential for teachers or learners to play by the rules of the blame game – denying responsibility and displacing it elsewhere. However, we believe that flourishing learning systems are open and confident and questioning, both of the wider cultural systems within which they operate and within their own internal systems and subsystems. Therefore blame is not the issue – differentiation is.

Our contention would be that this form is a case where the differentiation process was incomplete or had not taken place fully. It may not have been considered in enough detail at the point of planning education for all. Remember that differentiation is a concept that has to apply to all pupils – it is not just for those pupils who are labelled as having additional educational needs or requiring special education programmes. It may be that this form, and form three, indicate where there was further room for development. This is because the teacher is involved in a series of judgements and decisions at the planning stage about how they will broadcast learning of a given value. If it was not received at the same value then it could be because of processing errors by the learner. This means that judgements have to be made during teaching. In terms of differentiation, this raises issues about designing and employing strategies to minimize the chances of the rate of unintentional failure by paying closer attention to matching potential value at the planning stage. Differentiation may have intuitive elements but it has to occur within a planned framework.

This framework will be influenced by various factors. These will include the availability of information that the teacher has about different teaching and learning models and frameworks and how they can be applied. Learning can be hindered when teachers are involved in relationships with learners who require specific teaching strategies related to their learning needs but lack information. As a consequence teaching does not match need. Of course, similar problems occur when teachers become confused about whether certain models have to be applied in wholesale fashion to all learners or whether they can contextually be applied to some. The framework – and hence the success of teacher–learner relationships – will also be influenced by the quality of initial teacher education and further professional development programmes. Financial factors also impinge upon the framework as the availability or lack of specialized human and material resources can affect the quality of relationship.

Of course, the process of describing, defining and assessing the professional competence of the teacher learning influences the framework; as does who defines what the nature of high quality teaching and learning is and looks like. In most situations teachers do not define their own professional competence, government does. It is interesting to consider how teaching might differ if the main stakeholders in the process – teachers, learners and parents – were empowered to define what they perceive to be the optimum conditions for quality education.

Fundamentally, however, the framework will stand or fall on the teacher's understanding of the learning process. This also includes the possibilities that are offered to learners to enable them to learn about learning and to understand how they learn. As we aim to support the teacher in this area, we shall continue by looking at this in more detail.

# 4 Dynamic teaching, dynamic learning

In a chapter on differentiation and inclusion (O'Brien, 2000a), an illustration of a dynamic model of learning processes was provided. This three-dimensional model includes external and internal factors that influence a learner's ability to learn within an educational culture. It is referred to as dynamic to reinforce the view that teaching and learning are not static processes: they rely upon relationships. It was proposed that the model would alter in shape according to the learning needs of each individual. O'Brien argues that differentiation has to be seen as an inclusive concept in that it should apply to all pupils. It is not the reactive response of a teacher who suddenly notices that a learner is in difficulty and nor is it only to be seen as a consideration for pupils who are construed as having additional educational needs (AEN). A teacher is responsible for all learners that they teach and therefore differentiation must apply to all. Every learner should learn how to learn and learn about learning.

The key components of O'Brien's model are the four interactive factors that can impact upon a learner's ability to learn. They are:

- Pedagogical
- Emotional
- Cognitive
- Social.

These are not presented in hierarchical order – they are interrelated and interdependent, and operate as a framework for the model. In this chapter we shall look briefly at some of the components of the model before considering at a later point what a teacher can do in relation to differentiation. In order to differentiate the text and to synthesize your thinking, summary details of each section are supplied where appropriate.

The model (Fig. 4.1) begins by representing in a visual form how learning is affected by factors that take place within and outside of the head of the learner:

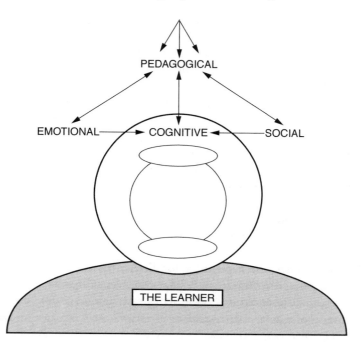

**Figure 4.1 Building the model**

In many ways, what you are about to do is similar to going shopping within the model – looking at various aspects of the model and selecting which of the areas are of particular relevance to you and the learners that you work with. Of course you may well need to go shopping more than once.

## Pedagogical factors

Yes, this involves *you*. The term pedagogy, although used in many countries, is not commonly used in the daily professional language of teachers in the UK. Pedagogical factors are factors that relate to the ethics of teaching as well as to the methodologies and content of teaching. It is the nature of this book that common and specialized pedagogy is being considered throughout but some factors that are highlighted in the dynamic model of learning processes will be considered here.

### Differentiation for autonomy

It has already been asserted that differentiation is a key feature of pedagogical practice. The process of differentiation presents the teacher with a variety of tools. Such tools lay foundations that allow learners to understand the potential for the availability of choices and to make them. One of the aims of education that is commonly highlighted in our discussion with teachers is that all learners, no matter what their learning abilities or disabilities might be, should become autonomous. At times the word 'independent' is offered as an alternative to autonomous, assuming that they have the same meaning and intention. Defining autonomy – a political, cultural, spiritual and philosophical concept – is a complex task. To attempt to unravel and analyse the dimensions that are inherent in the concept of autonomy would be an impossible task in this brief section. This is why only one element is referred to here: choice. A central consideration for any teacher who is planning for differentiation is the choices that will be offered to the learner. The choice-making that is provided through differentiation illuminates a vital stage in becoming autonomous as a learner and as a person. As a learner, the more choices that you can make the less you need to depend upon the control or direction of others. It could be argued that this also frees you from the position of being manipulated by others. As a person, learning to make choices can empower you to deal with dilemmas and make decisions that lead towards outcomes that you have judged to be of benefit to you – hopefully within an ethical framework where others can also benefit. Interdependence would be an ultimate goal in this situation, rather than a singular concern for independence.

The different dimensions of the educational aim of independence must be scrutinized because independence could, of course, arise out of immoral, unethical and unjust actions on the part of the individual. Our contention is that differentiation contributes to autonomy because it allows the learner to gain self-awareness, provides challenge and promotes awareness of choice. The learning that is provided by the teacher should encourage the pupil to, amongst other things, problem-find and problem-solve, to question what is offered to them as objective truth and to reflect upon the answers they can or cannot give when confronted by uncertainty. The learning must also challenge them to explore and question their own belief and value systems. This is most likely to be achieved through interaction with others than through isolated study. It is also more likely to occur when the learning system provides differentiation and education for all. The teacher, and the pedagogical environment that they create, really does contribute to shaping the quality of life for the learner now and in the future. They also contribute to an end that involves enabling all learners to become self-determining members of their communities at the level that they are most capable of achieving.

## Summary

In this section you have been introduced to four interactive factors: pedagogical, social, emotional, cognitive which affect the learner's ability to learn. In seeking to account for these factors, within a differentiated teaching and learning system, key importance is placed upon the need to synthesize these factors in order to enable the learner to develop autonomy and self-awareness.

## Differentiation by teacher

In some situations where learners are defined as requiring additional educational support, the response can be to provide a form of differentiation by teacher. Staffing is seen as the source of a solution to educational difficulties. As a consequence there is an increase in the amount of teachers present in the classroom. The new teacher may be another trained teacher but is more likely to be someone who has no specific training in how to teach. In the UK, the person in this role is generally known as a learning support assistant (LSA). These motivated and poorly paid paraprofessionals can be given the most complex of tasks to undertake as teaching assistants. Although some may be qualified in areas other than pedagogy, many will have no teacher training at all. However, many of them offer high quality teaching and learning (O'Brien and Garner, 2001). In this book we use the term 'teacher' as a term that includes LSAs. The appointment of a new teacher to a problematic situation is, fundamentally, a resource response.

Increasing the number of staff does widen the availability of tools for learning. However, it is a false assumption that increasing the headcount of adults is a guarantee of increased potential for learners to learn. There are causal and practical dimensions that are important here. The extra teacher has to be enabled to understand the cause of the learning difficulty and be able to provide education that will help the learner to overcome the difficulty. They will need training in being able to carry out their professional responsibilities. They will also need to work in a partnership where aims and objectives are clearly communicated. An increase in the presence of humans does not necessarily mean an increase in the quality of learning.

### *Oh no, not the reflective practitioner again!*

The concept of a reflective practitioner is important in relation to differentiation, as reflection is part of the differentiation process. Unfortunately, this term gets applied to so many different contexts, on so many occasions, that its currency is on the brink of becoming devalued. Schon (1991), in his work on reflective practice, proposes that there are different strategies deployed by teachers in problematic situations – those situations where learning has not gone smoothly and deciding how to make it work becomes 'puzzling'. Some strategies, he proposes, are informed by knowledge and allow a teacher to react spontaneously in a given learning context. Even though these strategies demonstrate 'knowing in action', a teacher may find it difficult to offer an explanation as to why they made a decision to use a specific strategy. He argues that, for a teacher to become reflective, the norms that inform decision-making or the theories that are implicit in teacher behaviour have to be analysed. The teacher has to create new understandings about problems by reframing them. Therefore, an element of hindsight can enable a teacher to detach from difficulties. They reflect back on them and hypothesize as to what was taking place. They can then test out new approaches in new situations.

One positive aspect of this type of 'reflecting in practice' is that it reinforces the experimental nature of teaching. It also encourages self-evaluation. This model of a reflective practitioner implies that teaching involves both intuitive and reflective skills. We do not wish to enter the debate as to what the balance between these two dimensions are or should be – is teaching based mostly upon automaticity that is gained through years of personal learning and development or is it mainly intuitive skill? Nor do we wish to engage in a discussion about the flaws in the application of Schon's model to an educational context that can be overprescriptive.

We would like to highlight that critical reflection is another central component in providing differentiation. Reflection on your own will provide for individual development and will hopefully invite joint review and reflection. Collaborative reflection, not just from teams within the school but also with the transdisciplinary network available to the school, adds to the expertise available to improve the quality of learning. Where teachers reflect upon their own practice, in teams, mutual solutions to difficulties can be sought.

Collaborative reflection can also engender a culture within schools where discussion about teaching and learning is given a high profile. How often teachers say to us that they never get enough time to talk about learning. As well as providing development for any learning organization, this collaborative approach also produces fertile ground for action research and the introduction of staff support teams. Through this process the beliefs, values, assumptions and stereotypes that may be endemic within learning systems are open to scrutiny. An open learning system, willing to gain the objective views of those who work within it, will develop in confidence and will allow teachers to take risks. This models learners taking risks too. If teachers are able to manage such systems, where risk-taking is validated by reflection and where reflection empowers them to extend their own thinking about ideology and practice, then learners will be the beneficiaries. We could take a much wider view of the necessity for reflection – many eastern philosophies and religions present the world as impermanent and everchanging. If we are to understand the nature of the world that we live in then the meanings that we create must remain under constant evaluation.

*Summary*
In this section we have looked at the varying roles that exist within teacher–learner systems and especially the role of paraprofessionals. The key importance of clear communication and communication systems, both formal and informal, has been highlighted. The role of *critical reflection* and *collaborative reflection* within all aspects of the system is considered crucial to the task of differentiation.

---

**REFLECTION POINT**

- What are the formal procedures or protocols within your school that enable you to reflect upon your practice?
- What do you think are the influences outside of your school that impinge upon your ability to reflect upon, and alter your practice?
- Think of a time when reflection enabled you to be better at teaching. What did you learn? What did you do differently?

---

## Emotional factors

---

**CASE POINT**

*The circus comes to town*

A man walked into a doctor's surgery one morning. He sat slumped forward in the chair that faced the doctor's desk. The doctor looked up from her papers, did not immediately recognize her patient, and asked, 'How can I help you? What is wrong?' The man proceeded to tell her about how desperately unhappy he was: 'I get up in the morning and look at myself in the mirror. I hate what I see. I look around me at the people in the world going about their daily duties and it all seems so pointless to me. Over the past months I have found that there are times when, for no apparent reason, I find tears streaming down my face. I cannot remember the last time I smiled. I have lost my appetite, I have terrible difficulty sleeping and the future looks so bleak.' The doctor explained that she could prescribe medication for this form of depression, but she had a much better idea. She explained: 'I have always believed laughter to be the best medicine. I have an idea . . . are you aware that there is a travelling circus in town? They are on tour and have artists of the highest international standards. In between each act there is only one clown. He is remarkable. If there is one thing certain in life it is that this clown will make you laugh. I have seen him

➤

---

myself and the laughter from the crowd is almost deafening. My suggestion is that you get a ticket for the circus and go and see the clown. It will make you feel so much better.' The man replied: 'I am sorry doctor, I am afraid that I cannot get a ticket to go and see that clown. It is impossible.' The doctor interrupted him: 'Yes you can, it may be full at weekends but there are tickets available for weekdays.' Her patient explained: 'No, you do not understand doctor . . . I cannot get a ticket to watch the clown because . . . I *am* the clown.'

There are a variety of meanings within this story. The meaning that we would like to highlight is that we cannot make judgements about what people need based upon assumptions or superficial knowledge of who we think they are. You need to see beyond what is 'in your face'. In being a teacher you may find that there are learners who present with challenging behaviour – it is challenging because it restricts their ability to learn or prevents new learning occurring amongst their peers. There are times when this behaviour can be aggressive and threatening – in your face in the real sense. However, we urge the teacher to see beyond the superficial and to consider what can be done to enable the learner to learn. The recognition of the seamless link between behaviour and learning has to be asserted. As with the clown in the story, we cannot assume that the external, acted-out behaviour that we see is related to how the pupil feels inside. We need to consider the reason why someone behaves in a certain way and how differentiation can support them in changing their behaviour. It involves complex analysis. One of the main ways of doing this is to use techniques that allow us to gain access to the inside of the head of the learner so that we can obtain an insight into their subjective reality – what the world looks like to them. There are some learners who construct a relentlessly hostile world around them; there are others who are unable to place their trust in adults. The reasons for this have to be explored so that their emotional state can become less fixed and more fluid. This is a part of the process of providing emotional differentiation.

The teacher will also recognize situations where a learner's initial response to new learning can be highly emotionally charged. It might result in abusive language and threatening behaviour or it might result in impulsive responses and an apparent lack of interest. There are times when the emotional response of a learner is intended to cause a confrontation with the teacher. In Chapter 1 we referred to the psychological reasons as to why this might occur. The teacher can emotionally differentiate by making a mental decision not to be enticed into such confrontations. This is akin to using a metaphor and applying it mentally at times when challenging behaviour is occurring. One such technique is to tell yourself that you must 'drop the ball'. You do not intend to play the game that the learner is trying to get you to play and so you apply a visual metaphor to prevent you from doing so. The situations where emotional difficulties restrict learning will be covered in more detail in Chapter 8.

## Summary

In this section the need to look at and beyond behaviour and to consider the one in relation to the other is focused upon. The importance of remaining fluid and flexible in your own thinking is highlighted. The ability to look at reality with a new eye, from the point of view of the emotional state and stance of others, is also presented as an important part of the differentiation process.

## Susceptibility

Learning challenges our notion of self. Whenever we engage in the process of new learning we are open to feeling susceptible as learning exposes our own vulnerability. A single task that involves learning can call into question our whole notion of who we are, what we are able to achieve and what we might feel able to do in the future. This claim may seem extravagant. However, if you think of the last time that you tried to learn something new and encountered a difficulty, consider the nature, duration and intensity of your emotional reaction. The context in which the learning took place should also be analysed, as your emotional response may have been context-specific. For example, if you felt pressurized to complete the task under the watchful gaze of someone who could already do it or were clearly expected to do it in a specific time and could not do so. You may have responded by becoming angry or you may have given up on the task in hand completely. In our training with teachers we have found that it is very easy for the intervention of an adult who can already do a task to cause people who are attempting a task to feel uncomfortable.

Despite the fact that teachers often have a sophisticated range of skills to call upon, a fear of doing the task incorrectly can cause them to become introvert, embarrassed and irritated. Leaning into the physical space of the learner, looking at their work, and walking away without commenting upon it can create this sense of susceptibility. It can also cause the physical reaction of the curved arm covering the adult's view of the work. The issue of the power that is invested in someone who knows what you do not know is evident in these situations.

Susceptibility can also become clear through the use of inappropriate questioning. For example, a teacher might ask 'why have you done it that way?' This may cause the learner to think that there is an implicit unspoken ending to this question which is '. . . because that is the wrong way to do it'. It may not have been the intention of the teacher for the question to be negative but from the inflection of the teacher's voice, the body language of the teacher, or previous experience the learner processes it this way. Asking questions is crucial in providing demand during a task and positive questioning can help to counteract learner susceptibility. Questions like 'Can you explain that further to me?', 'Why do you feel so strongly about that?', 'Have you noticed that . . . ?' or 'Tell me what you mean by . . . ? will encourage the learner to clarify their own thinking as well as offering them an insight into their own learning. For learners who experience emotional difficulties, susceptibility may become apparent before a task is attempted. The teacher might deal with this type of anticipatory anxiety through the process of differentiation by explanation – ensuring that all learners are clear as to what an activity involves and that all learners will be able to achieve success during the task.

## Summary

This section highlights how the actions of the teacher can affect the actions and learning outcomes of learners. We all, as teachers, need to be able to become aware of our own susceptibilities and how these might affect our practice. We also need to facilitate the development of this vital skill in learners.

## Learning experience

We all have an individual learning biography. This will have been compiled by us as individuals and will contain a vast amount of information about our learning history and experience. It will be processed and constructed by us. It will have a direct influence upon our current self-confidence and competence as a learner. How a person perceives her or himself as a learner will impact upon their personal constructs. This will have a direct link with how the person performs as a learner. This psychology of personal constructs will be dealt with in Chapter 5. A brief example will suffice here. Whilst working in a primary classroom in London, one of the authors met a nine-year-old girl who told him that she hated school because she could not learn. She said that she had always found learning difficult and she had reached a point where she did not care anymore. She had been permanently excluded from one school and was teetering on the brink of a permanent exclusion from her current school – mainly because of her challenging behaviour. Every morning when she entered the school she felt as if she was not only a useless learner but also a bad person. Here are some of the comments that she made when explaining her difficulties. They provide an insight into her own construct of herself as a learner and into the challenging job that her teachers have in teaching her:

- I am everything bad that you can say to me.
- I hate myself and what I do.
- It is difficult for me but nobody realizes.
- I should never have come to school.
- The horriblest person is better than me.
- I cannot do anything.
- I am a piece of crap.

The impact of past and present learning experience (in this case, in and out of school) is brutally clear. This girl and her family may need a level of psychological support that is not available through the school, but she is still the responsibility of the teachers when she is attending school. They have the complex task of changing her negative self-image through the use of differentiated learning experiences. By their own admission, they had not seen how the curriculum plays such an important role in emotional development and are currently setting individual targets for her to focus upon demonstrating to her that she can learn. When considering emotional factors that affect learning we cannot afford to ignore how learners view their past and present experiences.

*Summary*
In this section the importance of considering the learning biographies of learners, and teachers, is dealt with. A link is made to various chapters in which views of self are dealt with in greater detail.

---

**REFLECTION POINT**

- To what degree do you think that learners who experience emotional and behavioural difficulties want to behave as they do? To what extent do you think it is a choice that they make?
- How does the learning system in which you work gain insights into how the learners view:
  a) learning
  b) teaching
  c) the school?
- It is proposed that a learner's history is a component in creating emotional responses to new learning situations. How far do you agree with this? To what extent does a focus upon previous difficulties allow a learner to make a fresh start?

---

# Cognitive factors

## Styles and strategies
Chapter 7 deals with cognition in more detail. In recent years an interest has developed in learning styles and strategies. This is reflected in the increased availability of educational literature in this area. Learning styles illustrate how a learner processes information and makes judgements about their own learning capabilities. Learning strategies relate to how the learner reacts to teacher decisions about how the learning environment is structured. In terms of the notions of fixed and fluid thinking that appear in this book, learning style could be said to be more fixed than learning strategy which can be seen as fluid. There are 'tests' and checklists, some far more comprehensive than others, which aim to inform the learner of their main

modality in learning – auditory, visual or kinaesthetic. By answering a range of questions about their habits and preferences the person completing the questionnaire can establish whether they mainly learn through visual means, through listening, or through movement and touch. Whilst some of these tests may be crude, for example in that they separate modalities, the key point being made is that learners have a preferred modality for learning, as do teachers. In relation to differentiation, an analysis of the preferred learning modality of the teacher is important because it may be that a teacher who is a 'visual learner' may well teach mainly within this modality. This can be unhelpful when they are communicating to a range of learners who might prefer a different modality. This is a common critique of the 'lecture' format for teaching. A badly delivered lecture can over-rely upon one method of teaching, be underpinned by assumptions about how learners learn and may lack variety of content.

Flavell (1979) used the term 'metacognition' to indicate that the brain could do more than just remember and process information. For example, the processing involved when learning to drive a car is different to the processing once you can drive. The conscious elements of the brain can enable us to learn about learning and think about thinking. This he referred to as metacogniton and asserts that we can learn about our own cognitive processes. Through this process we gain more insight into our own potential as learners. Our contention is that learners should be provided with tasks which enable them to learn how to learn and to be aware of their own ability to think in an analytical and creative manner. We do not believe that there are any single exceptions to this. In a lesson with a group of young children, one of the authors asked the learners if they knew a popular children's joke: 'What would you do if you wanted to weigh a whale?' The answer, 'Take it to a whale-weigh station.' A discussion then ensued about what a whale-weigh station might look like, where it would be, who would work there and why. The task was to consider how to get a whale to the station safely and humanely and weigh it. One group managed to design a whale sling framework with a shower of water constantly pouring down from the top of it so that the whale could be transported across land. Another designed a portable station that could be submerged for the whale to swim into it. A focus upon the type of thinking and learning involved in such a task can provide information about the metacognitive abilities of children in the group.

*Summary*

This section focuses on cognitive factors in learning, especially in terms of differentiating to accommodate the optimum modalities of learners. The importance of fluid and flexible teacher–learner strategies is highlighted. The concept of metacognition was introduced emphasizing the importance of learning how to learn.

---

### DIALOGUE POINT

- Talk to someone about learning styles and strategies. How clear are they as to what they mean?
- With a colleague, plan a task that challenges learners to think in a creative manner. Discuss how they could improve and develop their own thinking. How could they evaluate what they have learned?

---

## Social factors

### Social inclusion

Learning is not simply a psychological process; it is a social process with social outcomes. What you learn and how you learn it provides information to you about your status as a person as well as a learner. The status that you derive from your education will depend upon how connected and included you feel in it and how intimate and grounded it was. The term inclusion here does refer to the philosophical commitment to enable all learners to learn within one diverse learning community and the manner in which a plan for a whole group can ensure that individual needs are not sacrificed. However, it is not our intention to explore global issues such as the fact that there are still millions of children around the world who receive no formal education at all – an example of the extremes of disconnected and distant learning. The concept of inclusion in relation to social factors involves:

- Being included in a learning system rather than being alienated from it.
- Being included in the learning that takes place within the system.

- Being included in learning about learning.
- Being included by having a voice that is listened to.
- Being included by feeling and knowing that you are included.
- Being included in understanding your identity as a learner and as a person.
- Being included by being empowered to make choices.
- Being included within your learning community.
- Being included within the wider community.

The feeling and knowledge of inclusion is heavily influenced by social factors. First, social interaction has to be seen as a component of a differentiated environment. You need peers and others to interact with so that you can extend your ability to learn. It has been proposed earlier in this chapter that, at an institutional level, collaborative problem solving will have wider positive outcomes than independent problem solving. This also applies at a classroom management level. Learners can benefit from interacting with each other as it also allows them to teach each other too. Of course, there will be issues for teachers who teach learners that have difficulties working in groups – the learner who is not wanted by a group or the learner who chooses not to work within groups. There are many techniques that teachers can deploy to differentiate social settings and groupings within the classroom. Jigsawing and snowballing are examples.

Jigsawing allows groups to gain information that only becomes complete when each group has joined with each other to form a body of knowledge. This allows groups to identify the roles that individuals and pairs will have within the group as well as enabling them to develop expertise in specific areas. Through communicating with members of the other groups the bigger picture is obtained. This might be used in an art lesson, for example, by different groups painting aspects of a whole group picture that is brought together and the totality of the process and outcome is jointly celebrated. This gives everybody a chance to experience the feeling of being an expert.

Snowballing is similar to the research technique that has the same name, where information is gained from one individual who then suggests another individual who could provide additional relevant information or viewpoints. This sampling technique can be applied to groups of learners in a classroom. Individuals can be used as informants, or where learners are less confident, it can be organized so that learners work in pairs. The snowball effect allows a progressive build up of interaction and information, until, again, a bigger picture becomes clear. A learning community will deliberately create a variety of situations where social interaction promotes opportunities for learning. It will also plan for individuals to receive positive interaction within this process. As we will see in following chapters there is a theoretical basis for social interaction being a tool for assessing and developing the emotional and cognitive potential of learners.

### Summary

This section deals with considerations around issues of status within teacher–learner systems. The notion of inclusion is considered and the varying scale at which inclusion needs to be differentiated is addressed. There are many strategies for building inclusion and status; two have been detailed here.

### Expectation

High expectation is a regular category that arises out of research into what makes effective teaching. High expectation can be implicitly transmitted by various means, such as the pace of the lesson, the incremental nature of learning content and the demands that are placed upon individuals and groups. Such implicit means of broadcasting expectation may not be picked up by all learners. There are times when the broadcasting of expectation has to be explicit. Where there are learners with behaviour difficulties, discussions about expectations for enabling all learners to learn are essential. However, spoken words can soon be forgotten and it is often helpful to display agreed expectations in a visual form. For certain groups of learners, in relation to well-matched learning outcomes, behavioural text may suffice. For others it may be necessary to display visual images or photographs of what the expected behaviour looks like. In this way, the teacher can recognize it when it is taking place, draw a learner's attention to it, and offer praise. For example, some learners may immediately understand the concept 'respect others' and what it means. For others it may be necessary to provide visual examples of how respecting others is achieved. The broadcasting of expectation is vital in contexts where learners move from teacher to teacher throughout the day.

## Summary

In this section the benefits of differentiating expectations as a means of structuring teacher–learner interactions was considered. The fact that different learners need different support structures around common and individual expectations was explored. The key point of making high expectations explicit is focused upon.

### Social class

We know that issues associated with social class – such as ingrained unemployment, lack of healthcare facilities, chronic poverty or immense wealth – can affect a person's ability to learn. This has to be taken seriously within schools. It is astonishing how some learners actually manage to attend school at all when their home circumstances are taken into account. This is not intended to convey an assumption that all children who have difficult home circumstances struggle to attend school. It is a reference to real life domestic conditions such as those where teenagers might be responsible for organizing the family for school while their alcoholic parent remains asleep, or where young children in large families sleep on the floor. How some learners complete homework in homes where domestic violence or categories of abuse are rife is also remarkable. The concept of education for all is brought into disrepute when learners who come from such backgrounds receive limited opportunity within systems where some groups are afforded more value than others are. In such a culture, minority groups such as travellers, refugees, children whose care is the responsibility of the social services, and the disabled, for example, can suffer negative consequences. They experience the rhetoric rather than reality of education for all.

This type of marginalization of groups promotes stereotypes and scapegoats. It criticizes and eventually rejects difference. It begins the process of removing opportunities for individuals to take up their rights and allows tolerance to have a greater value than acceptance. This allows superior groups to monopolize privilege and power and to establish preferential and protected identities. The outcome is exclusion and dislocation.

*Summary*

In this section the impact of socio-economic factors was introduced and explored. Awareness and consideration of issues concerning social inclusion and exclusion are seen as being of key importance in providing differentiation. A link was made between being marginalized as a learner and being stereotyped within society. Therefore differentiation is seen as being a key factor in preventing social exclusion.

---

### REFLECTION POINT

- What support does your school offer for pupils who experience difficulties at home?
- What support does it offer to pupils who have difficulties in terms of social interaction with others?
- To what degree is it your job to deal with such a problem?
- Does everybody agree? Why? Why not?

---

*Conclusion*

This chapter began with Figure 4.1 illustrating how learning is affected by internal and external factors. The model is represented in complete form as Figure 4.2 (see page 70). Look at the difference between the two figures. It is when all of the four factors are unified and integrated, in relation to the learning needs of a specific individual, that grounded and intimate learning can take place. The top of the triangle represents the point of connectivity for inclusion.

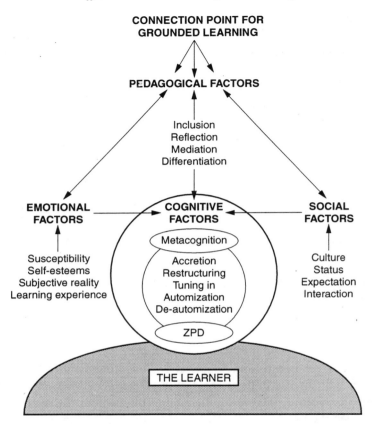

Figure 4.2  **A model of dynamic teaching and dynamic learning**

# 5 Personal constructs and differentiation

Let us now take you into an English lesson in an urban high school. A group of fourteen- and fifteen-year-olds are reading Shakespeare's *A Midsummer Night's Dream*. Various parts have been assigned to different readers who were selected by the teacher. The teacher has done this in a sensitive fashion. He has also explained to the learners that what they are about to read will be funny. One of the authors of this book is present in the room. He is observing the style and nature of the interactions of Paul, who encounters social communication difficulties. Although observing Paul, the observer's attention was diverted onto the class in general. The reason for this was that the teacher began explaining to the group that, after reading part of a scene, he would be asking questions of specific individuals. A sense of tension seemed to have been caused by this statement because he did not indicate which learners were going to be questioned. Everyone was on guard.

They began reading the first scene in Act 3. This is set in a wood where the queen of the fairies is lying asleep. A group of characters enter the wood. The teacher explains that their names are typical of characters from Shakespeare plays: Quince, Snug, Bottom, Flute, Snout and Starveling. The scene proceeds with the villagers meeting in the wood to rehearse a play called 'Pyramus and Thisby'. As they rehearse the play, Puck enters the scene and observes for a little while, before deciding to cause mischief. Bottom, who plays the part of Pyramus, has gone off stage, only to miss his cue to re-enter.

Kyle, who is reading the part of Quince, begins: 'Pyramus enter; your cue is past; it is, never tire.' The teacher, taking the role of narrator, reads aloud: 'Re-enter Puck, and Bottom, with an ass's head.' Kyle then reads in a voice that is trembling with fear: 'O monstrous! O strange! We are haunted. Fly, masters! Help!' The teacher replies by reading out the stage direction: 'exeunt Clowns.'

At this point, the teacher stopped the reading. He entered into a discussion of what had occurred in the scene, seeking to add understanding to the learners' appreciation of what was happening by setting exploratory questions. He was aware that the language that is used by Shakespeare needs to be processed so that both it, and the plot, can be understood before the learners continue reading the scene.

After several question to various members of the class he looked around and then asked Jay: 'When Bottom re-entered with Puck what had happened?' Jay did not answer. The teacher presented the question in another form 'Jay, try to think back to the story, when Bottom re-entered with Puck . . . what had happened *to his head?*' Jay took the cue from the teacher to look at the text again, doing so in a furtive manner. Looking thoughtful and glancing around nervously at his attentive peers, he looked directly at the teacher, before saying in an anxious voice: '. . . erm . . . (takes a deep breath) . . . has his head turned into his ass, sir?'

Why should this true and amusing misunderstanding happen? How can we hope to explain the unpredictability of human reactions in learning and teaching situations? Clearly a complete and accurate reading of every situation is impossible, but we are aiming to provide you with tools which will help shed light on such incidents.

---

### ACTION POINT

Before reading on, talk with a colleague and analyse why Jay may have produced this response.

- In your opinion what was going on in his mind? To what extent can you know?
- Do you think he is looking for laughs or is it a 'serious' response? Check your perceptions against our perceptions set out below. Remember nobody knows *the* answer, not even Jay. Compare your analysis with ours.

---

The analysis of learning errors enables teachers to be in a better position to aid new learning. It allows them to minimize or prevent opportunities of low value learning in the future. We recognize that for many of us such moments as the one described above are gems of human ingenuity and should be celebrated as such, which is the spirit in which this story is offered here. It is offered for analysis through an action point, not to belittle a learner.

Let us look again at Jay's responses and try to discover why he may have replied in this way. *A Midsummer Night's Dream* is an engaging play and is one of the more immediately accessible of Shakespeare's works, especially to younger audiences. Even so it is challenging in many ways such as in relation to language, imagery, knowledge, context and plot. In other words learners have to work hard at 'learning' it and teachers have to work hard at 'teaching' it. Many agree that there is a clear value and utility to be derived from experiencing the play in the many forms of media through which it is now available.

Jay and the rest of the class are being challenged by this teaching at many points, at many levels and in many ways. How can and does Jay seek to make sense of this dense piece of learning? We would say that he does this by relating it to previous learning. He uses what he knows in order to 'get a handle' on this new learning. To return briefly to the psychoanalytic theory presented in Chapter 2 he looks for ways of metabolizing his learning to make it more digestible.

He has heard the play read out aloud and is processing it as best he can. He has heard the teacher's explanation and is processing this also. He also remembers the teacher saying that the scene is humorous. He has heard the other learners' answers to questions and has heard the teacher using these answers to generate new explanations and new learning. He still has not quite made sense of it by the time that the teacher decides to ask him a question, in order to encourage his processing further. The purpose of being asked by the teacher to formulate your learning in the term of a rebroadcast to the teacher and the class is tantamount to the teacher placing the learner in the role of the teacher. The teacher is, in effect, saying 'now you teach me what you have been taught'. Further to this, the act of having to formulate an answer calls for a synthesis of learning. In this case, Jay has had to pull it all together very quickly. Of course this cognitive element is overlaid by an emotional element that is connected with self-esteems, group dynamic, teacher expectations and peer-group pressure for example. The learner is asked to assume a new role, as teacher, even for the briefest moment.

Owing to being placed under the spotlight, many learners experience answering questions verbally in class as extremely stressful, although it can also be rewarding for them. The style of questioning that the teacher adopts can exacerbate or reduce this feeling of being stressed. Fluid questioning, allowing for the development of thinking and the exploration of learning, is a powerful technique for differentiation. On the other hand, fixed questioning – often looking for straightforward answers that do not require further discussion – is often applied as a classroom management technique.

Jay needs to build an answer. He scans the pages again, reading quickly, catches sight of and remembers that one of the players is called Bottom. Bottom . . . where has he heard that word before? He moves on and reads that Bottom comes in with an ass's head. He ponders this as it is harder to make meaning from it. What is an ass in this context? Is this the part that is meant to be humorous? He considers the word 'ass'. He has heard it before, for example in the more common transatlantic usage. But has he heard this term used in any other ways? He reviews his experience and knowledge for clues, but draws a blank and has to return to the usage he *has* heard. But then given the first meaning you cannot have an 'ass's head'. So this leaves him with a problem which needs further thought.

He looks for a clue that will confirm this line of thinking and suddenly sees a link with the word 'Bottom'. He considers the text again: 're enters with an 'ass's head'. He checks out what he has got so far – a random collection of misinterpretations. Although they are essentially misinterpretations, learning and experience have informed them. Jay continues to work hard to synthesize an answer.

He now feels that he is arriving at an answer but becomes aware of a further problem. He realizes that there are issues and consequences related to saying a word like 'ass' to a teacher. Jay is the type of person who feels that you cannot talk to teachers like that even if they appear to have invited you to do so. A further problem – surely a teacher would never encourage you to say such a word to them?

The teacher, in trying to be helpful, then provides another question adding a little more detail about what had happened. He encourages Jay to focus upon what has happened to Bottom's head. There is also an expectation that the teacher is doing this because he wants an answer soon – placing Jay under further pressure. All of this has been happening at high speed and now there is only one answer that Jay can process and confirm in his own thinking which is verified against the text. He is not convinced this is correct, either cognitively or socially, hence his anxious voice. It is simply the best answer he can give in this context and at this stage, based on his past and current learning. Therefore he formulates the answer and informs the teacher that he thinks that Bottom's head must have changed into his ass!

A footnote to this analysis is to comment further on the value of observers and observation in the process of aiding good practice in differentiation. The observer may see and interpret actions and inter-action that are not available to the teacher. We emphasize here that teaching partnerships should be creative about who takes the 'teacher' role and who takes the 'observer' role, why and when. It is important always to remain clear as to which role each person takes and how these roles will complement each other. Clarity about how information will be fed back in a positive, helpful and non-threatening manner is important too. The reason for this is that effective role def-inition and mutual communication will ultimately improve the teacher–learner value.

We have argued that Jay's response, though flawed, was based upon high intentions, motivation to respond correctly in emotional, social and cognitive terms, as well as his previous knowledge, experience and learning. The question arising from this is *how* does he (and by inference how do we all) synthesize and formulate such experiences and learning into coherent systems of understanding?

## Eyeballing the world

In order to address this rather large question we now begin to explore a psychological theory, Personal Construct Psychology (PCP), and its associated principles and language. Of course there are many theories which could be presented, but we chose this one because teachers have found it informative, workable and offering information that is relevant to differentiation. At a later point details of two small-scale enquiries amongst teachers and learners will be presented. We have deliberately chosen not to present rigorous quantitative or qualitative large-scale academic research but to provide insight into new ways of looking within and without learning systems – something that a teacher can engage in within an action research project or school-based investigation. By using new tools and new ways of looking, teachers become more informed and thereby more able to question practice and beliefs in an open manner. We have argued previously that this is one of the main principles underpinning a healthy approach to differentiated learning in open and proactive learning systems. Having said this we have sought to avoid the following sections being dependent on advanced knowledge, grounding or experience in psychology. The main focus will be upon 'eyeballing' – looking closer at what is taking place, then looking again and again so that meaning can be made. Providing a very brief overview of a psychological theory means that we cannot provide full and detailed conceptual and theoretical explanations, which you will need at some stage, in order to further develop your thinking and understanding. To address this need, we include recommended reading regarding PCP in the bibliography.

## Personal constructs

We wish to look more closely at how people seek to understand, process, perceive and make sense of the world. It has been asserted earlier that everybody continually seeks to make sense of the world, everybody is capable of learning. We need to think about *how* they do this because the process of 'sense making' provides the raw motivation underpinning the human imperative to learn. There are many belief systems and theories available that propose to enlighten us as to how we can construct and develop the meaning of our world – the most obvious being religious or political systems. PCP, with a theoretical base that emanates from the work of George Kelly in the 1950s, is one psychological theory that deals with measuring how people see the world and make meaning of it. Kelly (1955) felt that everyone behaved like an amateur scientist in the way that they observed and experienced the world. Like scientists, we hypothesize about what is taking place, test our hypothesis, and then revise our views based on the results of our testing. Kelly felt that this construing and testing of theories was *the* basic human activity. He used the word 'construe' to describe an active process rather than just reacting to what is there. So 'construe' is deliberately chosen over, for example, a word like 'perceive'. We might better understand this idea of construing by considering associated notions lying behind words such as analyse, interpret, understand, translate or even believe.

It is a short step to move from construing the world around us to becoming aware that we all as individuals develop a system of 'constructs' or hypotheses, which we continually test and revise on the basis of whether they prove meaningful and useful to us or not. Let us consider the girl who is mentioned in Chapter 4. She sees herself as being completely useless and worthless and states that no matter whom we think of as being the most horrible person in the world – she is worse than that. This is how she has constructed a view of herself. She tests this out daily in her interactions with her peers and with her teachers. She may do so by being abusive, physically aggressive or refusing to work. Whatever her actions, they are all used to test out this constructed view of the world through the reactions of others. If people react by reinforcing her own view of how bad she is, by their words or behaviour, then her beliefs about what she is are confirmed. If people make an effort to convince her that she is wrong in her hypothesis about her self, and demonstrate that she can be seen in a positive light, then her hypothesizing will have to change to one that is more meaningful in relation to the responses that she receives. It might be a gradual process, but she may eventually believe that she is much better than 'the horriblest person in the world'.

## What are constructs?

One method of beginning to understand constructs is by thinking of words that we might associate with them. Examples of such words include models, frameworks, building, combining and assembling – all words that point towards things that are constructed physically or by the mind.

- *Constructs* in the sense used here are the associations we make to understand the world by testing it against our hypotheses. These associations are connected with the phenomena that constitute our world – elements
- *Elements* may be in the form of people, events, relationships or places, for example. For each 'element' we therefore associate a finite number of constructs. From this we can see that we can only have constructs in relation to an element.

Therefore personal constructs are the dimensions that we use to conceptualize and understand aspects of our second-by-second existence. They afford us all the ability to predict, to know what to expect, and to test whether events or relationships, for example, were as we thought they would be.

PCP proposes that we all check how much sense we have made of the world by seeing how well that 'sense' enables us to anticipate it. For example, someone might believe that people with thin eyebrows are aggressive. They may also believe that people with thick eyebrows are passive. The constructs here are thin eyebrows and thick eyebrows, passive and aggressive. Thus we all strive for *personal meanings*. To aid our understanding of constructs Kelly argued that it is useful to see them as having two poles: a pole of affirmation and a contrast pole. The previous example could be represented this way:

Thick eyebrows ⋯⋯⋯⋯⋯⋯⋯⋯⋯ thin eyebrows

Passive ⋯⋯⋯⋯⋯⋯⋯⋯ Aggressive

As there are two poles they are referred to as 'bipolar' constructs. They provide us with an insight into how meaning can be generated through contrast. Each person thereby has access to a number of constructs, which they use to evaluate the phenomena that constitute their world. Our contention is that this is exactly what Jay was doing in the English lesson – considering the constructs that make up his world, analysing them and providing an answer based upon the meaning that he had made.

## The value of finding out about constructs

Why should this psychological theory be useful in a learning system? Fundamentally it offers a method of enquiry for finding out what people believe, how and why. For example, I may want to find out about how one learner perceives other learners in my classroom. I may wish to find out how well a learner with a physical disability is being socially included. I may wish to find out how colleagues approach the teaching of a specific subject or how 'early years' teachers understand the development of young children. I may wish to analyse how a colleague carries out a specific role or how policies are being developed and implemented. The list is endless. Kelly describes ways of gaining and measuring personal constructs. One method is known as the triadic method and is described in the following case point.

## CASE POINT

*One method of gaining constructs*

A teacher is undertaking some action research in her own class-room. She is trying to find out how learners perceive each other. She is doing this because there are a wide range of physical and cognitive needs in her group and she is interested in finding out how children perceive difference and diversity. Once she has gained her information she intends to use it to apply a differentiated approach to organizing learners into groups. She has also assumed that she may have to provide some lessons that encompass disability awareness and wishes to check out if her assumption is correct. She is interviewing children individually and applies Kelly's triadic method. Here is a step-by-step breakdown of what she does:

1. The learner is asked to name a number of learners who are significant to them.

2. Each time a name is mentioned it is written down on a card. Only one name is written on each card. (These names are, in fact, the 'elements' that were referred to earlier.)

3. The learner is asked to arrange these cards into groups of three. The instruction is that within the group two must be similar in some way – but crucially, they must be different from the third. The learner, not the teacher, defines how these groupings are made and organizes the three cards: two are put together and one is left on its own. (The way in which they are alike and different form the 'constructs' that were referred to earlier.)

4. The learner is then asked to explain the similarities and differences. The teacher has noticed that the learner who has been selected as different is someone who has cerebral palsy. She assumes that this will be relevant. The teacher asks why the groupings have been organized in this way. The learner replies: 'These two are similar because they are quiet and this one is different because he talks a lot.' The similarities (being quiet) form the 'affirmative' pole of the construct and the difference (talking a lot) forms the contrasting pole – the 'negative' pole.

➤

5. The teacher then draws a bipolar diagram like this (choosing to use the learner's words):

    Quiet ································· talks a lot

6. She may then delve further into these constructs if she wants to. She can do this by adding a rating scale. Each element is rated on a scale defined by the two construct poles, which are set out along what is commonly called a 'Salmon line', named after the researcher who developed this application. If this is an area that she is interested in, she may decide to use a grading system, for example using numbers one to seven (with one being 'quiet' and seven meaning 'talking a lot') to see how learners identify each other within this category.

## Teachers and their constructs – how do they see learners?

Given this brief case point, we now wish to present some applications of these techniques that we have made within learning systems. As stated above, these are not presented within a framework of academic rigour and analysis, as this is not the intention. What we seek to illustrate is an enquiring attitude and one method of enquiry.

We were interested in how teachers construe learners who encounter emotional and behavioural difficulties (EBD). This interest is set against a global social and political impetus towards full inclusion and a critical debate about the parameters and limits of social inclusion and exclusion (O'Brien, 2001). Research in the UK suggests that young males – especially those of African-Caribbean origin and those who are identified as having additional educational needs – are over represented in exclusion figures. It also indicates that most permanent exclusions from school are likely to be boys excluded at ages fifteen or sixteen owing to perceived EBD (DfEE, 1998). Our interest was in how to elicit constructs from teachers about the learners they interact with, whose learning value (for themselves and the wider community) is adversely affected by their difficulties.

We proceeded by generating constructs from a small pilot group of teachers. They were female and male and worked in primary and secondary education. Issues of confidentiality prevent us from naming them or their schools. The basis for gaining constructs was a loose and free conversation using the triadic method described above. The interview proceeded by way of a free-form conversation that began with an explanation of PCP and the triadic method. Wherever possible this took the form of a narrative interview, with the interviewer encouraging subjects to tell stories and to assist the aim of clarifying and developing stories, as a way of delving into their constructs.

Almost immediately, each teacher made a distinction in their own minds between learners who 'were EBD' and 'were not EBD'. They had a range of names for the learners who were 'EBD' including disowned, disturbed, maladjusted, disaffected, disordered and naughty. The teachers were telling us that they had a range of constructs regarding those learners they construe as encountering 'EBD', apparently ones that are indicating what is 'wrong' or 'at fault' with them. They also had a range of constructs relating to learners who were not EBD. In their own minds they clearly differentiate between learners.

### What did they say?

By re-interviewing the pilot group and eyeballing the data, we were able to gather a common set of constructs and explore them further with a wider range of the teachers. This was done by the use of a rating scale. Clearly there were issues of research bias and prejudice to be considered. From this further work we identified twenty-four bipolar constructs relating to the element EBD. The affirmative pole is set out on the left and the contrast pole is on the right. A seven-point scale is used to separate the two poles, with 1 being closest to the affirmative or positive pole and 7 being closest to the contrast or negative pole.

1. Hold concentration      …… …… …… …… ……   Lose concentration
2. Compliant               …… …… …… …… ……   Non-compliant
3. Can be motivated        …… …… …… …… ……   Cannot be motivated
4. Recognizes boundaries   …… …… …… …… ……   No boundaries
5. Able to work in a group …… …… …… …… ……   Can only work alone

6. Predictable behaviour      … … … … … … …      Unpredictable behaviour

7. Rarely 'cusses'      … … … … … … … …      Frequently 'cusses'
   (a term for using
   abusive language)

8. Rarely acts out      … … … … … … … …      Frequently acts out

9. Stops talking if asked      … … … … … … … …      Always talking, regardless

10. Few noises when working      … … … … … … …      Lots of noises when working

11. Low physical aggression      … … … … … … …      High physical aggression

12. Appropriately demanding      … … … … … …      Inappropriately demanding

13. Does not personalize events      … … … … … … …      Always personalizes events

14. Manageable      … … … … … … …      Unmanageable

15. Appropriate responses      … … … … … … …      Inappropriate responses

16. Internal peace      … … … … … … …      Internal anger

17. Sense of inner self      … … … … … … …      No sense of inner self

18. 'Other' focused      … … … … … … …      'Self' focused

19. Flexible      … … … … … … …      Stuck

20. Mature      … … … … … … …      Immature

21. Elicits intuitive      … … … … … … …      Elicits intuitive sense of unease
    sense of well being

22. Trustworthy      … … … … … … …      Untrustworthy

23. Can help it      … … … … … … …      Cannot help it

24. Fillable      … … … … … … …      Never full

These are presented here only as an illustration of work on PCP with teachers. We are not suggesting that they produce any conclusions that can be applied generally or universally to construe learners who experience EBD. We are aware that there are many psychological, biological and social definitions that aim to provide – separately and in combination with each other – a way of understanding learners with these and other difficulties. What we are describing and illuminating is how the theory of PCP can be used in a small-scale research enquiry.

## DIALOGUE POINT

- Look at the constructs that the group of teachers has offered in relation to learners who encounter EBD. To what extent do you agree with them?
- Select some of the constructs and explore with a colleague what you think a particular construct actually means. For example, in construct number 12 what do you think 'appropriately demanding' means? To help you with this process we provide an explanation of what the teachers meant in construct 24: 'fillable' describes their feeling that some pupils cannot get enough of learning. Whatever they are given will never be enough to satisfy them and there is always a craving for something extra. By contrast other pupils can be 'filled up', can be satisfied very easily. What do you think of this view?
- To what extent can eliciting teacher views through the use of PCP become helpful in your school?

## Learners and their constructs – how do they see teaching?

There are serious questions to be asked about learning systems that only wish to hear the voice of teachers. What about learners: how are they given a voice in your learning system? PCP can also be applied as a tool of access to learner voice. In the following brief example we show how PCP was used to look at how learners construe the learning system in which they learn. This work took place amongst 500 learners, aged between thirteen and sixteen. The methodology was similar to that previously detailed. The intention is not to explore research design and methodology but to illuminate what you may find if you seek to look and listen in different ways to different parts of your learning system.

We were interested in eliciting construct systems around the element 'lessons I like' and 'lessons I do not like'. Not in terms of specific curriculum areas but in relation to the elements that cause learners to define and understand lessons in this way. Pilot interviews occurred with a random sample of learners. The learners identified over 150 constructs that were reduced to 51 through re-interviewing. Rather than present the complete list of constructs, we have selected some of them as they provide an insight into the voice and perceptions of learners:

1. Lessons are interesting ... ... ... ... ... ... Boring
2. Teacher thinks my ... ... ... ... ... ... Teacher thinks I talk too much
   talk is OK
3. We were told what ... ... ... ... ... ... We were not told rules
   the rules are by the teacher
4. The teacher is never ... ... ... ... ... ... Often sarcastic
   sarcastic
5. The teacher re-explains ... ... ... ... ... ... Never re-explains
   if we do not get it
6. The teacher likes us to ... ... ... ... ... ... Teacher does not like us to ask
   ask if we don't understand
7. It is rarely confusing ... ... ... ... ... ... It is always confusing when the
   when the teacher talks                        teacher talks
8. The teacher is fair ... ... ... ... ... ... Teacher is unfair
9. The teacher sets different ... ... ... ... ... ... The teacher sets the same work for
   work for different people                     everyone.

In the constructs they provided, there were four clear definitions of categories used to define and describe lessons that they like or dislike:

- Constructs relating to the atmosphere of the learning system.
- Constructs that relate to me as an individual learner.
- Constructs that relate to the learning group.
- Constructs that relate to the teacher.

### What do learners say?

What we were interested in were those constructs that learners particularly associate with lessons they like, the inference being that if they like the lesson the 'value' of the teaching and learning is likely to be higher than if they do not like it. On this basis our analysis suggested that twelve constructs were commonly associated with lessons they liked. From this information we were able to gain data as to what learners construed as being positive about learning systems. This allowed us to formulate what this group of learners might say as a collective answer to the question: 'What type of lessons do you like?' We have talked about voice and therefore, rather than list the constructs, we have chosen to present a verbal statement. Also we have reworded it slightly to fit in with the terminology that is common across this book, but no other detail or content has been changed.

> We prefer learning systems where the teacher–learner interactions are interesting and the class is quiet – but not all of the time. The lessons are regularly interesting and we learn a lot in them because of this. The teacher is in a constant mood, likes what they are teaching and is not too unpredictable. Learners get on with their learning amongst groups of their peers, not on their own. The learners listen when the teacher talks. The teacher and the learners respect each other. The teacher explains the rules so that the group can settle down quickly to work and know what they have to do. The teacher rarely shouts, is friendly but in charge, and marks work with helpful comments.

This formulation may sound too good to be true but is based upon our use, one use, of PCP research giving a voice to learners within a learning system.

---

**REFLECTION POINT**

Read the above quotation carefully.

- It is not represented as a valid or reliable representation of what all learners of this age group would say. However, in general, is this what you would expect learners of this age to say? To what degree does it have implications for practice?
- What do you think learners of a younger or older age group might say? Why? What assumptions cause you to make this proposition?
- In what ways do the answers to the above questions raise issues about differentiation?

In some ways the content of our formulation was not really the main point. We would ask what *you* currently know about the views of learners in your learning system. How do you know what you know? Is it based on assumption or have you gathered information? When did you last listen to the voice of learners? When did your learning system last listen? How is the listening carried out and why?

One last detail that emerged from this work was that we found that learners who found it harder to take value from lessons, those characterized as having a learning difficulty, tended to use the constructs by going to the extremes of the poles much more regularly. Our tentative hypothesis was that this might occur as a result of them employing inefficient construct systems that struggle to cope with new experiences. It may be therefore that some learners experience serial destruction and invalidation of their constructs through forms of perceived failure: by not understanding, by lack of motivation, by the behaviour and comments of teachers, peers and parents and by wider learning systems. Of course this is no more than a gut feeling, a hunch, and requires a great deal of further exploration and analysis. However, it does indicate the thought processes that create new routes for enquiry and differentiation.

---

**ACTION POINT**

This chapter begins with an analysis of a teaching and learning interaction. You were invited to complete your own analysis of this before moving on to read our analysis.

As learning is a cyclical process we ask you to re-engage, with a colleague, in interpreting the classroom scenario that follows. What answers do you arrive at when you try to interpret what could have happened to produce this outcome?

We have not attempted to provide our own interpretation; it is your joint interpretation that is important.

---

## Renaissance man

Another real-life example takes us into a classroom where a teacher is teaching a history lesson with a group of learners who are eleven years old. The teacher has been using the Italian Renaissance as an example of cultural change and innovation. She cites details of famous places and people, focusing on the life and times of Leonardo da Vinci – her favourite artist. She talks about his upbringing, his decision to become a vegetarian and refers to him as 'one of the smartest guys who ever lived on earth'. The teacher hands out images downloaded from different Internet sites to show sketches he made of flying machines, combat devices and machines for travelling under the sea. She then divulges to the class that not only was he an outstanding scientist and engineer but he was also a famous artist and sculptor. The class is introduced to, and talks about, some of his paintings. For every painting the learners explore, the teacher knows the dates when they were painted. She has selected one in particular to focus upon: *La Gioconda*, better known as *The Mona Lisa*.

We are swiftly approaching the territory where the teacher's evident enthusiasm is in danger of creating information overload for the learners. Luckily, one of the learners interrupts. She points out that the woman in the picture is smiling and asks what she is smiling about. Another learner argues that she is not smiling – claiming that she is worried or nervous and that is why her lips are so tense. A debate ensues.

The teacher enjoys this discussion and allows it to run its course. Then, moving on to another stage in the lesson she begins to illustrate the importance of Christian imagery to painters at this time. Not surprisingly, the artist whose work is chosen to illustrate this is also Leonardo da Vinci. The class looks at his painting entitled *The Last Supper*. In an excited voice the teacher tells the group that the artist began this painting in 1495 and that it took years to complete. The learners are staggered, they can not imagine spending so long on one piece of work. How did he do it?

The learners were set a task of writing a small obituary, printed in an imaginary Renaissance newspaper, recalling the life of da Vinci. The learners were informed that they could include anything they wanted to in this account of his life and achievements. Various material and technological resources were to hand and the learners set about the task with collective interest. The teacher moved between groups offering nuggets of historical information. As a way of drawing the lesson to a close the teacher gathered the whole group together to recapitulate the content and learning points of the lesson. Various members of the class were asked if they would like to read their work aloud. Some talked about his relationship with his father;

others provided evidence of his genius in many areas, and some chose to focus on the detail, quality and innovative style of his paintings and anatomical drawings. A small number even attempted to copy sketches or paintings. The teacher was very pleased with the teacher and learner value of this lesson.

There were a few minutes of the lesson left and so the teacher decided to ask a series of linked questions. We have noted details about questioning previously, with teachers using questioning strategies in very specialized forms, often based on the needs of individual learners or groups of learners. In this instance the teacher was seeking to get the whole group of learners to give examples of Leonardo's famous works. She saw this as an enjoyable rounding-off activity, offering everybody the chance to participate and assumed that it would not be too complex. She began by asking the following question: 'Can someone tell me the name of a painting of a young and beautiful woman with a sort of smile on her lips?', seeking to describe the work, but without giving clues about its title. The script continues:

Teacher:     'Yes, Latrice, you have your hand up – can you tell me the name of that painting?'

Latrice:     'It is called the Mona Lisa and was painted in the fifteenth century by Leonardo da Vinci and now it is in Paris in a gallery. I think it is behind bullet-proof glass.'

Teacher:     'That's right. Well done, that was very good. And can anyone name another famous painting by Leonardo da Vinci?

(*Group silence*)

No . . . well think about other paintings we looked at earlier in this lesson . . . anyone?

(*Continued silence*)

No? OK. I'm now thinking of one in particular. He started painting this one in 1495. Can anyone name

that painting? Anyone know the answer now?
*(More silence)*

No? Right . . . I am sure that you know it. Think about
the last days in the life of Jesus . . . think very carefully
. . . what was his last meal called?

*(There is another long pause while the class thinks)*

*Suddenly Josey puts her hand up.*

Teacher:     'Ah, yes . . . good . . . Josey?'

Josey:        'Was it called burger and fries miss?'

# 6 Applying fluid thinking

## Making connections

Thinking is an associative process and activity. We may intend to think about one subject and find that very quickly we seem to have ended up thinking about something completely different. This can cause difficulties for those who encounter emotional trauma in that one activity or interaction, such as listening to music or hearing certain noises or seeing certain people, may set off a train of thoughts about a previous painful experience. This can become a barrier to new learning. Thinking is also associative in that most people need to engage with others in order to develop their ability to think in an analytical, systematic or imaginative way. This reciprocal interaction, involving mutual communication and mediation offered by another person, enables hypothesizing to occur and new ideas to be developed or planned. It may also provide modelling of how mediation can help to provide new learning. This type of interaction, and the mediation that is involved, is central to the concept of the 'zone of proximal development' (Vygotsky, 1978) which is explored in Chapter 7.

Tensions can be created when we try to think about things on our own and find that our thinking is fixed, or stuck. The tensions increase when we are left to think on our own, in stressful situations, when we find that we cannot generate any solutions and become overwhelmed by problems. This can become processed so that we feel bad about ourselves and this may have a negative effect upon relationships with others, especially the people who try to help us in our thinking. Fixed thinking can result in negative self-related and other attributions. Fluid thinking can provide positive self and other, related, attributions. There are people who prefer to be in situations where they can improve their thinking by 'bouncing' ideas off others. This system of mutual development and reflection is especially relevant to teachers as it can improve their professional skills.

Those teachers who are new to the profession will recognize the feelings associated with the very first time they were in a classroom, on their own, responsible for managing the learning of a group and expected to perform to a high standard. Some may have been excited about being given this responsibility while others could have felt anxious about it. Of course, some may have felt a combination of both emotions. However, they soon found that it is a regular professional experience for teachers to be on their own, in a position where they have to make quick decisions and execute routines. It is at this point that their attitudes, beliefs, values, personal and professional skills, and their ability to think on their feet are available for all to judge.

Although all teachers need to make quick mental decisions about the context that they are in and the outcome that they desire, we would assert that this emanates from a planned process of grounding teaching and learning – differentiation. Although the contexts can vary greatly, the teacher has to connect with them instantly. For example, a teacher may be teaching a lesson according to a specific plan when something occurs that requires an immediate reaction: perhaps a learner refuses to work, makes racist or sexist comments to a peer, or asks a question that challenges the teacher's subject knowledge and understanding. For connections to be made – perhaps about the reasons for such behaviour – a teacher has to think in a focused manner.

### What is the secret?

The concept of the reflective practitioner has been explored previously. One model of reflection involves historical analysis and futures thinking: looking back at what happened and looking forward to how it could be improved next time. This is an important part of the process of differentiation. It represents what could be termed planned differentiation. No matter how well planned a situation might be, learning is a dynamic process involving humans and there will always be unpredictable responses from learners. This unpredictability necessitates a reflective response from the teacher that involves 'thinking on your feet' or 'differentiation on the hoof' as it is often referred to. It can be argued that this is where the intuitive and charismatic teacher comes into their own – always flexible and responsive, never flustered by questions or actions that seem to take the learning plan in a different direction, excelling amongst the wondrous unpredictability of teacher–learner interactions. Some teacher interventions allow the learner to lay the foundations for a new learning route. Colleagues talk of spontaneously enabling the learner to take the learning to somewhere that they are interested in going to rather than the route that the teacher had originally planned. Others might assess the situation and take time out from the main learning agenda only to return to it later.

We could frame a situation where a learner asks a specific question or behaves in a certain manner as 'problematic'. This is not to say that learners should not ask for clarification or demand enrichment from their teacher – far from it. 'Problematic' in this context has a positive overtone in that is enables learning to move forward. It is problematic in that it represents a technically unplanned moment when the teacher is called upon to act without a script, supposedly to be intuitive. It also places the teacher in a situation which, for some, results in a high level of creativity and for others in an immediate sense of stress. Why should this be so?

First, we draw your attention to the reactions to change that we have highlighted in Chapter 1. Interactions by learners cause the learning environment to change. The teacher is central to that environment and so she or he changes too. This notion of reciprocal change is most important as it focuses our attention on the fact that in any teacher–learner interaction, the feedback the adult is open to represents a new learning experience for them. They have to deal with the twin processes of being a 'teacher' and a 'learner', a role reversal that can occur many times during a period of teaching. This may be seen as threatening for the teacher, the script suddenly changes and improvization is required. We could polarize two possible reactions to learner interventions. One teacher may respond creatively: not threatened and confident, they apply fluidity of thought. Another may feel stressed and threatened, imagining that their response is under the spotlight, available for all to see, and this can promote fixed methods of thinking and behaving. We know that when we are under stress we are least able to detach from situations, think beyond what is happening and make clear connections. Stresses can be one of the main causal factors in producing fixed thinking.

The reflective practitioner is assumed to be able to make connections and think on their feet so that learning contexts and outcomes can be implemented either as planned or with adaptation. Some teachers seem to be highly skilled in diffusing challenging behaviour and responding positively to challenging questions. They seem to be confident, self-assured, have a sense of proportion regarding the incident, and possess an overwhelming and unswerving sense of trust in the learners. For these teachers, the problematic situation is most certainly one that they somehow perceive to be positive. So, what are they thinking during these incidents and how is it affecting their behaviour? This comment from a teacher demonstrates that colleagues are aware that some teachers seem to make conscious decisions to behave in certain ways when situations become problematic. A teacher remarked, when referring to a colleague who seemed to thrive in contexts where learners experienced emotional and behavioural difficulties: 'If he ever walks into your room with his hands in his pockets, smiling at everyone and calmly looking out of the windows . . . get out of there as fast as you can . . . the school is on fire and he is modelling calm behaviour!' Another teacher, talking about a colleague who seemed to react instantly and successfully whenever a potentially difficult situation arose, said: 'I have looked in her bag for the magic dust that she must sprinkle over the children when nobody is looking . . . but have never been lucky enough to find it.'

---

**REFLECTION POINT**

Think about yourself as a teacher.

- To what extent do you think you are mainly intuitive or do you depend on structures?
- To what degree are you a balance between the two?
- How do you respond to 'problematic' situations? Are you consistent or to what degree does it depend upon the context?
- Is it really about a form of magic – or to what extent is something else at work?
- Is it about charisma – or to what extent is something else at work?

### Beyond the magic dust

The myth of a form of magical dust that a teacher spreads onto a problematic situation to make everything right has both positive and negative connotations. It implies that teachers can be in control of problematic situations and can strive for resolution when potential difficulties arise. However, it also suggests that there is a bag of tricks, a secret touch, that some teachers have and others can only dream of. We propose that this book will help to move you beyond the concept of magic dust and analyse the focused thinking that takes place in these situations – connective thinking that *all* teachers can participate in. This focused thinking is a form of differentiation in action, taking place at speed, which allows the teacher to make sense of what is taking place when problematic situations occur. It can also ensure dignified outcomes for the learner and the teacher alike. Our assertion is that what might appear to be highly intuitive must have a framework of thinking and questioning that surrounds and underpins it. This thinking and questioning will have been informed by much of the thinking that reading this book will have provoked in your own mind.

We propose that the thinking will be prompted by four main questions that illuminate all situations where decisions have to be made. In this context we apply it to problematic situations so that resolutions can be sought. It is essential to emphasize that we do not assume that this thinking should and can only be applied to problematic incidents. Of course, it is as relevant to the analysis of experiences where things are going well as it is to problematic ones. We have selected problematic incidents because, in our work with teachers, it is often situations that were puzzling, problematic, threatening or apparently unfathomable that they wish to explore. The questions will have involved a great deal of thinking before the problematic incident occurred. The answers that a teacher gives to the questions will direct their behaviour during and after the incident. Having looked at the questions we will then consider two real life scenarios.

**Why?**

**Why?**

- Who am I?
- Who is she or he/who are they?
- What is happening?
- What could be a solution?

**Why?**

**Why?**

## Four questions – a problematic situation

*Who am I?*
The teacher's response to any problematic situation will be linked to how they perceive who they are, what they do and how they do it best. Factors that will have an impact upon this self-definition include –

- a view of what pedagogy is
- an attitude about how this can be put into practice
- a perception of professional and personal status
- a concept of what learning is
- a view on how learners should learn and behave.

For those who operate from a position of fixed thinking some elements within their own model of who they are and what they do cannot be challenged. This results in predictable responses. For others, their model enables them to respond in a fashion that will place the needs of learners above their own, and cause their model to change. This can be achieved because their personal and professional identity is not threatened by potential problems. Their trust in themselves and the learners to reach solutions reinforces their identity and aims to reinforce a positive identity in the learners too.

*Who is she or he? Who are they?*
The teacher's view of a learner will also inform their response and intervention when situations become problematic. If a teacher carries emotional baggage in relation to their own past experience with individuals or groups of learners then the possibility of negative

attributions, projection and even revenge, in extreme cases, could rear its ugly head. If a teacher engages in a relationship with learners that constantly allows for new interpretations, then resolution replaces retribution. Responsive relationships are less likely to create a context where a teacher will build up to a time when they decide to assert their own status and authority by belittling a learner, or adopting physical restraint at an inappropriate time, or as a punishment – which is completely unethical and unacceptable. The problematic situation where a teacher believes that a learner 'deserves' to be humiliated because of past demeanours is likely to lead to confrontation not resolution. Information that the teacher has gathered, even informally and subconsciously, about learners whom they regularly teach, learners that they hear about through comments from colleagues, and learners with whom they have no regular contact, will influence how they attribute the motivation of the learner. There is no doubt that the perceived motivation of the learner will influence the behaviour of the teacher. The reverse is also just as true of course.

### *What is happening?*

This may appear to be the most obvious question of the quartet. However, this highlights an assumption that we *really* do know what is taking place, at all levels, during any incident or interaction just because it is taking place in front of our eyes. The teacher needs to make instant judgements about what is taking place in a problematic situation (and also when things are going well) and this is not easy to do. It might involve making inferences about why a learner is behaving in a certain way. These judgements will be informed by who the teacher thinks they are and how confident they feel in the situation. They will also be informed by who they think the learner is, and what they believe the motivation of the learner to be. All of this will provide information that enables decision-making. Whatever the formulation, it will require the teacher to adopt a stance which allows them to detach from what is taking place in order to gain a better view of it. It is difficult to make rational judgements when you are stressed or unable to see beyond what is directly in front of you. The assessment of what a teacher believes is happening, and why, will direct their response.

### What could be a solution?

Problematic situations, just like positive situations, differ in their frequency, duration and intensity. They may involve 'low level' provocative questioning or behaviour. They could also involve the use of abusive language, acting out, put downs, loud attention-seeking behaviour and attempts to de-skill teachers. Others, far more serious, may include scenarios where a learner, or a teacher, is in physical danger. Yet the desired outcome should be resolution – a form of resolution that is fundamentally based upon retaining the basic human rights of all persons who are involved. A teacher has the complex task of holding in mind an idea of what the solution will look like from all angles or for all the people involved *before* they begin interactions for resolution. You may recall the cases in Chapter 2. One of them details a stressed teacher's reaction to a girl in her class whom she has had enough of. She wants the girl to be taken to a local special school. She wants no excuses. If you read this again you will see that the teacher describes a step-by-step solution to the problem, viewing it as a 'good' solution to the problem. In reality however, it is only a solution from one point of view – the teacher's. In the terms we have introduced earlier it is a fixed solution. It relies on others doing what the individual felt powerless to do and therefore sets the individual up for future failure.

We need to break down the larger question into smaller ones. What will be the solution when we arrive at it? Remember that it is inevitable that there will be a point when some type of solution will occur. What are the costs and what are the benefits from this solution? Who incurs these costs and benefits? Who is expected to do what, how and why? How can we ensure that everybody's dignity remains intact? The list of questions continues. We are simply encouraging you to triangulate your thinking in order to consider solutions. This means viewing the situation and the solution from more than one point or perspective. This enables you to ground your response within the information that you gain from looking from various angles. This is not an easy task, but it is an essential one in terms of open and active differentiation.

### CASE POINT

The following two cases will provide a setting for a problematic situation, as defined earlier. The outcomes will contain an example each of fixed and fluid thinking. Each will show how the four questions could be answered and how this influences teacher response. They will be written as if the teacher is talking.

*It's a pig's life*

A teacher in a primary school is teaching a group of ten and eleven year olds. The group contains learners from a variety of faiths as well as those who belong to no faith community at all. The group also contains learners from different cultural groups. Denise is the teacher and Leon is one of the learners in the group. Leon has recently undertaken an IQ test, initiated by his parents, as they believe that he is gifted. Having received the result of the test his parents have informed the school that he is not gifted – he is a genius! Leon regularly asks Denise questions in class. The group has been looking at aspects of different faiths. Last month it was the five pillars of Islam. This month it is Hinduism and Denise is trying to engage the group in a discussion about reincarnation. When she was at university, Hinduism was one of her specialist areas of study. Her task is to optimize the teaching and learning value, so that all of these learners can understand the complex causal relationship between the cosmic law of Karma and the concept of the eternal transmigration of the soul – who ever said teaching was an easy job! The group is talking about how people might live a good or bad life. Then, using school as an example, they talk about how good behaviour can receive rewards and bad behaviour can receive punishment.

Denise then introduces the idea of the soul being affected by good or bad behaviour and uses the word 'karma'. She asks Sonal, a Hindu, if she knows this word; what have her parents told her about it; what does it mean? Sonal says that she knows nothing about it, has never heard of it and explains that her parents do not even go to the temple. Suddenly Leon interrupts:

➤

'Miss, I have heard about that. They believe that you get punished by God for bad things and that you are rewarded for good things . . . that your soul gets a new body depending upon how you live your life now.' There is no stopping him, he continues 'I visited a temple last year and . . .' Denise is about to reinterpret what Leon has said so that the learning can become intimate for other learners, but Leon continues, '. . . the priest said that if you live like a pig then you will definitely come back as a pig. Your soul comes back in a pig's body.' Denise stops him at this point and tries to engage the group in a discussion. Amarjeet, a Sikh, asks for clarification: 'Miss, does that mean that if you behave bad you get a bad body in your next life and if you behave good you get a good body?'

In terms of teaching and learning we are now approaching a problematic moment. Denise has already stated that, in relation to the concept of reincarnation, the best body to have is that of a human. She may well be concerned about having to explain a complex conceptual idea to a group, when not all of them might understand it. However, she may also be concerned about oversimplifying a concept so that some learners who might be able to explore it do not get the chance to do so. An intervention from Leon adds to the problematic scenario. He engages in some teaching himself and speaks to Amarjeet: 'Yes, you are right. As long as you lead a good life you can get a better body next time. That's right isn't it miss?' Denise is about to attempt to slow the pace of the learning, to involve other learners, and to answer Leon's question when he suddenly has a 'penny dropping' moment – he sees a potential problem inherent in the concept of Karma. Immediately he calls out 'Miss, if that is right . . . it is really unfair on animals. How can a pig lead a "good" life so that it can come back as a human? What is good or bad behaviour if you are a pig – and how do you know?' The teacher is under the spotlight. It is time for Denise to respond.

In relation to the four questions here are two possible outcomes. They characterize, and maybe at times also caricature, fixed and fluid thinking.

*Fixed response*

- *Who am I?* I am a qualified teacher. I have been teaching, successfully, for ten years. I hold a senior position within my school. I have both a degree and a personal interest in phenomenology and comparative religion. I have spent a long time planning this piece of teaching and learning.
- *Who is he?* He is a genius of course. Well, at least that is what his parents keep telling me. I know that he is able because of my own teaching and assessment of his learning, but . . . a genius? Leon is a pleasant boy but he can be very annoying with his constant questioning. He can also be extremely arrogant with his interventions about how much he knows. Smart kids like him are so irritating. There are times when I think he really believes that he knows more than I do. No wonder he does not have many friends. It is typical of children like him. I know because I have met about five of them in the last six years. Anyway, never mind who I think he is – who does *he* think he is?
- *What is happening?* I need to teach this topic at a level so that ten and eleven year olds can understand it. The plan for doing this is involves a small introduction from me; grounding some of the ideas in their own experience; asking some children, especially Hindus, what they know and think; finishing the discussion and spending most of the lesson in groups finding out different pieces of information. The discussion has gone on for too long. This means that we might not get the group activities finished before break time. Yet again, Leon is hijacking the discussion. He is not giving anyone else a chance. He has now taken the discussion into areas that I did not want to go into. This is absolutely typical of children like him. It may also be that he is testing me out, trying to see what I know?
- *What could be a solution?* The lesson must go according to plan. Leon's ridiculous question about how a pig might lead a good life is irrelevant to everyone else except himself. I shall

take the discussion back a few stages, and then organize the learners into groups. I shall make sure that Leon does not go near any learners who find this topic difficult, as he will just humiliate them. I might give him some work to do and engineer it so that he does it on his own – after all, that is what gifted learners prefer.

*Fluid response*

- *Who am I?* I am a qualified teacher. I have been teaching, successfully for ten years. I hold a senior position within my school. I have both a degree and a personal interest in world religions, in understanding how humans behave individually and in groups. I have spent a long time planning this piece of teaching and learning. I have been quite ambitious in expecting learners to understand this area, but that is what teaching is all about – unfolding the world before the learners to see what sense they can make from it. That is why I enjoy it.

- *Who is he?* Leon is someone who loves information. He cannot get enough of it. He is almost hyper-inquisitive. He is very well informed about many areas of the curriculum and has an excellent memory. I know that he is a very able boy because of my teaching and assessment of his learning. He is a boy who regularly achieves optimum learning value from my teaching. In fact, sometimes when I teach something and I am aware that I could have done it better, he still seems to achieve optimum learning value from it. As a consequence, I have been concerned that he might become self-conscious of his own ability or even become bored and I do not want him to under-achieve deliberately. He often asks questions and it tests my management skills to ensure that his needs are met alongside those of others in the group.

- *What is happening?* I have been talking about an area that fascinates me. I cannot wait to see how the learners will react. I have made an assumption that, just because someone comes from a certain faith community or background, they will know the answers. I was wrong. Leon has actually helped me out. He has helped to move the learning forward. He has also modelled what I want to happen later in the lesson –

supportive peer interaction. I am surprised by his question because I know adults who would not ask such insightful questions. It is very impressive that he can think so analytically about complicated concepts. I cannot ignore his question but I do want to allow other learners to become involved.

- *What could be a solution?* If I thought that I could not answer Leon's question, then I would say so. However, I know two short Hindu stories that I can tell. They may give Leon an answer and enable other learners to remain connected, or even become more connected, to the learning. It also adds variety to the presentation of the lesson. After the stories I shall ask Leon if they have helped to begin to answer his question. I shall engage other learners in the discussion too. When we do organize into groups, I shall put Leon in a group where he can have a specific role. When I arrive at his group, probably the third group that I will get to, I shall have a brief individual discussion with him. I shall also thank him for his enthusiasm and help.

---

**CASE POINT**

*The headache*

It is a sunny afternoon. A teacher and an LSA are working with a group of learners who are fourteen years old and involved in a PE lesson. The teacher has been in the profession for three years. This is his first year teaching in a special school. The school is for learners who experience emotional and behavioural difficulties. Some of the learners from this school spend time at a local high school that prides itself upon being inclusive. It has made proactive efforts to offer full time mainstream education to an increasing number of learners who used to attend local special schools. It also offers integration opportunities as well. This PE lesson is taking place for a small group because the rest of their peers are at the local high school. There are eight learners, a teacher and an LSA playing badminton. One of the learners, Tanika, was angry before the lesson began. Her anger increases every time she misses the shuttlecock with her racket. She accuses

➤

---

others of laughing at her and refuses to play. She says that they are all much fitter than she is. She accuses the PE teacher of deliberately embarrassing her by making her play badminton and runs off. The LSA has worked in the school for fifteen years. She has witnessed this type of incident many times before. She knows it can become unpleasant, even violent. She adds another dynamic as to how the learners perceive the role of the teacher. The LSA 'broadcasts' to the whole group advising them that Tanika is looking for attention and that everyone should ignore Tanika. She hopes that this will encourage Tanika to return to the group.

Dave, the teacher, is concerned about this as Tanika is standing in the corner of the room, waving her racket around and singing a song aloud. The words of Tanika's song begin to change. Now she is singing about another learner in the group and being abusive about his mother. The problematic scenario is building up. Dave decides that something must be done quickly. Tanika likes Dave. Three weeks ago he spent some time talking to her after he found her sitting on the floor crying. She thanked him afterwards. The LSA offers to take Tanika out of the room. Dave thinks that this might make matters worse. He decides that the first action to take is to remove the racket from her. He walks towards Tanika who is waving the racket aggressively and swearing. Looking right into his eyes, Tanika shouts at Dave 'You come near me and I'll smash this racket over your head.' Dave replies 'No. I know that you will not do that. Give the racket to me and we will sort out the problem.' Tanika warns him 'One step closer and I'll hit you. I don't care. I have had enough of this school and I have had enough of you. I hate you.' Tanika then begins to use abusive terms to describe Dave. Everyone else has stopped playing badminton; they are enjoying this form of free theatre. Dave walks closer and repeats his request 'Give me the racket Tanika.' Immediately Tanika moves forward and hits Dave over the head with the racket. The racket, bent and damaged, falls to the floor. The other learners look at each other in disbelief. The teacher is under the spotlight. It is time for Dave to respond.

*Fixed response*

- *Who am I?* I am a trained Art teacher. I currently have a terrible headache. I got bored very quickly in mainstream education. I wanted to move schools to work with learners who have problems. I wanted to do this because I think that I am good at it. I like to teach PE because I enjoy sport myself. I want to pass this enthusiasm on. I knew it would not be easy moving to a special school, but I was up for the challenge. I have never been as physically tired as I am in this job. I feel that I constantly have to show other colleagues that I can do this job. I have heard rumours that they feel that I have not had enough experience of mainstream schools before coming to teach in a special school. I have to prove to them that I am capable.

- *Who is she?* Tanika comes from a family of six. She is obsessed with how she looks. She manipulates people all the time. One day she likes you, the next day you are her enemy. It is love or war with her. A few weeks ago I was the best teacher in the school, now she hates me. Two of her brothers used to attend this school. Both were excluded. She has been excluded from three mainstream schools already. It seems unlikely that she will last the duration of this school year. It will only take one more major incident and then she will have to go. It seems to me that a family pattern is developing. That is a shame. It appears that she is just like her brothers.

- *What is happening?* This lesson is about cooperation skills. I have tried hard at the start of the lesson to emphasize this to the group. The lesson was only under way for a few minutes when Tanika started to be difficult. She even told me that the lesson was rubbish. She did the same last week. I approached her for the racket, I was not aggressive, but still she hit me very hard over the head. I cannot let her behave like this towards me, especially in front of another colleague and in front of other learners. It caused me physical pain.

- *What could be a solution?* What will my colleague think? What will she say about me to other colleagues? What will the group think? What will they say to other learners in the school? I cannot afford to appear that I am not in charge otherwise they will all be hitting me with objects. The fact remains that a fourteen-year-old girl attacked me. I do not come to school to be physically attacked by the learners. They may have difficulties but this is unacceptable. I shall have to get her out of the room and to the headteacher's office. She will have to be excluded from the school. I will need time to think about what will happen after that. If the headteacher does not exclude her I might have to refuse to teach her.

*Fluid response*

- *Who am I?* I am a trained Art teacher. I currently have a terrible headache. I got bored very quickly in mainstream education. I wanted to move schools to work with learners who have problems. I wanted to do this because I think that I am good at it. I like to teach PE because I enjoy sport myself. I want to pass this enthusiasm on. I knew it would not be easy moving to a special school, but I was up for the challenge. I have never been as physically tired as I am in this job. The unpredictability of the job makes it exciting as well as exhausting. I pride myself on the fact that I have never met a learner that I do not like, and I assume that this will always be so during my whole career.

- *Who is she?* Tanika comes from a family of six and she is the youngest. She has had many difficulties in early childhood. Her father left the family recently. This has caused her moods to fluctuate. They were already unpredictable, but now it seems as if she can go from calm to furious in three seconds. Two of her brothers used to attend this school and some teachers are keen to remind her of this. She is labelled as a victim of the family that she comes from. She says that she wants to do well at this school and I believe her – it just seems that she cannot sustain it at the moment. Her individuality is often expressed through the way that she dresses. She has a good sense of humour and is very protective of any younger learners in the school who get into difficulty. She can engage in mature and well-informed discussion.

- *What is happening?* I need to ask questions about what I did. Maybe I should think about how I introduced the lesson? Perhaps the aims were clear to me and not to the learners? I think that my aims for an art lesson would have been much more precise. Perhaps I should have listened to what she said when she warned me not to come near. She was breathing heavily, agitated and using abusive language – maybe I should have given her some space. It may seem strange but perhaps it was my behaviour in not taking her threat seriously that caused her to hit me? She says she hates me. I will not take that personally. I am not sure if I said 'please' when I asked for the racket. Perhaps that would have helped? There may have been other factors that were involved in the build up to this incident. She may feel upset that she has not been given the chance to attend the local high school. This might reinforce her own negative view of herself. She is also aware that some of the other learners in the group are far more athletic than she is. She is right. Perhaps I should be more sensitive to that. Maybe she is also upset that it is sunny and she wants to be outside.

- *What could be a solution?* A whole variety of interactive factors may have caused this to happen. As I have looked extensively to assess why this has happened, then I also need to look extensively at the solution. I cannot change the fact that a decision has been made, at senior management level, that means Tanika cannot attend the high school programme. However, I could raise the wider issue of what it must feel like to be 'left behind' and what we are doing as a school to deal with this. Perhaps next time we can play badminton outside. It might give everyone a bit more physical space? One matter remains simple and in some ways beyond my control. The school rules clearly state that this type of physical attack is unacceptable. The school accepts that the learners have difficulties but has made it clear that physical attacks will not be tolerated. Luckily, from my point of view, they treat each situation individually. This could mean that this incident might not become the one that sees her thrown out of the school. I do not think it is serious enough for that.

I may have to remove the whole group from the room and wait until Tanika is ready to come to the headteacher's office with me. Afterwards, I will need to let the rest of the group know what the solution is and why this specific decision has been made. When we get to the headteacher's office, or the headteacher comes to us, I will not be demanding that Tanika should be permanently excluded because of what she did to me. After all, what other educational opportunities are there for her if she is excluded from this school? For her, realistically, the options are part-time education or no formal education all.

---

**REFLECTION POINT**

- How far do the notions of fixed and fluid thinking apply to your own practice?

  How far might they apply to the practice of your colleagues? In what ways can you see them aiding the process of differentiation?

- If these cases were focusing upon the learners rather than the teachers how might they have answered the four questions from their perspective?

  Do you think they would have used the same four questions? If not, what others might they use?

- Often teachers talk of learners as having high or low self-esteem. How far can you tell which of the two learners in these case studies has the highest self-esteem? What evidence do you have for making this judgement?

- To what extent is the concept of self-esteem helpful in enabling you to understand the learning that is taking place? Please keep your answers to this question in mind for Chapter 8.

---

# 7 Models of learning

It seems that all human beings have an innate desire to learn new skills, knowledge and applications. We just cannot help it. As newly born babies we are predisposed to learn to do things that help us to survive as well as to become more independent. For example, we learn to grasp, discriminate, indicate preferences, make choices, feed, talk, crawl and walk. Sometimes of course there are internal and external factors which adversely affect this disposition. We also learn to use crying as a way of indicating a complex range of emotions. It is often the carer's task to establish what a cry is actually communicating – could it be boredom, pain, emotional distress, hunger, physical discomfort or tiredness? This is a task that involves differentiation.

We have written elsewhere about the notion of teacher value and learning value and have sought to analyse different forms of outcomes that may arise from teacher–learner interactions. We do this in order to be able to focus more clearly on the task and process of differentiation and grounded learning. At this point we wish to return to these teacher–learner interactions in order to consider them again from another standpoint.

## Teacher and learner energy

As teachers we have probably all come across individuals or groups where the transfer from teacher to learner proceeds very well indeed. The learners just seem to 'get it'. This is to the extent that teachers have said to us something like 'this learner can teach herself' or 'that group can just get on with it'. However, we would not want to downgrade the level of teacher input which structures and underpins this feeling of running on 'auto-pilot' which the teacher and learners experience. We have even had some exceptional teachers say to us, often in a humorous and self-deprecating way, that they feel certain groups

---

**REFLECTION POINT**

Recall a successful teaching learning interaction that you were involved with recently. Make sure it is one where you took the role of teacher:

- How do you think that particular learner learned in that particular situation?
- Broaden your own thinking: consider how you think learners in general learn. How do they do this? How do we all do this?
- What theories and models do you carry around in your head that enable you to think that learners can and will learn? To what extent can you articulate them? To what extent do you articulate them to learners? To what extent do you articulate them to colleagues? To what degree do you think that your colleagues carry similar or different models? To what extent do they or can they articulate them?
- Having read Chapter 5, write down some typical constructs that you would associate with learners and learning. How can these help you to help them to learn?

---

or individuals learn despite what teachers do and say.

We now wish to stand back from the notion of teacher and learner value and look closely at this relationship again but this time with different eyes. We want to look at the power or energy that is put into the interaction before learning can come to life and can be seen to be taking place. At the beginning of this book we mentioned power and it is worth stating here that we are not using it in a political or physical sense at all.

One power scenario is where the teachers feel that they are working in a highly efficient teacher–learner system, whereby the amount of effort, energy or power (call it what you will) put into that system is readily and efficiently translated into learning outcomes. Having facilitated these high-value teacher–learner interactions, some teachers may modestly downplay their part in structuring this very efficient 'energy' transformation. In these highly differentiated interactions most of the energy transformation (not most of the input) from teaching into fully grounded learning, is enabled on the learner side of the interaction. He, she or they can use a given amount of teaching 'energy' to go a very long way as learners.

This efficiency of transformation raises another point that teachers have often made to us, being one of many questions that seem to be unanswerable: whether they 'taught' a given thing or whether the learners 'learned' it. We would say that most usually both are true. The one generates the other. However, consider the following:

- A baby aged eleven months takes her first faltering steps. Did she learn this skill or was she taught it?
- A child aged eighteen months hears another child crying. Instead of copying the emotion and crying too, he walks over to the other child and tries to offer comfort and sympathy. Did he learn this emotional response or was he taught it?
- A child aged two speaks a three-word sentence for the first time. It contains the naming of a familiar object, a familiar person and the use of a verb. Did he learn to speak or was he taught to speak?
- A child aged three recalls and explains what she did when she went swimming last week. Did she learn how to remember or was she taught it?

We do not doubt the influence of parents, carers, key adults and social factors informally imparting knowledge and skills as 'teaching'. In fact we would support a view of learning that emphasizes the crucial importance of social interaction. However, the point being made is that, as adults, we do not seem to conceive these important life events in a high energy 'teaching' mode. We do not seem to think in terms of 'I will teach you to walk, talk, sing, or to have a sense of humour or empathy'. What seems to happen here is that we naturally expect high efficiency learning to take place, from the loosely structured (low energy) teaching input of significant adults. These highly efficient transfers appear to link in with a natural disposition for learning and usually follow developmental markers in early life.

There is a whole range of situations when the teacher energy and learner energy is equally efficient. The first may illustrate a characteristic of more formal learning systems. Here there is an expectation that learning can and will take place, given the correct modes and strategies of transmission. In terms of an energy model these interactions present as more balanced or equal transformers of teaching energy into learning outcomes. Both parties work hard at transforming teaching energy into learning energy. It shifts and changes, ebbs and flows, moves forwards and then meets resistance before moving on again.

There are also interactions that are characterized by inefficiency, for whatever reasons. In this scenario, teachers (and learners) may feel more negative about what is taking place. We may hear teachers say that a particular learner or group of learners 'do not seem able to learn'. They might say things like 'they just do not get it', or 'it just goes over their heads' or even more negatively 'it goes in one ear and out the other'. If we step back and look at this teaching learning system then it can appear that the teaching energy stays as teaching and is inefficiently transformed or translated into learning by the learner or learners. It does not become intimate learning for them. This can lead to exasperation on the part of the teacher, at which point emotions may come to the forefront which can result in learners being blamed for what are perceived as deficiencies within them – a deficit model. The same response can be applied to the wider teaching learning system too.

## Avoiding the 'tourist' approach to differentiation

We now wish to look more closely at what can happen in the disconcerting situation where the teacher–learner transformation is inefficient. We have noticed that in these fixed or 'stuck' situations the teacher response may typically be to put more energy into their part of the teacher–learner interaction. What the teacher tends to do in such situations is to try to 'rev up' the teacher power. An example of what we mean could be gained from thinking about the behaviour of a tourist, trying to be understood in a country where they do not speak the language. Imagine a common scene in which a tourist is trying to discover the way to the nearest hotel. In this case, the tourist is an English speaker, looking for a hotel in a village in Mexico. What follows is a teacher–learner interaction between two people who do not speak the same language, a situation that occurs in learning systems all over the world. In this context, the teacher has an agenda they wish to put over as a learning outcome. The non-English speaking person is the learner, who is going to receive something from the teacher (a specific request in a foreign language) which they will be asked to transform efficiently into a learning outcome: a reply to the question about the proximity of a hotel. This will be delivered (the mode of teaching used), in a foreign language that the non-English speaker cannot speak. What teacher–learner value would we bet on in this situation?

The tourist's need is for a hotel and so the question asked is a valid one. Owing to the need and the pressure derived from the desired outcome, we are often prepared to suspend normal teacher–learner value decisions in such situations. We also abandon whatever models of learning we usually adhere to. Instead, for some reason, we simply 'rev up' the teacher energy. This works at the level of believing that if we can put enough power or energy into the teaching side of the inter-action then the recipient will somehow understand and learn. Not only will they miraculously learn to comprehend a language that they have never understood before in their life, they will suddenly master its semantic complexities. As always in teacher–learner interactions there are many inherent hopes, risks and assumptions subsumed within the apparently simple teaching plan. In this context it is assumed or hoped that the person being asked, randomly selected off of the street, will know the name of the closest hotel. It is likely that hope extends further and that they will know if it has vacancies or not and will be able to supply clear directions to it.

If this initial teaching plan fails then we must have a fall back plan to turn to. This plan is likely to be based upon subtle yet powerful methods of differentiating the teaching, in order to rev up the teach-ing energy. This typically could include some of the following highly personalized incremental strategies:

- Asking, in English, if the other person speaks English.
- Ignoring the reply given in a language that you do not under-stand.
- Continuing to speak in English, but differentiating by speak-ing very slowly.
- Articulating words more clearly, as if this will aid under-standing.
- Suddenly developing a condescending tone of voice.
- Missing out some words and changing grammatical order.

This could result in an interaction that begins with 'hotel, me want, you show?'

- Speaking loudly.
- Using over-exaggerated and random hand gestures.
- Developing a fixed grin and nodding furiously even though you are confused.
- Shouting.

The underlying belief is that once teaching has been revved up in this way it is hard to see it failing. It really should do the trick!

---

**DIALOGUE POINT**

Talk to a colleague about the tourist example.

- What type of differentiation is being applied in this interaction? To what degree is it likely to work or not to work?
- What could the tourist have done to improve the situation?
- To what degree would you say that elements of this tourist approach to differentiation – and revving up teaching – take place in your learning system?

---

It is not coincidental that the actions and needs of the learner seem to have been ignored or forgotten in our example. We might rev up the teaching as much as we can but if it is not grounded within the experience of the learner then it is doomed to failure. In this scene it is the teacher who is under pressure and this translates into the learner also being placed under pressure. In effect the learner is given an impossible task. The teacher may claim to have differentiated in a number of ways but it can be seen that they are only differentiating the teaching without attempting to ground the learning. This style of 'tourist differentiation' cannot be expected to work. At the beginning of this interaction the key to the errors built in from the outset is the pressure the teacher feels. This emotional response to a stressful situation is likely to produce fixed rather than fluid thinking. Inevitably there is also a severe over-revving of teaching power. It is at the point that teachers feel most pressurized that they need to differentiate but at these times it is hard to do. Hence there is a need for principles, planning and structures already to be in place. These structures add confidence when we are in fixed situations because they enable us to respond flexibly. Pressure can be threatening and can also have negative effects upon the self-confidence of the teacher and the learner.

In teacher–learner systems that are clearly inefficient, the way forward may revolve around ways of putting more energy in. It may also require reflection upon designing and implementing ways of utilizing that energy in different forms and in different ways once it has been put it. We would never entirely discount putting more energy into the system as a solution to inefficiency but as a single strategy this can become a problem. There are clear ironies, at a social and emotional level, in a teacher who is encountering inefficiency in their teacher–learner interactions being told that they need to put more energy into the system. They may well be working extremely hard and such a comment can be processed as negative criticism. Quite understandably, anger and resentment can be the outcome.

This situation is most often highlighted to us in teacher–learner interactions where learners present challenging behaviour. The behaviour can be personalized by both learners and teachers. The teacher may become resentful of working hard in a relationship where the learner does not seem to respond in proportion to the amount of energy put in by the teacher. In reality, some teachers do emphasize the difficulty of being in relationships where they give everything and the learner seems to give nothing positive back in return. We have to accept that this can result in the teacher eventually developing challenging behaviours too. We would argue strongly that the principles of differentiation have not been followed through if this is how teacher–learner interactions develop and continue. It is a complex task to ensure that every learner is afforded their right to a differentiated curriculum in relation to learning and behaviour.

When the 'energy' in the system is very inefficiently transformed then teaching very quickly becomes problematical. No matter what the teacher does it does not seem to result in efficient learning. The teacher might know what they are doing but they do not seem to know what the learner is doing. The focus in solving the problem will in part lie in returning to analysing teaching, because the teacher implicitly knows more about this. However, we are arguing here that analysing learning may prove to be equally and possibly more productive in terms of providing differentiation. Certainly we feel the balance needs redressing in order to equip teachers with the necessary tools to look more holistically at teacher–learner systems.

It may be that a teacher's theories or models about learners and learning are actually only models of teaching and this is why teaching is placed under the microscope and focused upon in an unbalanced way. Therefore it is important to consider in detail models of learning. Again, we choose to select one particular model of learning for this purpose. Having a model to hand may better enable us to rev up learning as well as teaching.

## A model of learning

We have mentioned an innate and basic human disposition to learn. It could be argued that a basic disposition to learn also has an accompanying basic human disposition to teach – the corollary of learning. We consider that all initial learning takes place as a series of incremental accumulations and applications. Slowly these build up, perhaps into construct systems whereby learning becomes integrated. When a piece of learning occurs we can reflect upon how we 'got it'. We have learned something, we 'know it', but how did we come to 'know it'? What happened?

Thinking about how you learn and how learners learn is essential in the process of providing differentiation and grounded learning. As a teacher in a learning system, learners and learning are your direct professional responsibility. Considering how they learn is part of this responsibility. It is also fascinating. It ensures that the teaching and learning system that you develop is inclusive, responsive, confident and able to question within and without itself. It also ensures that the teaching learning system does not suffocate individual and group development, remaining open to change, and offering respectful learning experiences for everyone, learners and teachers alike.

It is our intention to invite you to explore models of how pupils learn and to consider how the teacher–learner system can be made more efficient. This should be able to counteract situations where inefficient revving up of teaching, or the use of the tourist approach to differentiation, are seen as solutions to teaching or learning difficulties. This thinking about learning will be analysed by taking three separate strands or pathways of thinking. In effect these are differentiated learning routes, or learning pathways as we have seen them named in some curricula.

Strands 1 and 2 will be considered in this chapter and will be combined in one unified model at the end of the chapter. A summary of the main points from each strand is provided at the end of each part in order to augment your thinking further. Strand 3, relating to the emotional context of learning, will be considered in the following chapter.

## Strand 1: The social context of learning

The psychological underpinning of our approach stems mainly from our interpretations of the work of Vygostky (1978). We were attracted to the fact that Vygotskyian psychology offers an optimistic view about human capabilities. Differentiation is about everyone being seen as learners, learning for all, not just some. Some teacher–learner systems currently over-focus upon the *difficulties* that learner's experience, rather than their *needs*. A focus upon the difficulties of learners can reinforce deficit models where the process of teaching can be perceived to be too difficult with specific individuals or groups of learners. This emphasis upon difficulty can have an overwhelmingly negative effect upon how a learner's potential is defined by teachers – a key component affecting teacher optimism in learning and teaching, which is crucial for differentiation.

Vygotsky proposes that human learning potential is created socially, for example in the process of upbringing and education. He asserts that the most important index of a child's development is not what they can presently do, their *actual level*, but what the child may be brought to do, dependent upon new social experiences and learning, this being their *potential level*. A differentiated approach to teacher–learner interactions ensures that learners are brought to the point of optimizing their learning potential. It is therefore through inclusion, collaboration, interaction and differentiation that learning can become embedded. A learner needs a teacher. We have emphasized that the influence of the teacher is absolutely vital, especially dependent upon how they develop a pedagogical attitude and approach. This will determine how they understand learning and how they provide learning opportunities. Vygotsky's emphasis upon learners constructing understanding through social experience has immense implications for the task of teachers. Immediately, it establishes them as mediators of learning and the learning environment. It demands that they are interactive with learners and enable learners to be interactive with each other. It also encourages them to become more analytical about the emerging needs and capabilities of learners. We have proposed that to do this, to consider elements which interact and combine to produce the totality of the learning process itself – albeit academic – various social, emotional, cognitive and pedagogical factors must be analysed. The interconnectedness of these elements is illustrated in Chapter 4 and considered throughout this book.

### What is the zone of proximal development?

Vygotsky noted that the difference, or distance, between a learner's actual and potential level, what they now know and what they can be brought to know, could be described as the 'zone of proximal development' (ZPD). This encourages teachers to see functions and processes within the ZPD as being in a state of maturation – they may not be fully learned today, but they can be tomorrow. It also encourages them to assess the abilities of learners and to evaluate their teaching in relation to learner progress. As regards assessment it also presents teachers with opportunities to assess within the ZPD as well as establishing what the ZPD is. Many would argue that knowledge of the ZPD with its cultural, cognitive, emotional and social interrelationships is a far more reliable predictor of potential than an IQ test.

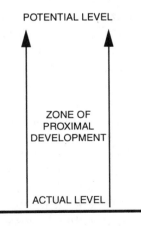

POTENTIAL LEVEL

ZONE OF
PROXIMAL
DEVELOPMENT

ACTUAL LEVEL

**Figure 7.1 The ZPD**

In order to move from actual to potential levels, we as learners and teachers need to be able to think of ourselves in a way that is different from the way we are now. This is achieved by interacting with other people, who know what we do not know (teachers). As we have highlighted throughout this book, 'teachers' may be peers or parents or carers who can become involved in collaborative learning. Collaborative interaction involves trust and risk. We can begin to conceive of all pedagogically-based interactions as a series of teaching experiments. The teacher's immediate task in a learning interaction is to determine the amount and nature of the pedagogical interaction required for the learner to be able to create a new piece of learning. Beyond this the task is to promote generalization of learning in a fluid manner.

Our contention is that efficient and effective high value learning and teaching can very usefully be framed in Vygotskian terms. We have stated that teachers, consciously and subconsciously, make decisions about the learning and teaching needs of their learners. This occurs through a planned and systematic process of applying the tools and processes of differentiation as well as the more spontaneous on-the-spot fine-tuning of the moment. We propose that all teachers must be doing this all of the time for all of their learners.

For the purposes of providing grounded learning we propose that this process can be formalized in this staged way:

1. Each teacher must carry a notional idea (correct or not) of the *actual level* of the learner, in relation to specific baseline assessment and feedback from previous learning.
2. Each teacher must have a notional idea about where they want the learner to get to, subsumed within implicit or explicit knowledge of where they believe the learner can get to, over a specified time period and given specified resources. We view this as a *potential level.*
3. Each teacher will have a notional plan of 'best interactions' that the learner needs to experience, in order for them to learn. These best interactions will also include the types and levels of support they will need to receive from other teachers and learners who know what they do not yet know. Thus the teacher carries a notional view of how the learner will progress within the *zone of proximal development*, through the process of mediated and supported learning.

This is, in fact, a pragmatic description of the everyday, minute-by-minute, reality of teaching. It carries with it implied notions about match, a match that relates to teacher and learner value. Practically speaking what teachers must be doing is carrying some form of 'reference map' to help them navigate with and on behalf of their learners. Whilst highlighting the existence of such maps, rather than commenting on their accuracy, detail or efficacy, it follows that the more accurately this map can be constructed, the more effective the teaching and learning that is likely to take place. These mental maps are another way of describing and understanding the ZPD.

---

**REFLECTION POINT**

- How far do you agree with the concept of the ZPD? What advantages can you see for different types of learners if their potential is conceptualized in this way?
- To what extent do you agree with the description of the minute-by-minute reality of teaching that we have proposed?

---

### A staged process of learning

The work of Vygotsky enables us to look in an optimistic manner at the dynamic process of teaching and learning. Vygotskian theory has been further explored and developed in a process model (Tharpe and Gallimore, 1991) which provides the basis for our analysis of a staged process of learning, which all teachers and learners go through.

### Stage 1

The learner is not yet able to conceptualize the learning in the same way as the teacher. They have to be taught so that they can learn. As the teacher and learner interact there will be a steady decline in the teacher's responsibility for task performance as the learner begins to 'get it'. As this occurs, there is a reciprocal increase in the learner's level of responsibility for task performance.

### Stage 2

The learner is able to carry out a task with and without assistance from others, but the performance is neither fully developed nor automatic. The learner is working hard to master the content of the learning, to gain control over their learning, to make meaning from it. What was once completely guided by others is beginning to be guided and directed by the learner on their own, though with many opportunities to re-engage the teacher.

## Stage 3

The learning task performance is now fully developed and automated. The learner has 'got it' or the learner 'can do it'. Whatever the learning task or activity involves is in the process of becoming fully integrated as learning. The teacher task is almost complete.

## Stage 4

Automization and de-automization. The learner is now fully independent of the teacher, though the teacher task may well be to validate the learning in some formal way. Over time and for a number of reasons, skills or knowledge that we do not use are lost or have to be relearned in a new context. What we could do once we can no longer do, without re-assistance – teaching. This leads us back to the earlier stages through the ZPD, in what can be seen as a continuous feedback loop. Our lifelong learning will require continual movement back through any number of ZPDs and will always describe our route from not knowing to learning.

It follows from these four stages that the rate, frequency, intensity and type of teaching interaction that will move learners from their actual level to their potential level can be held within what is termed as the ZPD. This notion of a ZPD informs the hypothesizing that teachers undertake when 'mapping' out learners' learning needs. Packaged within this we can identify the bare bones of the learning process, which it is possible to reduce to the forms described below.

1. The representation of a problem.
2. Problem construction and problem solution, implying the ability to acquire and use different intellectual capacities.
3. Evaluation and developing control over learning.
4. Loss of learning owing to reasons such as forgetting or emotional trauma, for example. This requires a new representation of the problem so that it can be solved.

Lastly we have presented below yet another way of looking at the underlying structure of the teacher–learner interactions. This may possibly describe the next interaction you will have with a learner:

- The production of a problem so that general relationships can be clearly identified.
- Modelling of relationships.
- Transformation of relationships.
- Creation of new problems and tasks.
- Control over learning actions and applications.
- Evaluation of applications of learning.

### Strand 1: a summary

So what is contained in this first strand of thinking? First, an optimistic view of learning potential and capability. Allied to this is the idea that learning is essentially a social activity and that learning takes place *between* two or more heads rather than *within* one. Then we have the idea of teachers having a mental map of learning in mind for their learners whereby they know the actual or current levels of learners and the potential level they wish them to achieve. The planning and strategizing that takes place on a minute-by-minute basis can be encapsulated within the notion of a ZPD. The teacher is an active and intentional mediator. Rather than transmitting teaching they mediate learning.

Secondly, learning can be seen to proceed through four stages. These stages show a gradual transformation from the learning being with the teacher and then being transferred over to the learner. If optimal learning is not achieved or is lost or forgotten, whatever the reason may be, then the work done within the ZPD is carried out again, refocused and redefined. As a consequence the learning stages are entered again. In helping learners to re-enter and re-apply, teachers also mediate ways of knowing. It is exceptionally important to recognize that no learners or teachers have failed in this process, they are always moving towards their potential. If they did not 'get it' then the ZPD needs recasting or redefining. This can be done in relation to areas such as learning pace, style, strategy, input or aims and objectives.

Thirdly, the bare bones of this process are presented, in two slightly different ways. As is evident, the process moves from being entirely teacher focused at the starting point to being entirely learner focused at the end point, though validation and overall responsibility must remain with the teacher. Gradually the learner transforms this learning, is able to take control of it and evaluate its utility and value.

---

**DIALOGUE POINT**

One of the best methods of illuminating the processes that have been described is to engage in a dialogue with a learner during a learning activity – this could be a colleague, but it may well be more productive if it is a learner in your own classroom.

- Talk with them about what they are doing and feeling from the moment that a task begins. Record in some way what is said and done.
- How do they describe their involvement in, and understanding of, the learning process?
- To what extent can this help you to understand learning and teaching?
- What have you learned?

---

## Strand 2: the cognitive aspects of learning

We know that many factors combine and interact in a complex manner to inform learning, but for ease of analysis, exploration and understanding we are choosing to separate them out. Therefore, as the details presented in Strand 1 were essentially social, Strand 2 is essentially cognitive. It is best to see them working in partnership rather than in isolation. This partnership also includes the issues associated with Strand 3, such as emotions, behaviour and self-esteems.

### Knowing how we learn

How do we learn? How did you learn to read and understand text? Did you learn it in the same way as other people? These and other such questions remain difficult to answer. Superficially, it would seem both logical and reasonable that professionals involved in teaching would have a clear and sophisticated understanding of learning. We could also assume that they have a clear underlying conceptual model to help them in this difficult task. But is this so?

In our work with teachers we have found that this can be a false generalized assumption to make. In our experience teachers are very aware of the variables that can promote or prevent learning from taking place. They also demonstrate clarity about learning outputs: these being seen as measures of teaching input but also, by some teachers, as measures of whether learning itself has taken place – yet conceptually the two are not the same. For a variety of reasons, some teachers can also fall into the trap of describing coverage – what a learner has done – when they were intending to describe what a learner has learnt.

When searching for a model of learning we found surprisingly few (only one so far) which in any way came close to describing the processes involved. The work of Norman (1978) provides such a description in a 'Tentative Model for Complex Learning'. We would argue that this model has various merits in describing the process of learning that takes place whenever we learn anything at all, though we also recognize it has some evident limitations. For example, it is solely a cognitive model. For the present, however, we are holding other factors to one side.

If this model works then it should be describing the process that will happen, and is happening, as anyone seeks to understand and re-understand it as a model. In fact, the process of learning about this model should help you understand how you learn. The model, if it is to be of use for the purpose intended, should provide answers to questions that will enable us to know 'how' it works, 'why' it works and how we can know that it works. Put simply, understanding and applying the model should provide an insight into learning processes.

### A model for complex learning
Coincidentally, this is also a staged model involving four stages:

### Stage 1
Here the emphasis is on accumulation of new learning. The teacher has a piece of learning in mind for a learner or group of learners. Learners will take in this teaching through the process of *accretion*. Let's pick up on this term accretion, as it is a very important term within the model. It is useful to consider a working definition of this word. Accretion can be described as a process of growth, an organic process. It also applies to the process of the growing of separate things

into one. This conveys exactly the fundamentals of the teacher–learner interaction as we view it.

As learners are actively involved in this act of accretion – achieved by taking in new information through sensory channels – they do not engage in other forms of learning at this time. The speed at which learners move through this stage is relative to learning need and difficulty.

The pace and modes of accretion should be made clear to the learner. The teacher can reduce frustration or anxiety by explaining to the learner which are the key senses required for a specific piece of learning. If not, there can be a tendency for the learner to take in the whole of the new learning in order to transform it. This can result in sensory overload and failure. This may strike a chord for readers in terms of recalling the psychoanalytic theory presented in Chapter 2, where we described having to take in new learning, process and digest it. At this stage, as accretion is taking place, you will often hear learners saying ' could you just give me that again' or teachers checking out the accretion process by asking ' do you want me to go over it one more time'. Teacher–learner interactions at this stage are all about dealing with amounts of new information that are mediated in terms of teacher–learner value; energy transformation; the ZPD; and actual and potential levels. Essentially at and during Stage 1 teachers are saying to learners ' take this'. This relates to the modelling discussed in Strand 1.

### Stage 2

Once accretion has begun to be successful, the accumulative part of the task is less prominent. The learner has something new and can begin to think about it and act upon the subject matter. This is called the *restructuring* phase. Let's think about restructuring at this point. This notion of structures and frameworks may well take you back to the work on constructs described in Chapter 5 which is an important link to make and illuminates how you are restructuring your learning as you read this chapter. What happens in restructuring is that learners transform the teaching into the internal structures and constructs that they have formed from their previous learning and experience. Learning begins to become intimate and grounded. It becomes known. It connects with the learner and becomes part of the learner. But of course it is still new and raw and remains still to be worked on.

At this stage, in order to think about, act upon, manipulate or transform what is being learned, the learner does not need to add to how much they 'know' about what they are learning. They may want to check a detail, test something out, but they would not want fully to re-enter the accretion stage. They do not want to go straight back to the beginning of the learning process. This would get in the way of digesting or processing the learning. It would make learning more distant at the time when they are seeking to make it intimate. An example may be useful at this point.

Let us return, very briefly, to the Shakespeare lesson on *A Midsummer Night's Dream* that was detailed in Chapter 5. The joint reading of scene 3 provides the accretion stage. The teacher then seeks via questioning to initiate a moving on, as part of the lesson, to the restructuring stage. The teacher first models 'here it is' and then moves on to 'now do this with it'. At the point of changing teaching style this marks the watershed of changing phases or stages in the lesson.

The movement between stages in the learning process when handled skilfully and sensitively by the teacher is a watershed – not a waterfall.

It is very important to note that, in this example, the teacher did not ask the learners to restructure by repeating the accretion stage. It would be unusual simply to read the scene again and expect the learners to have moved on to restructure their learning. This is because we believe that this teacher is in touch with the structure and stages of the model that we are making explicit here. His own learning is intimate.

### Stage 3

This is where the learning arising out of the previous two stages of accretion and restructuring is given an opportunity to become enriched and personally meaningful to the learner. The learner is invited to make the learning more intimate. The learner is less reliant on the teaching and it is at this point that the learner is most likely to experience insightful learning, typified by the Eureka principle or what we call 'penny dropping moments'.

When we have worked with teachers and learners we have noticed a very powerful buzz of excitement as the emotions surrounding achievement in learning are set free through success. You will, no doubt, have witnessed the same tangible excitement. Penny dropping moments are happy moments for learners and teachers alike. Learners might raise their arms in the air, smile or indicate that they have 'got it' by shouting. We must also recognize the emotional impact of not getting it, of the penny not dropping. Older learners can usually deal with this by recourse to their own inner resources, though their self-confidence may be dented for a time. Younger learners can find this lack of success personally challenging and undermining. If it happens regularly, it can have a devastating effect upon them. We must always be open to the effect on self-confidence that a long series of experiences where they never seem to 'get it' will have for learners.

Learners at the point of 'getting it' may often need to check their learning out by returning to previous stages briefly. Returning to Jay in the Shakespeare lesson, we can see that the humour in his answer was a product of some of the other learners being in Stage 2 of their learning. Jay was not at the same stage and, though concerned about it, did not see his response in this light.

### Stage 4

At this stage the learners learning becomes increasingly 'known' and automatic and the learner is becoming fully independent in this area. This enables the learner, in effect, to 'play' with the knowledge or skill. They can *practise* and develop short cuts. They can merge or discard constructs. This stage also includes natural wastage, whereby through lack of practice or application or through forgetting or due to trauma we lose previous learning. Automatic learning now becomes de-automized.

As a reader of this section you will have been involved in a process of change in your learning. Through accretion and restructuring you will have made sense of the model and will be in a changed learning state. You have been given something, you have taken it in and maybe you have experienced thinking 'yes I can see that, I think I understand it, but I'll just check it again'. The example of Jay's learning in an English lesson aimed to support you in this process, offering a step towards a penny dropping moment. By now, you should be thinking 'yes I've got it, I understand, I begin to see what it means'. This should enable you to apply it to your own experience. However, you may need some practice to feel assured and confident that you have learned.

If this has *not* happened yet, then as an independent learner you are likely to re-enter the learning stages in a manner suited to your learning needs. You may decide to read it again or you might disengage from the text so that you can think about it again. You may keep it in mind until you can talk to someone about it. In doing this independent learners tend to automatically refocus which stage of this learning model they want to re-enter in order to learn more efficiently. They know where they need to go in order to improve the quality of their learning. What we notice with many teacher–learner interactions however is that the teacher overfocuses on the accretion or practice stages. That is Stage 1 and Stage 4. They particularly tend to rev up the accretion or the practice.

In our work with teachers in a variety of settings we have found that all areas of learning appear to fit into this model – though clearly being such a fundamentally cognitive model restricts its breadth of application. Teachers have reported being able to use this model to aid their analysis of how learning might occur and to develop their practice as a response to this. They have done so in relation to a wide range of learners with diverse learning needs. We are always mindful to emphasize the need to reflect upon components that the model does not incorporate, such as self-esteems, motivation, the link between behaviour and learning and other key social and emotional factors.

### Strand 2: a summary
We can review this section and point to a model of complex learning which claims to fit all learning situations – this is another big claim to make. The claim does have a qualifier in that the limitations of the model have been made clear too.

### On your bike
Let us consider one example that many readers will have experience of – learning to ride a bicycle. Most would agree this is a complex piece of learning and therefore teaching this skill must be similarly complex. The situation that we are proposing is one where the teacher can ride a bicycle and the learner cannot. The teacher has to plan the lesson and the method of differentiation. They decide the best way to teach this skill is to go to a safe grassy area and to find a slight incline. A common method of teaching this skill is adopted: the learner sits on the bicycle and the teacher, holding the saddle, runs with the

learner and bicycle down the incline, keeping the bicycle as upright as possible until the bottom of the incline is reached. This is work at Stage 1, the accretion phase. The learner accretes the complex and new sensations and experiences of maintaining balance on two wheels.

The teacher knows that after this stage it is not helpful suddenly to move to activities associated with Stage 4. For example, they would not expect an optimal learning outcome if, after having arrived at the bottom of the hill, they asked the learner to perform the task again with their arms in the air or to practise wheel spins. Instead Stage 1 is repeated but at a certain point the teacher judges that they are able to take their hand away from the saddle. The learner experiences that this has happened and may become anxious. The hand may have to return quickly to the saddle so that balance is regained, but the teacher is starting to reduce their control over the learning. They repeat this process many times. Gradually the teacher is able to take their hand off the saddle for longer and longer. Soon the learner is able to ride several metres down an incline on their own.

What about the learner's perspective? Initially, the teacher controlled all of the learning. When the initial support was no longer there the learner may well have fallen off many times. However, they repeat the process and again use internal cognitive and emotional resources, admittedly intermittently. The learning then moves to Stage 2. The learner structures and restructures the feedback they are receiving. They have nearly 'got it', but not quite. They can balance when on the move but they cannot start or stop without falling off. These skills are also addressed and introduced slowly over time. At last the out of breath but proud teacher will see the learner use their own resources to ride the bicycle. The learner, excited and delighted, naturally practises and fine-tunes their skills, not without a few spills and anatomical grazes in the process. Gradually automaticity is established.

Some learners who might not ride a bicycle again for many years are likely to need similar re-instruction the next time they try and ride a bicycle. Yet others never forget these deeply processed and structured skills.

**REFLECTION POINT**

Think of all the teacher–learner interactions you are involved in.

- To what degree are there any you can think of where this four-stage model does not seem applicable? What makes it so?
- Think of examples where it is applicable. How far it is possible to identify each stage? To what extent can this help you with your teaching?

## Bringing it all together

This chapter has presented two optimistic pedagogical formulations or models. One is grounded in a social interactionist view of teaching and learning, the other presenting a dynamic cognitive model of the process of learning. Putting them together into a unified model provides a useful basis for beginning to think about learning. This in turn provides further opportunities to think about teaching, to enable the teacher to dig deep within the principles and practice of differentiation.

This unified model can be mapped on, in real time, and applied to any learning system. We have deliberately chosen not to illustrate the inherent complexity of this unified and integrated model in a diagrammatic form as this may alienate some readers from the text. Instead, in keeping with the spirit of the book we have chosen to present them in other differentiated forms, including the use of examples and by breaking them down into smaller areas. An illustration of the two models superimposed upon each other would represent a visual bombardment; therefore we represent them, in text form, next to each other for comparative purposes. You will remember that the models in both strands have four stages or phases.

The limitation of presenting the models in this way is that they appear to be linear when in fact they are circular and cyclical. These stages are presented in linear form for convenience of access only. In effect when we get to the end of Stage 4 then we move back to Stage 1 for the next piece of learning. It works as a loop. The ZPD represents the totality of the context within which this teacher–learner interaction takes place.

| Social learning model | Cognitive Model |
|---|---|
| Stage 1  Assistance provided by teacher<br>peer, colleague, other | Accretion<br>Incremental learning<br>New learning |
| Stage 2  Assistance provided by others decreases<br>Assistance provided by self increases | Restructuring<br>Discovery, invention<br>Application<br>Getting it |
| Stage 3  Increasing internalization of learning<br>Intimate learning<br>Rechecking with teachers | Automization<br>Enrichment<br>'Got it'<br>Penny dropping moment |
| Stage 4  Automaticity achieved<br>Life-long learning | Tuning<br>Practice<br>Playing with<br>Short cuts |
| De-automization | Forgetting<br>Trauma |

### There are always more questions to ask

If Stage 4 is not achieved then this does not represent failure for teacher or learner. The models are provided to enable you to analyse which area may need adjustment by asking questions such as, Was the teaching learning interaction accurately placed within the ZPD? Is the baseline information, upon which the actual level is based, accurate or not? Is the potential level a true reflection of what can be achieved on this occasion? Does it need to be thought through again and redrawn to become achievable? To what extent are you as teacher overestimating or underestimating the difference between actual and potential levels for this learner or group of learners? What forms of teacher assistance are being provided? Who else could do this? Do peers support each other during learning? What is the balance of your teaching learning interactions? What range of strategies and approaches are focused upon accretion? How and why are learners given opportunities for restructuring? At what point do you ask learners to practice learning? How do you know that they have internalized the learning? How do you provide enrichment tasks? How do you differentiate them? Who do you provide them for?

You will be able to think of many more questions, the model is provided less for us to detail questions but to enable you to generate grounded questions within your teacher–learner system, therefore it is not our intention to detail the full range of them here. We provide some in order to emphasize that the principles and practice of differentiation are also cyclical – questions are generated, answers are offered and new questions are generated. Questioning enables us to clarify our own thinking and to become aware of our own assumptions, values and beliefs.

Asking one question can set off a whole series of other questions that can help us to analyse and improve our own practice.

'Can you tell me the way to the nearest hotel please?'

# 8 Self-esteems and emotional differentiation

This chapter continues with the notion of focusing upon particular strands or themes as covered in the previous chapter. Here we consider Strand 3 relating to the emotional context for learning and its relationship to differentiation. For reasons that will become clear we are particularly interested in issues that surround the concept of self-esteem as well as commenting upon teaching and learning experience, the nature of self and our personal susceptibilities. We closed the last chapter with a large claim, namely that the cognitive process model which was presented will apply to all learners and all learning contexts. We open this one with what might appear to be another large claim – *self-esteem does not exist.*

By making this claim we are not intending to devalue emotional factors relating to personality or self-concept, for example; we are simply pointing out that self-esteem itself is not 'real', it is a construct, a descriptive and explanatory construct. It does not exist in the form in which we constantly hear it applied and used in teacher–learner systems. It is used to describe and explain a combination of factors with multiple variables and outcomes that are relative and contextual. Definitions and explanations of self-esteem do not seem to help us to become more analytical and sophisticated in planning for emotional differentiation. We find it difficult to make substantial progress in defining or measuring it because it does not exist. We may want it to exist and therefore we talk about it as if it is real. We create and adopt tools to measure it, when these tools often highlight a relationship between thinking, feeling and behaviour. However, the identification of such a relationship does not explain causation and nor does it prove that self-esteem exists as a singular characteristic of an individual.

At times, we have tried to engage in discussion with teachers about self-esteem and asked challenging questions of each other. In many situations it is like trying to discuss the concept of a person's soul or spirit. What is it? Where is it? What influences it? How do we know about it? How can we alter it? One general outcome of such discussions and debates is that many people see self-esteem as a concrete concept – there is a belief that all people have a self-esteem that is high or low depending on how we feel about our 'self', especially in relation to how others perceive us. Self-esteem appears to be located on a linear scale ranging from high to low. Clearly we do not dismiss the importance of emotions in relation to learning and we are not saying that emotional factors do not exist.

For example, we would accept that a learner aged seven who wishes that they were dead does have a devastatingly negative image of their self and worth. In this example, if the teacher believes that the seven year old has low self-esteem, perhaps at rock-bottom level and as a singularly defining characteristic, then what routes can they design to offer learning for that child? Herein lies a serious difficulty. If you buy into the 'low self-esteem culture' then it is most likely that your teaching routes will only be defined within the parameters of the child's negativity and despair. This may distort your thinking and planning and will impact upon your operations within the zone of proximal development (ZPD). As detailed elsewhere, you are always seeking to act in the most open, creative and positive manner on behalf of learners within the ZPD, not to enter into their negativity, no matter how bleak this may appear. If in this situation we do not seek positive support and solutions, we are in danger of becoming as emotionally paralysed as the learner . What value would you bet upon in such a relationship?

We are proposing that self-esteem is a weak construct and should be defined in terms that demonstrate that it is responsive to different persons and contexts. This is another situation where differentiation is necessary – in this case we need to differentiate the construct. This allows us to explore it in relation to concepts that are concurrent throughout this book, value, flexibility and scale being especially relevant. Thus, if we are looking at emotional responses to teaching and learning we need a fluid rather than a concrete construct. This can be achieved by a minimum alteration to the word that makes an optimal alteration to the construct. Consequently, this chapter deals with a debate around *self-esteems* as against *self-esteem*.

We select self-esteems as we feel that differentiation in this area needs to begin with a workable proposition that can operate above the level of what has become almost a cliché. A term that is used so often that its meaning is rarely called into question. This follows the ethos underpinning this book in asking you to question and requestion your own practice and the practice within your teaching and learning system. Not in the form of negative questions but in a positive manner to sustain, create and engender a respectful teaching and learning environment for all.

When working with schools, learners and parents or carers we often see planning that speaks of the learner's self-esteem – it is always the learner's self-esteem that is under the spotlight. When self-esteem is raised as a difficulty it is low self-esteem that needs to improve. It is rarely high self-esteem which needs to move higher. The focus is usually on repairing brittle, broken and fragile self-esteem. This poses the question as to what self-esteem is, how and where it becomes so vulnerable to collapse, and whether it is possible or perhaps worthwhile to define it as a whole. To become analytical and for teachers and learner to benefit, it is more helpful to eyeball the concept in a different way. Redefining it as self-esteems offers the learner and the teacher a more meaningful insight into a complex constellation of factors that are fluid and changeable. Self-esteem has become a catchphrase involving the casting of a wide net that trawls everything into it, resulting in a sometimes chaotic and often ill-defined mass. It is a concrete, solid and problematic construct, unlike self-esteems, which are holistic. Our task is to try and break down the self-esteem monolith in order to bring a fully differentiated focus to bear on the reality lying beneath the label. To do this we need to look closer at self-esteem so that we can understand why a more fluid concept is required – a concept that enables us to gain more data about learners and their emotions.

## Self-esteem – what is it?

Clear and succinct definitions are not that easy to come by. Often people turn to dictionaries for precise definitions but interestingly it is difficult to find a single entry for the hyphenated term in many dictionaries. Therefore we are reduced to looking at them individually. Common definitions are as follows:

*Self*: individuality, essence, oneself.
*Esteem*: think favourably of, regard as valuable, positive opinion, respect.

Definitions of self-esteem involve combinations of these notions, along with other self-centred associations such as self-concept, self-confidence, self-worth and self-respect. The notion of self-esteem is linked to these, there is a correlation between them, but it also appears to be different from them too. This is particularly evident in its usage and application. In our view it has become a shorthand form of interchangeable 'common speak' for a watery set of indistinct notions which are not useful to the process of differentiation. In fact, at some levels, differentiation is fundamentally hindered by the concept of self-esteem. We see self-concept as a clearer notion and most definitely one that supports the thinking that is associated with differentiation. Certainly there are espoused psychological theories around self-concept. In this chapter, self-concept is used to describe how a person sees her or himself.

Let us begin by thinking about the self. Here we are inviting you to think for yourself about what the notion of 'self' means to you. How does this relate to your 'selves' as teachers thinking about the other 'selves' with whom you regularly interact – that is, learners?

## Three views of self

The concept of self is confronted and investigated in many sacred and philosophical writings from diverse cultures and traditions. Some traditions identify a conscious self that is often described in physical terms. Others see the concept of self as an illusion. There are religious doctrines that assert that there is only one permanent and everlasting true self, often described as God. Self is also a concept that is considered beyond philosophy and religion. We are interested in presenting what psychologists have said about self. The earliest concept of 'psyche', from which the word psychology derives, contained a notion of the self or soul that continued beyond death. We shall consider three psychological views of self. All that we offer are the very briefest of tastes of these different forms of thinking about self. Their outline is presented to orient your thinking. Each area has a wealth of material and literature associated with it that certain readers might wish to explore further. Our purpose is not to produce a textbook explanation of such theories and thinking but to highlight rich areas to provoke and stimulate your questioning. For this reason we have chosen the work of three well-known psychologists who offer differing perspectives. We present them in a non-judgemental fashion. We must emphasize, however, that they are all male views of self.

### Carl Rogers: self and organism

Rogers divided the person into *self* and *organism*. The self is the 'I' or 'me'. He postulated that everyone has an ideal self. The ideal of what they would like to be.

The organism is the real world as seen and experienced by the 'I' or 'me'. Differences between these two can create deep-seated anxieties and result in conflict and a lack of congruency. For example, a learner may believe that they are the best linguist in the group. This is how they construct their self in relation to the speaking of foreign languages. However, when the teacher assesses written and spoken language, the learner might be in the lowest 50 per cent of the group. This is the information gained from the real world. There is a gap or discrepancy between how the learner perceives their 'self' and the feedback from the 'organism'. Such a difference can move, through learning, to congruence and accommodation over time. In more serious situations than the example given, therapy may be required to enable the discrepancy to be dealt with. Given the right situation and support everyone can be led to resolve these personal crises *for themselves*. They can be seen to regard themselves positively. Rogerian therapy is known as Client Centred Therapy. It has also been used as a model for mutual support therapy groups.

### John Bowlby: attachment theory

Bowlby developed attachment theory which he saw as social, emotional and behavioural characteristics resulting from an individual being in close proximity to their main caregivers. From this we construct working models based upon our experience of these absolutely critical relationships. This happens from the moment of birth and recent research would suggest it could happen before birth. Our early experiences provide powerful underpinnings to our sense of self and the way we operate within and upon the world. There are different types of attachment, such as secure attachment. There are also attachment behaviours, for example a baby crying to gain the care and attention of a main caregiver or to express anxiety about the unavailability of a main caregiver. These attachments facilitate us in playing, learning, socializing and in growing and developing emotionally. He thought that early patterns of attachment persisted throughout life. In positive situations attachment could result in an individual feeling a profound sense of self-worth and becoming confident in developing relationships with others. Bowlby proposed that secure attachment can result in a higher level of curiosity, risk-taking and determination in learning – being able to deal with perceived failure through persistence to get things right. In negative situations, such as insecure attachment, phobias and self-doubt could develop. Attachment is developmentally represented inside the head of the learner.

### Sigmund Freud: id, ego and superego

Freud described the self as being made up of three component parts: *id, ego* and *superego*. The id is unconscious. It is present from birth and provides us with instinctual, impatient and impulsive urges to receive gratification. The ego is preconscious. It acts as an intermediary between the instinctive urges of the id and the outside world. The superego forms an internalized inhibiting force of control. This is an internal representation, for example, of parents or caregivers or teachers who may wish to impose cultural and societal morals. It is similar to the concept of a constraining conscience that can create feelings of guilt. It negotiates, mediates and differentiates. Freud proposes that there is a constant tension between the primitive forces of the id and the inhibiting control exerted by the superego, with the ego seeking to mediate between the two. Freud asserts that everyone develops coping mechanisms to help deal with their own concept of self not being gratified. These he refers to as defence mechanisms. For example, painful memories and experiences can be repressed or denied completely – as if they never happened or are not happening. At times, the feelings associated with one person or event can be projected onto another person or event.

---

**REFLECTION POINT**

Consider the three views of self.

- Bearing in mind the brief nature of the explanations, how far would you agree with any of them?
- How far can any of them help you to understand your 'self' as a person and as a teacher?
- Now consider a learner that you teach – how far can any of these theories help you to understand any of the learners that you teach?
- Now consider your colleagues. What do you know about their thinking in relation to 'self'? How could you find out?
- To what extent would it make any difference if you had strong views one way and a colleague had strong views informed in a different manner, about learners you both work with?
- What systems does your learning system provide to enable learners and teachers to understand and develop their own concept or sense of self? What other systems could they offer?

---

Whatever self is, you will have your own ideas and views about it. Whichever factors mould, make, inhibit, enable or facilitate development of the self exist among the development of the selves of the learners you work with. Of course they were, and some would argue that they still are, continually around in the development of all of us as teachers.

After this brief consideration of self we know turn to esteem. The esteem part of the equation is probably easier to understand, dealing as it does with self-respect and a sense of inner confidence, value and worth.

## Some characteristics of self-esteem

We have asserted that the construct or concept of self-esteems encompasses a holistic view of self. Self-esteem asserts the opposite – a monistic or one-sided view. It implies a singular characteristic that changes in a linear manner from low to high. It is a singular notion, as are self-confidence and self-respect. It has an evident hierarchical aspect to it.

Maslow (1954) proposed a hierarchy of human needs. At the lowest level are physiological needs, such as hunger, thirst, sex and sleep. One level above this is the need for safety – avoidance of pain, fear, illness, cold and wet, for example. At the next level is the need for belongingness and love. Above this is esteem – meaning self-confidence, worth, strength, capability, feeling useful and necessary in the world. Finally, at the top of the hierarchy is self-actualization. It can be seen in this structure that as human beings we cannot move up to the next level unless and until lower level needs have been satisfied. Therefore someone cannot have their higher-level needs met unless their basic human needs, such as eating, drinking and sleeping, are being met.

In this hierarchy of our needs, esteem is second from the top. We can see that notions, definitions and the sheer scope the term esteem covers are getting larger and larger as progress is made from one level to another. In this view there can appear to be a developmental element to thinking about self-esteem which in turn is often associated with behavioural and emotional disturbance. We hear this most commonly expressed with regard to learners who present with challenging behaviour, where planning to address their needs seeks to improve or build their self-esteem. Certainly it is felt that self-esteem as a singular entity can be measured, for example through self-esteem inventories, which in turn may enable a degree of labelling to occur.

## Some characteristics of self-esteems

It seems evident to us that if we are to be more accurate in differentiating and bringing about grounded learning, then we need a term that represents what takes place in the real world. One of the authors recalls a learner that he recently taught (O'Brien, 2000c). This learner was labelled as having 'low self-esteem'. He describes the learner as having low self-esteem in one area, reading, and high self-esteem in another, burglary. Whilst his self-concept was poor in relation to literacy, it was high in relation to illegal activity because he received peer group adulation for it, and his peers were important to him. This is provided as an example of considering self-esteems – looking at how learners feel in different contexts – rather than making assumptions based upon one universal, constant and concrete concept of self-esteem. The point being that the casually applied label that 'this learner has low self-esteem' may restrict opportunities to see what it is that makes someone feel good about what they do in certain contexts. If we transfer this concept to the curriculum then we can see the benefits of viewing a learner in terms of their self-esteems.

Consider the teacher planning which seeks to improve self-esteem. How can a teacher know when self-esteem has been improved? What evidence can they seek? How will a teacher conceive indicators of the totality of a vague and ill-defined notion of self-esteem when the learner somehow demonstrates it? It could be proposed that vague planning and lack of clarity in goal setting do not enable a teacher to raise a learner's self-esteem. The problem is seen as being located with the teacher and their practice rather than with an understanding of self-esteem: it is the teacher's fault. We see the problem as broader than this – self-esteem is a phrase and an explanatory construct that, although it feels intuitively right, promotes fixed rather than fluid and holistic thinking. Worse than this, because it is such a global term it can be a constant negative theme in a learner's career.

The curriculum is multidimensional and therefore a learner's experience of it is not flat. In this context we define the curriculum as all learning that takes place in and through the school. A learner's experience and emotions undulate according to their own perception of their ability in relation to achievement and attainment in different curriculum areas. Even within one specific subject area a learner can have multiple esteems.

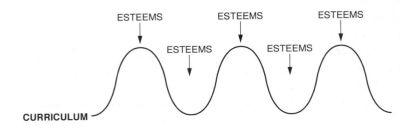

Figure 8.1 Curriculum topography and learner self-esteems

Consider this example. A teacher comments or writes that Suki encounters various learning problems, sometimes she acts out, especially in practical lessons in science, and she can be emotionally fragile. With this type of behaviour and her family difficulties, a link is made and the judgement is that she has low self-esteem. The next learning plan includes broad targets to improve her self-esteem. A support professional fills in a self-esteem inventory in interview with her. Suki objects to this interview taking place and the outcome is that she *has* got low self-esteem. The plan from now on has to be to build and improve her self-esteem.

How can this be done?
*By?* Making her feel good about herself.
*How?* By making her feel good about herself.
This is not the most analytical or helpful starting point for planning.

At the planning meeting there are two nonplussed members. The drama teacher sits scratching her head as, in the last lesson, Suki once again took the lead in choreographing a dance, which will be performed at an open evening to be held in three weeks time. The other teacher who is bemused, the learning support assistant, has been working with Suki on a collage in art lessons, where she has been able positively and creatively to express feelings about some of her family relationships, though this remains a tender and fragile area. Suki's brother died two years ago. Her father left the family. Suki feels the loss. However, she has even discussed with her teacher the possibility of displaying her collage in the school entrance area.

Has Suki got low self-esteem or has she got variable self-esteems, in changing and different contexts? In this example it would appear that she presents with a range of self-esteems according to the differing facets of her personality, individuality and sense of self. Doubtless these have arisen from a complex combination of past experiences, learning and development and current susceptibilities. She evidently has high and robust self-esteem in the context of dance, extending to creative leadership and group management. She has growing self-esteem in the area of her artistic expression and representation. She may have low self-esteem in science but we cannot assume that she has low self-esteem in every aspect of the science curriculum.

This has pinned down the actual work that needs to be done in understanding the experience of learners within and beyond the curriculum and differentiated the original casually applied label. Yet ideally we would suggest a further progressive focusing on the actual esteems themselves within these areas which need developing and working on. How can they be scrutinized and targeted? What has to be done, how can it be planned for, taught and evaluated, to show that a focus has been placed upon Suki's esteems?

This is why we must take another look at self-esteem and recast it as a complementary and more inclusive concept. This will encourage a more holistic view and one that matches the complexity of individuals and the processes of teaching and learning. Self-esteems is a circular concept which describes a continuous and multidimensional approach. If it was linear there is a temptation to leave it alone once it is high. If it is cyclical then high or low it can always be developed further. It can add to definition and understanding of needs and help to identify areas that require further support and differentiation. These factors or facets of the self exist and coexist in a complex manner and it is better to think of them in terms of interaction and inter-relationships rather than overidentifying a block of self-esteem with certain behavioural presentations. Lastly, this more qualitative approach to the complexity of esteems can address and combat the negativity and stereotypes that are the outcomes of a process of bulk labelling. The difference between the two concepts is summarized below.

| Self-esteems | Self-esteem |
|---|---|
| Holistic | Monistic |
| Circular | Linear |
| Complex | Singular |
| Flexible | Fixed |
| Insights | Labels |
| Multiple focus | Single focus |
| Positive power | Negative power |
| Destination | Navigation |

## Mapping self-esteems: lost in space?

What we are proposing here is a conceptual shift from self-esteem to the complementary and inclusive notion of self-esteems. This is in fact really a mapping exercise. Just as the curriculum has its own topography, an undulating landscape, so do esteems. The notion of self-esteem feels rather like the description of a small-scale map of a region. It can be likened to a space journey where you are in one part of the galaxy and wish to travel to another part. Given the vast scale of the universe, the first task in finding the planet you seek would be to arrive at the right portion of the galaxy. For this purpose you want a general map rather than a detailed one. You would not need a map of downtown Manhattan, even if arriving in this part of New York was your ultimate goal.

Instead you would want a map with sufficient detail only to locate you in the correct sector of the solar system. This map must deal in an easy to manage form with vast detail and scales. Therefore information has to be prioritized and fine detail, which causes confusion to the bigger picture, is discarded. Once you arrive in the correct corner of the universe then the map that helped to get you there is no longer useful. At this point, you still do not want a plan of individual streets and blocks within a city. You scale down again and use a map that has selected data that can help you locate one particular planet.

So the process goes on, you continually select and reject data at different levels of detail in order to home in on the target area. When you arrive in the city of your choice you are no longer using a map of the solar system to help you navigate. Using this image, let us call that original map 'self-esteem' and consider that it was useful for a given purpose. It is no longer useful for the fine detail of differentiated teaching and learning. It was useful to navigate with initially, to get you moving in the right direction. It worked well to help you in the process of arriving but it operates at a macro level and is no longer employable at the scale at which you are now seeking to work. In fact to use it still would be negligent. Now we need a map that can deliver much more exact locations in fine detail. These are the maps of 'self-esteems'.

They describe the detail and interrelations of the emotional ecosystems of individuals. A self-esteems map lays out all those factors that contribute to a sense of self, all with a sense of topography. It provides the shape, feel and flow of the surface in relation to the underlying structures. This is what we need to have an understanding of when seeking to provide emotional differentiation. We cannot hope to do this successfully if we are not aware of the question and impact of scale.

We believe that the notion of self-esteem is not useful because it predisposes us to look at the wrong scale. In fact, it causes us to look only at one scale. Although the purpose may be right, the map is wrong. This can leave us seeking to address subtle and powerful issues almost from a position of remote control. This maximizes the space between teacher and learner and is unlikely to bring about intimate learning. In its place we propose using the right tools for the job by dealing with self-esteems, a map to help locate the heart of the issue. Let us be clear – self-esteems will get you to your precise destination, whereas self-esteem will only offer navigation.

### Positive and negative power

In this section we are using power in the sense of political and physical power. We consider negative power rather than positive power, as this is a regular concern of teachers that we have worked with. We remind you that teachers have self-esteems as well as learners, though we tend to hear more about those of the learners than we do of the teachers.

---

**REFLECTION POINT**

Look back at the examples given in Chapter 2 of statements made by teachers about learners.

- What would you say about the self-esteems of the teachers and learners included in these comments that raise issues about stereotyping?
- On what basis would you make these statements?

---

Negative power seems to be an orientation arising from low self-esteems in individuals, whether they are teachers or learners. This presents itself in a variety of forms within teaching and learning systems. In younger learners it may present as overt acting out behaviours. In older learners it can be a motivational presentation, in which they want teachers to know that they are disaffected and to experience their disaffection. Having access to some control and predictability is something that we have seen, through considering personal constructs, as being very important to us as individuals. The power underlying these acts of control or attempts to gain, regain or retain control can be perceived as either positive or negative. Not only do individuals exert positive and negative power but so do groups and systems.

Negative power in teachers as well as learners is likely to arise as the result of some key areas of esteems that require further development, attention, resourcing or differentiation. Adults tend to present with different forms of negative power within teaching and learning systems. Obviously, on a societal level, adults may fight, riot and engage in war, and these may be seen as the more extreme forms of negative power. We are referring to more subtle signs and indicators than this that we can learn to recognize and address through emotional differentiation.

Throughout this book we have spoken of open questioning being the basis underpinning inclusive and fully differentiated teaching and learning systems. We have to recognize that teachers and learners may employ questioning in a negative manner. Where this happens occasionally and in a balanced manner it is a natural by-product of human interactions. Where it happens routinely it is a sign that things are not as they seem. One linguistic indicator of this that we see a lot is in the polite use of the word 'but'.

## I like it . . . but

Imagine that one teacher has an idea or a plan. A plan to which they have given much consideration. They take it to another person, possibly a more senior person in the teaching and learning system, for consideration. The other person replies, 'I like it . . . *but*'. The other person may register the 'but' in various ways, another common phrase being 'I hear what you are saying . . . *but*'. Sometimes the 'but' is signalled and inferred by the pause only. How will this make the teacher with the new idea feel – about their 'self', their value, and about their idea? We are conscious that in drawing attention to this practice we are not aiming to prevent the term from being used from a positive basis. We are concerned with the power and status issues that might be inherent in the use of the word or the negative feelings it raises in relation to how it might affect a person's self-esteems. It is difficult to say to another adult that you do not like their ideas about teaching and learning, so the message can be sweetened with ' I like it . . . but'. If the idea or plan as a whole is not applicable, achievable or realistic then what is really needed is a conversation about aspects of their idea that might be useful within the teaching and learning system that they have responsibility for. This will impact upon their sense of worth and represents emotional differentiation in action. Of course, the same principle applies to learners, especially where the 'I like it' is subsumed by the message associated with the ensuing use of the word 'but'. Inevitably some teachers and learners will process 'I like it . . . but' as 'I do not like it at all'. We all exercise negative and positive power at times and the joint aim of teaching and learning systems is to minimize the destructive force that this can represent and maximize the creative force that positive applications can unleash.

Why should teaching and learning systems be particularly prone to variability in self-esteems on the part of teachers and learners? Of course they are not. All systems suffer from this, but the act of teaching and learning is very closely linked to basic life experience and evokes profound reactions in all concerned with the process. Teaching and learning is above all an emotional activity and this is why we need to plan for emotional differentiation. We fool ourselves if we ignore, deny or remain unclear about the degree of raw emotion that runs deep and strong in every learner teacher interaction. Some teachers have said to us that they are subject teachers and subject teachers only; it is as simple as that. Nothing could be further from the truth or from the reality of their professional work. The following are learner's views of the emotional hothouse that is their classroom or school. They know who is 'in' and who is 'out'. They can identify who is good and who is bad. They regularly reassess who is top and who is bottom in the pecking order. They know who is friendly with whom; who is not friendly with whom; and who should never be allowed to get friendly with whom. They can tell who likes what and who does not like what, who is trustworthy and who is untrustworthy, who can survive and who cannot survive – and this just describes their view of teachers!

## DIALOGUE POINT

Discuss with a colleague this view of your learning system being powered by emotions, for teachers and learners.

- To what degree do you agree or disagree with each other about the role that emotions play?
- Think of positive examples of emotions being harnessed to good effect in teaching learning interactions. In what way were they harnessed and by whom?
- To what degree is negative power employed in your teaching and learning system? Who does so and why?
- How far can you identify the underlying self-esteems that this use of power came from?
- To what degree can you identify positive uses of power employed in your teaching and learning system? Who does so and why?
- How far can you identify the self-esteems that were associated with this use of positive power?
- To what degree can areas of negative power be changed into areas of positive power?
- Identify what could be done:
  (a)  by yourself
  (b)  with a colleague
  (c)  with a manager
  (d)  with a partner
  (e)  with learners.
- When and where will you begin?

The power within teacher–learner interactions is based upon the teacher having an agenda, knowing something and having the responsibility to impart this to the learners. We have written about the basic human predisposition to learn in other places within this book but we are not naive enough to suppose that learners always want to learn what is being taught at the time that it is being taught. Therefore teaching and learning also involve power issues. As well as this, in most teacher–learner systems there are usually more learners than there are teachers at any given time. Often, a single teacher has a group to teach and is responsible for every individual's learning. The learners may not share the teacher's agenda and individually, or communally, through their internal group dynamic, may have other agendas to attend to instead and to learn from. Therefore there are fundamental management and responsibility issues that fall upon the teacher rather than the learners.

Having set up a scenario of more negative learner interaction, we are keen to point out that we feel there are strong emotional factors at play in all teaching and learning systems and in fact in all human interactions, whether they be efficient or inefficient, positive or negative. What differentiates them is the outcomes for the learners and teachers.

Even where the teacher–learner energy transformation is high we propose that the same emotions are and have been present, but they have been harnessed and held in a different, more positive manner. They are differentiated in a way that sustains and develops personal esteems rather than attacking, degrading or demolishing them.

This emotional management task is felt very keenly by teachers but is just as relevant for learners. What adds further power to teacher–learner interactions is the potential at the outset for some form of conflict to be the result. We are not saying that teacher–learner interactions are typified by conflict. We are highlighting that when emotional management and differentiation issues are raised and tested, especially at the initial stages of interaction, the emotional stance of both parties becomes challenged and success may hinge on reactions to the possibility of conflict.

We have to investigate this further in order to understand what is taking place now that our mapping has located us at the very core of self and esteems.

## Emotional management and differentiation

If, as we assert, there is a flow of emotional power in every single teacher–learner interaction this can produce stresses in each person. Stresses in the sense used here are seen as both positive and negative, whereas stress, another example of a monistic and broadly applied term, has become more clearly associated with negatives. These stresses arise from the conflict potential inherent in one person exerting teaching and learning responsibilities over a group of others.

When you, as a teacher of varying experience, next teach a group of learners of varying experience nobody knows exactly what will happen next. Think about it. You have an idea or a plan, and they have an idea or a plan too. Nobody knows what will happen or is happening until interactions unfold in real time, in front of you and them. From one perspective this could be seen as offering the potential for existential terror as everyone prepares for 'take-off'.

The experience is potentially stressful. The ways in which we cope with these stresses are complex and interesting. The following is one description of what you may experience in the act of teaching, and what learners may experience in the act of learning. When combinations of stresses are present what might be seen as negative reactions are most likely to be experienced. This is especially true when self-esteems are under threat. We need to be aware of how we react to such stresses because it is at this time that we are most likely to be the recipient, or the user, of negative power.

### Physiological reactions

The liver produces glucose to fuel muscles so that energy is readily on tap. Hormones are released to aid conversion of fats and protein into sugar to fuel the muscles. One of the most powerful of these is adrenaline. This increases heart and breathing rates and blood pressure, and muscles become noticeably more tense. Saliva and mucus in the mouth may dry up (note that people addressing groups often have a cup of water to hand). Endorphins, natural painkillers, are then released. Surface blood vessels expand and contract. The spleen releases more red blood cells in order to carry and convert increasing amounts of oxygen. What we have described here, as many readers will have realized, is what is typically known as the *fight-flight response*: this is an innate or automatic response.

We cannot help this from happening to ourselves if we feel under threat. We are not suggesting that it follows that all teachers will feel these reactions all the time but the potential is always there. The potential stresses of teaching are not only associated with these types of interactions. We have had many teachers admit that they never sleep very well at the end of vacations when the start of a new term looms. Many of us will also admit to the stresses of teaching even causing us to experience worst-case scenarios in our dreams.

### Psychological reactions

These can be many and varied. One key factors is decision paralysis. This is a difficulty in making key decisions at a time when, owing to stresses, a person needs to be able to make very clear and rapid decisions. The type of difficulty that would be problematic if you were, for example, employed as an air traffic controller. This is a serious point and highlights why people who work in situations where there are potential for multiple stresses practice and simulate their decision-making processes under extreme conditions: the armed forces, the police, and airline pilots are examples. This paralysis is linked to difficulties in retrieving relevant information from memory and the consequence can be thinking that becomes fixed and fixated. A person's ability to prioritize becomes impaired and choice-making about possible alternatives becomes stuck. Thus, we need to remain alert to what is going on under the surface for individual teachers and learners, groups and systems that will affect learning and behaviour. We are then in a better position to support each other through differentiation.

### Emotional responses

Once again the 'health warning' needed here is to underline that these are also variable and that different individuals react differently to different stresses. But for those whose emotional reactions evoke negative responses and lowered esteems in key areas, there is an increased potential for experiencing feelings of guilt, apprehension, tension, fear, anger, aggression and displacement.

Teaching and learning systems, and the individuals and groups who are part of them, develop ways of 'holding' these emotions. This can be positive and can operate at informal and formal levels. Emotions can be held and differentiated through all of the usual aspects of collegiality that we find within all systems. These would include socializing, celebrations, cliques and factions, which can be representative of positive and negative power flows. A typical method that is common to many teaching systems is what amounts to 'coffee-cup-counselling'.

### Coffee-cup-counselling

This is a well-developed system for dealing with teacher negative feelings and lowered self-esteems and for enabling emotional differentiation. It maintains the concept of 'group' but without adult fear of being seen to need direct support or counselling. It is useful and has purpose because it is provided in-house, at very regular intervals, in a non-threatening manner. It thrives upon informal and non-judgemental peer-support systems rather than external experts and so, from the perspective of the users, it remains relatively safe. Also, it is free.

It carries its own signals, language, personnel and counselling space and typically operates as follows. It is break time in teaching and learning systems all over the country. A teacher arrives in a staff room looking a little exasperated, takes a cup and proceeds to make some coffee. At the same time they open a conversation towards other colleagues by saying something like 'I have just been teaching Jimmy . . . do you know what happened?' They proceed to sit down with the coffee and this is a signal to their colleagues that they wish to talk about a negative interaction with Jimmy. Colleagues may have their own cup of coffee, signalling that they are available to be engaged as peer counsellors. They will make a choice as to whether they wish to be part of the discussion. If they do, they can join in the exchange, offering sympathy, advice, commiseration and at times lightening the load by offering humour. They can also offer helpful and practical advice. The benefit of this occupational counselling is that it is easily available and the signals are so widely recognized. So much so, that it is rarely recognized, in the form we present it here, for what it really is. A problem will not be overly analysed and self-esteems are not called into question as such; it is not turned into an issue, a 'teacher danger' situation, as the teacher is not the focus of debate. It is usually dealt with in a manner which is understandable and which adds to the collegiate bond and group perceptions. This bond is often strengthened by the mutual exchange of problems. One negative outcome of such counselling could be that, given the fact that there is no time for critical analysis, it can become a forum for the labelling of learners and the transmission of assumptions.

In conclusion, we have dealt at some length with self-esteems as an important factor in aiding your analysis and understanding of emotional differentiation. We have sought to place this, unusually, within a context of looking at the self-esteems of both teachers and learners when dealing with issues of emotional differentiation. For too long it has been a one-way street with low self-esteem solely accorded to learners, almost to the point of becoming another negative and self-determining label.

---

### CASE POINT

This case is presented in different segments – it is differentiated. Each segment has an associated and hypothetical action point. We would like you to imagine that you are the teacher responsible for Susan.

*Part 1*

Susan is a very happy and bright little girl. She has many friends and is socially adept. She has always achieved in all aspects of her learning. She lives with her mother, father and younger brother. Susan has problems with mobility and other physical activities though she is very independent minded. She is eight years old and her ninth birthday is ten weeks away at the end of November. She has a condition that is commonly known as 'brittle bones'. She weighs eleven kilograms and is 60 cm tall.

Despite having problems in attending school owing to the many broken bones she has suffered from, she has always been seen as 'an achiever' – not a pejorative term relating to her disability but a positive term relating to her learning. At the beginning of a new academic year things change drastically. She is now seen as moody and sullen and emotionally fragile. However, despite some problematic behaviour her work has not suffered. Her teachers meet to address these issues. There is a strong feeling that Susan has developed low self-esteem since the term began. Previously it used to be high.

*Action: Given this admittedly limited information what would you suggest that could provide wider differentiation for Susan?*

*Part 2*

A plan is constructed and put into action. In three weeks time it is evaluated and it is not working. Susan is becoming more and more volatile, though she is still managing to do well in

➤

those lessons that she is able to stay in. On one occasion she explains to a learning support assistant that she would rather be dead. This very worrying information is fed back immediately to you. The situation is disconcerting and very puzzling – her self-esteem has reached rock bottom with alarming speed.

*Action*: *As the teacher responsible what do you do next to address this very worrying situation and why?*

### Part 3

A meeting is organized with Susan's parents. They need time to make arrangements firstly to change her father's work shift pattern and then to organize her younger brother's care arrangements for the afternoon. The meeting is arranged for ten days later.

*Action*: *Who else would you want to attend this meeting? Why? Is there anyone that you would not want to attend the meeting? Why not?*

### Part 4

At the meeting you discover that Susan's parents are very worried too. They have never seen her like this. It is very sad as her ninth birthday is only five weeks away now and she will not even discuss a party. They wonder if the mood swings might have a hormonal aspect. They explain that they have discussed with the parents of another girl in her class something they think is called 'precocious puberty'. These parents said that it was a very early onset of puberty. This may be affecting her self-esteem. If you invited someone from the medical profession to the forthcoming meeting this can be addressed directly at the meeting. If not, then such worries and the associated information should be looked into. You know nothing about this but you are aware that a doctor will be running a clinic in the school in six weeks time and make a note to discuss this likelihood with the doctor.

*Action*: *Information is collected before and during meetings. What other information will you decide to collect in this meeting? At what*

➤

*scale are you looking? Why have you decided to look for this partic-
ular information?*

### Part 5

You decide to collate a family history. Susan's father is 46 years
old and works in car production. He is an 'automobile engineer'
and works shifts. He has quite an abrupt manner in the meeting
and cannot see the point of such questions. He makes it clear
that being asked such questions makes him feel as if he has a
problem. This is unfair, as he had made every effort to get to the
meeting to help Susan. Susan has problems, not him – and what
are the teachers going to do about her problems? Maybe she
needs a referral to a doctor or someone like that? The parents
have their own thinking on what is happening, it demands an
urgent response, but you have told them that you will check out
this information about puberty in six weeks. They claim that in
the meantime her self-esteem will have gone off the bottom of
the scale.

Susan's mother is 45 and works in a bar part-time. The two
parents have to struggle, given their working hours, to make
sure that someone is always around to look after the children
when they come home from school. The children? Yes, there is
Susan, of course, who has to wait to get a special bus home and
arrives at one time and then there is Charlie, who is seven years
old. In relation to his health he is fine – as his father explains
'brittle bones is hereditary but Charlie hasn't got it'. Charlie is a
concern of the school that he attends owing to his increasing
emotional and behavioural problems. His wife continues 'Yes,
problems with Susan, problems with Charlie and then of course
there is Darren.' At the mere mention of his name, mum begins
to cry. Dad comforts her but looks angrily in your direction.

*Action: This appears to be a classic A or B situation. What will you
do next? Will you take route A and change the line of questioning?
Or will you take route B and continue the line of questioning whilst
recognizing the emotional impact it is clearly having on both adults.
Will you ask who Darren is?*

➤

*Part 6 (Route A)*

You decide to stop this line of questioning and follow another.

*Action: What do you now ask? Why?*

*Part 6 (Route B)*

You decide to carry on. You express your sympathy, explain that it was not your intention to upset Susan's parents and acknowledge that it is difficult for them. You reinforce that your aim is to help Susan. You reassure them that if necessary you will contact the doctor by telephone at any point during the meeting.

You pick up on the mention of Darren. You ask who he is. Susan's mother continues to cry and says that he was their other child. He also had brittle bones and he died several years ago. That is why the family left the house where they used to live and moved to a new city for a fresh start. Darren would have been eighteen but he died just after his ninth birthday. It was a traumatic experience for the whole family, everyone loved him so much and life has not been the same since. In about five weeks time it will be the anniversary of his death.

*Action: Think large scale and small scale – what have you found out? What do you do next and why?*

# 9 Teaching and learning: a real world analysis

This chapter provides you with three case studies: we present two of them. The third is currently 'virtual', as it will be offered by you and does not exist in this text. The two that we have chosen are deliberately complex in their nature and there will be many answers to the open-ended questions that we pose after you have read them. They are presented to you in the belief that, having read all the previous chapters, you will be at an advanced stage in your own learning in regard to the details presented in this book. You may be at a stage that is equivalent to the processes of restructuring or enrichment. We invite you to begin the process of practising and analysing these skills, as you will eventually apply them in your own teaching and learning system. This is a similar process to the one that you were engaged in in relation to analysing the case point regarding Susan in the previous chapter. The aim of presenting very precise and detailed case studies at this point is to help you to synthesize your own thinking so that you can then extend it further and move on to immediate applications. For this reason outcomes are not given or even hinted at, but details of contexts are. It is also the reason why the questioning in the reflection and dialogue points is more detailed and demanding.

These case studies encourage you to engage in individual and mutual critical reflection. Earlier in this book we proposed that reflective processes enable a teacher to deconstruct and reconstruct their own practice and to analyse the organizational and cultural factors that influence teaching and learning. Effective reflection does not only focus upon cognitive issues, as you will have seen by now, but it also looks at emotional and social issues. As you are aware, reflection is a strong indicator and an essential component of a system that values the principles and practice of differentiation. Through a process of reflection teachers and learners can look at what they do and the context in which their actions and interactions take place. In keeping with the spirit of this book, all case studies are real, though certain details have been altered in order to respect confidentiality.

A wide range of teachers can use the case studies provided: those in initial teacher education at university or college; those who are participating in professional development courses; and those who are engaged in school-based in-service training. They are offered as tools for balanced observation and critical analysis of practice. Through looking at the practice of others, we can begin to understand our own practice. Each case contains background information and it will be up to the reader to judge to what extent, if any, the background might be relevant to the learning context. A descriptive 'teaching and learning scene' is provided for each teacher–learner interaction along with a running-record style of commentary, relating what actually happened at the time. The detail of this commentary highlights the level of data required to differentiate. Many teachers may be able to remember teacher–learner interactions in this level of detail. Various methods of recording and analysing data are available to teachers and these need differentiating too.

There then follows a series of questions that we hope will inform your analysis. You will want to consider how the balance of pedagogical, emotional, cognitive and social factors are weighted in each case.

## Case One: Ben and Horace – a music lesson?

### Learner profile

Ben belongs to a family that does not have much money. His father has been unemployed for three years. His mother is able to do occasional part-time work. Ben is an only child. In the past year there has been some family involvement with support agencies, as Ben once arrived at school and stated that his back was very sore from sleeping on the kitchen floor. This claim was found out to be true. Ben has been assessed by an educational psychologist and a psychiatrist and appears to be quite an enigma to them also. There is talk of Ben having a social and communication difficulty, possibly associated with high intelligence, although this has never appeared on a formal report. Ben likes food and music. He likes to collect things – his current favourite is collecting ring-pulls from cans of drink. He seems to be a loner. His teachers have described him in various ways, from 'charming' through to 'aggressive' and 'difficult to teach'. His parents rarely seem to say anything positive and refer to him as 'clumsy', 'stubborn' and 'not interested in what other children of his age are interested in'. They say that he seems to enjoy the company of adults rather than children.

On one occasion, in a meeting at the school prompted by Ben's aggressive behaviour, his mother described him as being 'evil from the age of four months'. Ben is seven years old and describes himself as 'clever but bad'. He does not seem to like making or holding eye contact. There are times when he will answer a question in a way that seems to show a great depth of general knowledge, yet at other times he will ask questions like 'Is it true that tall people are older than small people?'

### Teacher profile

Horace takes his job very seriously and is good at it. He is not convinced that Ben has a diagnosable communication difficulty and feels that his lack of empathy for others and his apparently pedantic attitude are simply what Ben is like. Inside, he feels that learners like Ben should be in special education of some description. However, he has never expressed this view to his colleagues, as he feels that it would be seen as unpopular and against current inclusive trends in education. He admits that his relationship with Ben is reaching breaking point since he feels that his meticulously planned lessons often result in him being involved in further confrontation with Ben – even though the lesson was intended to prevent or minimize such difficulties. Horace has worked hard and invested a great deal in a new individualized reward system as part of a behaviour development programme for Ben whereby he can gain privileges for behaving in an acceptable way. This too is problematic because other learners complain that Ben receives rewards for doing what he should be doing – behaving as they do. They say it is not fair. Horace has explained that being fair means treating everyone differently, but inside he feels that the other learners in the group feel hard done by.

### Context

Horace has initiated many strategies to deal with the challenges that Ben presents in terms of his learning and behaviour. However, everything still seems to be problematic. Ben seems to be highly skilled in manipulating and destroying any system that is set up for his benefit.

In this lesson Horace has decided to catch Ben being 'good' as many times as is possible. It is one of Ben's favourite lessons, and Horace's too: music. Ben is one of a class group of 30 learners, but the group splits in half for music, with fifteen in the music room and the rest of the class in the art room. Horace feels that the organizational arrangements that result in a smaller group may enable this lesson to be a very positive experience for Ben. Horace has also made a special individual reward system for Ben. It has a soccer player kicking a ball towards a goal. There are ten stages until the player scores a goal. Ben can receive a sticker for each stage. When he scores a goal he receives a reward. Ten goals and Horace will write to Ben's parents to say how well he is doing. Horace sees that as a valuable reward. All other learners in the group have access to the school reward system which also involves being given stickers for good work and effort.

## Teaching and learning scene

Horace is the teacher and Ben is the learner. They are the key players in this scene. Ali is another learner who plays an important role. Horace has arranged the chairs in the room in one large circle. He asks each learner to select a seat within the circle. Immediately, Ben argues with Ali because Ali has chosen a chair that Ben wanted. Ali sits firmly on the chair. Horace has to intervene and asks Ben to sit elsewhere. To his amazement Ben does exactly as he is asked. Remembering one of his main individualized objectives for Ben, Horace immediately thanks him for not fighting with Ali and for sitting on a different chair. Horace explains that the group is sitting in a circle because all of the singing or playing of instruments will take place within the circle. Clearly the circle is the place to be if you wish to obtain optimal learner value from the lesson. Glancing around the group, Horace states: 'if you leave the circle then everyone will ignore you. I can only give rewards to people who are in the circle'. Ben becomes angry, he stands up and shouts at Horace stating that Horace is pretending to speak to everyone else but, in fact, is addressing his comments directly to him. Horace knows that on one level this is actually true but explains that the rules always apply to everyone. Amazingly, Ben accepts this explanation and sits down. Immediately Horace thanks him for sitting down and explains that Ben can receive a sticker for his reward chart. Ali, sitting across the circle from Ben, is not too impressed with this and asks 'Why can't I get a sticker, I'm sitting down?' A chorus of protest follows, until Horace agrees to give everybody in the group a sticker for 'sitting down nicely'.

Horace is concerned that the situation may deteriorate and so he begins the activities very quickly. He asks the learners to name the instruments from which they will be allowed to choose. Ben is able to identify and list them all – even those from other countries that were only introduced to the group last week. This seems to have brought Ben back on task. Horace then explains that each person will be asked to leave the circle, choose an instrument and return to the circle. He asks who would like to choose first. Ali is cued into the system of putting your hand up to gain the teacher's attention and therefore it is no surprise that the first hand in the air belongs to Ali. He has the privilege of choosing first. Ali returns to the circle with the instrument that everyone wants – an African 'talking drum'. Ben kicks his chair over and leaves the circle. He is shouting and claiming that he never gets a chance to play that instrument. When other learners try to ask him to stop this disruption, Ben tells them that he is 'bad' and that bad children do what they like and if they want to try to make him come back then they will have to fight him. Horace invites him to return to the circle and reminds him that he played that particular instrument two weeks ago.

This time Ben ignores Horace and begins to wander around the room. Horace invites the other learners to choose an instrument. Despite attempts by Ben to stop them, everyone, except Ben, has an instrument and is sitting in the circle. Horace begins a routine that everyone is familiar with – a percussion conversation. He keeps saying loudly what great fun everyone is having and Ben slowly edges back to the circle. Whilst the musical conversation is in progress Ben chooses an instrument and rejoins the circle. As the group continue with their syncopated dialogue Horace announces loudly, 'Thank you Ben for joining the circle, well done. That deserves a sticker. That is your ninth, one more and you score a goal. Please do not say that you are bad – you are good. Look what you are doing; you are in the circle and taking part.' Ben looks towards Horace . . . and smiles.

The next activity is about to begin when Ali decides to initiate a discussion about the concept of justice and equity. Why has Ben been given a sticker for coming back into the circle when, from Ali's perspective, he should have had his earlier sticker taken away for leaving the circle in the first place? Before Horace can explain, Ben spits at Ali and becomes abusive. Horace, raising his voice, instructs him to stop. Ben does not comply and begins to kick Ali. Horace stands in between them to try to avoid any physical harm and to redirect Ben's attention. He asks Ben to put his instrument on his chair. This time Ben throws his instrument across the room and climbs onto a table. He threatens to kick anyone who comes near him. Horace, using a strategy that he has learned from a course, tells Ben what he wants him to do rather than what he does not want him to do: 'Ben, get down from that table now please, you could fall and hurt yourself.' Ben says that he would like to fall and hurt himself, it would be a good thing to do. Horace continues, 'if you do not get down from on top of that table, I will not be able to give you a sticker, you will not score a goal and I will not be able to write home to your parents.' Ben replies: 'Get real. I don't care about your stupid stickers. I hate football. I don't care about a letter home. I hate my parents. If you give me a letter I'll tear it up.' Horace stands and waits.

---

**REFLECTION POINT**

Look at all or some of these questions below and reflect upon your own learning in relation to them. In considering these questions please note that they can also be used systematically to look at your own teaching and learning system.

- To what degree can you identify the stages that the lesson moves through? Could you justify these choices to a colleague? What strategies were used to deliver the learning and what types of differentiation were used?
- What constructs did the teacher hold about Ben? What evidence do you have for this answer? What evidence can you gain that Horace was trying to change Ben's personal constructs? To what degree has he been, and will he be, successful?
- What was in Horace's mind with regard to the ZPD for the group, for Ali and for Ben? How do you know?
- How would you judge the teacher–learner value in this case study? How can you gain evidence to rate the value?

➤

- Where was the teacher–learner energy transformation taking place? Was it mainly on the teacher's side or was it on Ben's side? To what extent could it be defined as being equally balanced? How does Ali's behaviour alter the dynamic?
- How well do you think that Ben dealt with the stresses of the learning interaction?
- How well do you think that Horace dealt with the stresses of the teaching interaction?
- Did anyone display positive or negative power? When and why did they do this?
- To what extent do you think that issues of gender influence the interactions? Why?
- What role was Ali playing? Why?
- To what extent do you think Horace dealt competently with the use of an individualized reward system for Ben?
- How well do you think he dealt with the implementation of rewards for Ben and for the rest of the group?
- How well do you think Horace organized the structure of the lesson? To what degree might you have modified or adapted what was taking place and why?
- How do you envisage the rest of this lesson continuing? What assumptions cause you to visualize such a scenario?

## Case Two: Yuka and Ella – There's a war going on out there

### Learner profile

Yuka is fourteen years old. She appears to enjoy school. Her school reports often remark about how thoughtful and sensitive she is but consistently encourage her to speak up in class discussions. She used to represent the school in various sports but lost interest six months ago. Her behaviour has changed quite drastically in the last three months. She now seems unwilling to engage with what is on offer to her at school. Last week she told a teacher that she felt as if the whole world was against her. She has become withdrawn and her mother is worried that she seems to be losing weight. Yuka is in a group of 26 learners, sixteen of whom come from a lone parent family. However, her mother often expresses the view that a lone parent family is better than two parents who are unhappy. Yuka's father was violent.

Teachers are concerned that her grades are not as high as they should be. In a recent self-assessment, Yuka described science and foreign languages as her favourite subjects.

## Teacher profile

Ella has been teaching history for many years. Owing to the nature of the group, there is another teacher in the classroom offering learning support. Initially, the teacher just worked with one learner. However, Ella suggested that the two teachers should develop the curriculum rather than label and single out particular learners. Consequently, on the basis that two heads are better than one, Ella has become more ambitious in the teaching strategies that she adopts. She feels that history should develop investigative skills and enhance a learner's understanding of what life must have been like in different times. She also feels that learners should be offered an insight into those aspects of historical investigation that are not always given a high profile in the public domain. For example, in this topic she has looked at the role of women during the war and raised awareness of the contribution of black soldiers. She wishes to move the learners beyond the notion that history is all about dates, events and timelines.

## Context

The learners have been studying the First World War. Ella is aware that some of the learners still do not seem to understand what being a soldier must have been like even though, last week, they read and talked about the poetry of English, Scottish and American poets of the time. In discussion with the learners about what they had learned in the last lesson, they fed back to the teacher that the war poet Wilfred Owen suffered shellshock and trench fever and that he was killed in action just before the war ended. They recalled another war poet, Siegfried Sassoon, as brave and many mentioned that his brother died in the war. Almost everyone remembered that his nickname was 'Mad Jack'. This was not what the teacher had expected. For her, these learning outcomes were subsidiary. She had intended to illustrate, through the use of poetry, the painful images of young men 'dying like cattle', with 'froth-corrupted lungs' amongst 'demented choirs of shells'.

She wanted them to understand the physical and emotional conditions that resulted in soldiers committing suicide in the trenches. It was the horror of war and the warnings and insights that the poets gave that she intended to teach – yet the learners had seemed to learn something else, mainly peripheral biographical information. This represented a problem because next week the group would be writing a diary. Each person would have to imagine that she or he is a soldier in the trenches. They will be assessed on this piece of work. Ella now knows that some learners will find this difficult. She has decided to take a risk in order to meet her aims and objectives. When the learners arrive in the classroom there will be no chairs for them to sit on. All of the tables will have been gathered into the middle of the room and covered with a dark cloth. Music will be playing but almost at a subliminal level.

Ella feels that by creating this sort of atmosphere the learners will remember what they are about to experience and hopes that she can turn her teaching aims into their learning outcomes.

### Teaching and learning scene

Ella is the teacher and Yuka is the learner. They are the key players in this scene. Yuka's group arrives in the classroom. Immediately they sense that something different, perhaps interesting, is about to happen in this lesson. They are asked to stand away from the centre of the room. Already there is a buzz of excitement. What is under the cloth? Why is it there? What is the music and why is it playing? Someone notices that there is a large box in the corner of the room and that it too is covered. He asks what is in it and what is it for? Ella explains to the class that the answer to these questions will be given later, but first she must explain what will take place in the next hour. The learners are reminded that they are studying the First World War. They recall what they have done in previous lessons. The teacher explains that the class will be split into two groups. She also explains that the first task is about listening, looking and emotional feeling. One group will be asked to take metal pans and a selection of drums out of a box while the other group will lift up the cloth and gather together in the small confined space under the tables. The tables will be covered by the cloth so that they are in near darkness. Then, those with the drums and metal pans will stand around the tables and make as much noise as they can. They will be allowed to scream and yell as if they were in pain or in fear.

This task will take place for three minutes. Those under the cloth are asked to think about how they feel amongst the darkness and noise and, if possible, to imagine that they are in cramped conditions in the trenches. When the task ends those who have been under the cloth will emerge and will write a series of words about what the experience felt like. Then the groups will swap roles and the same process will occur. Ella explains further that the words that have been written down will become the basis for a poem that each person will write. Then volunteers will be 'hotseated' – they will read their poem and be interviewed by the rest of the class. Finally, they will look again at the poetry that they read last week and talk about what it means now that they have engaged in this task.

The expectation in terms of learning and behaviour are made clear. In Ella's words: 'I know that some parts of this lesson might encourage some people to behave in an immature way – especially when a large group will go under the tables and the cloth. I expect mature behaviour and this is why there will never be a teacher involved in the task with you. To be honest, there are some groups that I would not try this activity with. You are a mature group and this is why you are doing it. Enjoy it.'

The lesson begins in a noisy way as the two groups clarify what they have to do. At the instruction of the teacher, one group crawls under the cloth while the other group collects the instruments. Ella reminds the group of her expectations and some of the giggling emanating from under the cloth stops. There is a protracted silence that is suddenly broken by screams and crashes. Yuka has a drum but is not using it to make noise. Whilst those around her scream and shriek at the top of their voices, Yuka just stares at the floor. This part of the activity is over. The learners crawl out from underneath the cloth. Some look terrified. Immediately they are sent to write down their feelings. Ella congratulates everyone for engaging in the task in such a mature manner.

It is now time for role reversal. The new members of the group who will be under the cloth rush to secure their places – all except Yuka. She refuses to participate at all. Ella temporarily stops the lesson and calls Yuka to one side. She explains that if this part of the task is not completed then Yuka will not have a poem, will not be able to appreciate war poetry and will find next week's task more difficult. Yuka politely explains that the world war took place a long time ago and holds no interest for her – she suggests that it has no relevance to her or to life in the new millennium. Ella tries to persuade her to participate but has no luck. She decides to become more assertive and explains that this is what is expected of all learners in the group, it is the content of the lesson, and Yuka has to participate. What would happen if learners selected what they would and would not do in lessons? Yuka refuses, again doing so in a non-threatening manner but with the same argument. The teacher says that the reason given is not acceptable and that she must participate. Suddenly, a few tears roll down Yuka's face. She turns to Ella and says 'No matter how many times you ask me or tell me to go underneath that cloth, I will not do it. You will not understand but I am frightened.' Ella explains that this is actually the intention of the task, to instil fear, to empathize with the soldiers. Yuka explains: 'No, I can't say to you why I'm frightened, but I am. I am not going into the dark under that cloth. You can say what you like but I am not.' At this point Ella makes an on-the-spot decision and instructs the others to continue with the task. She speaks quietly to Yuka saying that she will have to see her after the lesson is completed. They can continue their conversation then.

---

**DIALOGUE POINT**

Choose a colleague or colleagues you are confident in working with or those whom you rarely work with. Choose questions, or develop your own, that allow you to focus on aspects of the case that interest you. Discuss with your colleague your views on these points, trying to justify them as you work through each point. You may wish to reference details presented in other parts of this book or other books. The aim is not necessarily to agree or disagree with the views we have presented here, but to engage in open and professional debate, questioning and critical analysis.

- To what degree can you identify the stages that the lesson moves through? Could you justify these choices to a colleague?

➤

- How well do you think that Ella's lesson plan matches the processes within the learning models that have been presented in this book? For example, to what extent does it allow for accretion and restructuring?
- What strategies were used to deliver the learning and what types of differentiation were used?
- What constructs did the teacher hold about Yuka? Can you know? What evidence do you have for this answer?
- What was in Ella's mind with regard to the ZPD for the group and for individuals? How do you know?
- How would you judge the teacher–learner value in this case study? How can you gain evidence to rate the value?
- Where was the teacher–learner energy transformation taking place? Was it mainly on the teacher's side or was it on the learner side?
- How well do you think that Yuka dealt with the stresses of the learning interaction?
- How well do you think that Ella dealt with the stresses of the teaching interaction?
- Did anyone display positive or negative power? When and why did they do this?
- To what extent do you think that issues of gender influence the interactions? Why?
- To what extent do you think that Ella was successful in broadcasting her expectations?
- Why do you think that the learners had not learned what Ella had planned for them to learn in their previous lesson? On what evidence do you base your answer?
- How far do you imagine that this type of group activity would enable her to meet desired learning outcomes?
- Why do you think that Yuka would not participate in the part of the task that involved being covered by the cloth? What assumptions or evidence informs your answer?
- Do you think that the teacher should have insisted that she participated? Why or why not?
- How might you imagine their conversation to have continued after the lesson, in private? What information or assumptions cause you to imagine such a conversation?

# So . . . where to now?

You are invited to supply the third case study. It will concern a learner that you know and a teaching and learning scenario that is problematic – remembering that framing something as problematic enables you to look for both meanings and solutions. It will challenge you to eyeball the situation in detail, looking at it from varying scales, perspectives and angles. Looking, hypothesizing and then looking again. Asking question after question. This enables you to use the book in a self-help manner on behalf of the learners that you teach. This process of analysis is cyclical, and the case study format, when interpretations and solutions are sought, can be used as a template for other learners that you teach and will teach in the future.

Having worked through your case study and this chapter with its applications you have now completed a piece of learning. There was an *actual* level of what you knew and who you were when you began reading the chapter and there is a *potential* level which describes who you are now or who you have become as a learner. This process applies in relation to the book itself. You began with an actual level and the book will have engaged you within your own ZPD. As a learner you will be the best judge of the teaching and learning values implicit in this book. You are also the best judge for you, of whether we got your ZPD right, amongst a community of the ZPDs of other readers. You will be able to make a judgement about how successfully the book has been successfully differentiated. So where to now?

There has been a lot of use of simile, metaphor, case studies, anecdotes and examples in this book and this has been deliberate. This has been done to differentiate the ideas, concepts, notions, details, debates, questions and arguments that we hope this book will inspire. You will have noticed that there are many images used in this book. Images which relate to power, energy, transformation, value, responsiveness and flexibility, for example. These are useful images to allow you to conceptualize teaching whether you see it as an art or a science or a craft. Now you need to consider how to put your own thoughts on the principles and practice of differentiation into action. What you will do to harness your own mental energy once you have completed this book.

One final image that may help you in this task is to visualize the teacher–learner system as an interlocking series of gears. We are aware that the image of gears may present you with a mechanical picture and reinforce a view that individuals are merely cogs within a bureaucratic machine. This is not the intention – we ask you to focus upon the process, the fluidity within the cyclical movement, as that is crucial. This is highlighted in Fig. 9.1, which chooses to illustrate and select some of the gears. Of course, in different contexts there will be many more gears including clusters of schools or school partnership networks. However many there are, they do not move independently of each other. When one moves all the others will be affected. They can be seen as gearing down from the broad policy of government to the teacher and the learner. This is one way of viewing the system. Another, which is more learner-focused, is to view it as gearing up from the needs of the learner. This raises a fundamental issue of who the key movers and stakeholders are in teaching and learning systems both large and small scale. If we are driven by change, where we are on the receiving end of change that was initiated elsewhere, we may offer resistance. Resistance quickly turns to resentment. Forced change can be demoralizing; it attacks esteems and can make people feel powerless rather than empowered. It can feel like the use of negative power. People talk of being 'worn down' or 'worn out'. The process of change will be more productive where partnerships based upon equity exist. Where individuals contribute to change. Therefore, we propose that this model should begin with the learners and teachers and move up. Certainly, this will be the view of the processes within the model that will create inclusive systems.

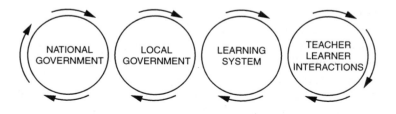

Figure 9.1 Movement within learning systems

### Scaling change

The task you now have is to choose to work at a level that can bring about positive change. Use positive power to enable differentiation. As mentioned in the self-esteems work, having regard to a sense of scale is vitally important in such a task.

You may have to work in, on and between differing levels of scale – one impacting upon the other. Some of these scales will include:

- Learner to learner
- Teacher to learner
- Teacher to teacher
- Teacher to parent
- Parent to learner
- Teacher to smaller organizational systems
- Small system to small system (e.g. department to department, faculty to faculty)
- Small system to whole system
- Whole system to same level whole system (e.g. school to school)
- Whole system to local government system (superordinate system)
- Local government system to national or federal government system.

## And now some closing words of wisdom

We wish to close this book with some words of wisdom. Learners we have taught and spoken with at different stages in the development of our own thinking about differentiation gave the words to us. Their words, the words and wisdom of young learners, have in turn informed our learning, casting the learner in the role of teacher and the teacher in the role of learner, in a continual cycle of change. A cycle that involves learning and teaching, and continues by relearning and reteaching. A cycle that one of the learners describes. We use their words to offer insight into the principles and practice of differentiation and the nature of teaching and learning:

When I am learning I feel as if I am always going round in circles. You just keep going backwards and forwards and round and round but then suddenly you realize that you have learned something.

I learn best when I know what I'm learning and how I'm going to learn it and why I'm learning and what it means and how it fits in. I like it when the teacher tells me the rules and gives me lots of interesting ways into it and a chance to talk about it and think for myself and to check it out.

I always know when I am with a good teacher. Even if your learning is bad they just seem to know ways of how to make you better at it. I like teachers that do that. I like being better at learning.

# Bibliography

Aboud, F. and Alemu, T. (1995) 'Nutritional status, maternal responsiveness and mental development of Ethiopian Children'. *Social Science and Medicine,* 41, 725–32.

Ayers A., Clarke, D. and Murray, A. (2000) *Perspectives on Behaviour: A Practical Guide to Effective Intervention for Teachers* (Second edition). London: David Fulton.

Bannister, D. and Fransella, F. (1986) *Inquiring Man: The Psychology of Personal Constructs* (Third Edition). London: Croom Helm.

Bennathan, M. and Boxall, M. (2000) *Effective Intervention in Primary Schools: Nurture Groups* (Second edition). London: David Fulton.

Bowlby, J. (1979) *The Making and Breaking of Affectional Bonds.* London: Routledge.

Corbett, J. (forthcoming) *Supporting Inclusive Education: a connective pedagogy.* London: RoutledgeFalmer.

Croll, P. and Moses, D. (2000) 'Ideologies and utopias: educational professionals' view of inclusion'. *European Journal of Special Needs Education,* 15 (1), 1–12.

DfEE (1998) *Truancy and School Exclusion Report by the Social Exclusion Unit.* London: The Stationery Office.

Flavell, J. H. (1979) 'Metacognition and cognitive monitoring'. *American Psychologist,* 34, 906–11.

Freud, S. (1984) *The Theory of Psychoanalysis.* Harmondsworth: Penguin.

Gipps, C., McCallum, B. and Brown, M. (1999) 'Primary teachers' beliefs about teaching and learning'. *The Curriculum Journal,* 10 (1), 123–34.

Guiney, D. (2000) 'The individual education plan', in P. Benton and T. O'Brien (eds) *Special Needs and the Beginning Teacher.* London: Continuum.

Hart, S. (2000) *Thinking through Teaching: A Framework for Enhancing Participation and Learning.* London: David Fulton.

Hedegaard, M. (1996) 'The zone of proximal development as basis for instruction', in H. Daniels (ed.) *An Introduction to Vygotsky.* London: Routledge.

Hornby, G. (1999) 'Inclusion or delusion: can one size fit all?' *Support for Learning*, 14 (4), 152–7.

Kameenui, E. J. and Carnine, D. W. (1998) *Effective teaching strategies that accommodate diverse learners*. Upper Saddle River, NJ: Merrill.

Kelly, G. A. (1955) *The Psychology of Personal Constructs*. New York: Norton.

Klein, M. (1988) *Envy and Gratitude and Other Works 1946–63*. London: Virago.

Lunt, I. and Norwich, B. (1999) *Can Effective Schools be Inclusive Schools?* Perspectives on Education Series. London: Institute of Education.

Maslow, A. H. (1954) *Motivation and Personality*. New York: Harper and Row.

Mortimore, P. (ed.) (1999) *Understanding Pedagogy and its Impact on Learning*. London: Paul Chapman.

NCH (National Children's Home) (2000) *NCH factfile 2000*. London: NCH.

Norman, D. (1978) 'Notes towards a theory of complex learning', in A. Lesgold, J. Pellegrino and S. Fokkena (eds) *Cognitive Psychology and Instruction*. New York: Plenum.

Norwich, B. (1996) *Special Needs Education: Inclusive Education or Just Education for All?* Inaugural Professorial Lecture, Institute of Education, University of London.

O'Brien, T. (1998a) *Promoting Positive Behaviour*. London: David Fulton.

O'Brien, T. (1998b) 'The millennium curriculum: confronting the issues and proposing solutions'. *Support for Learning*, 13 (4), 147–56.

O'Brien, T. (2000a) 'Providing inclusive differentiation', in P. Benton, and T. O'Brien (eds) *Special Needs and the Beginning Teacher*. London: Continuum.

O'Brien, T. (2000b) 'Increasing inclusion: did anyone mention learning?' *REACH, The Journal of Special Needs Education in Ireland*, 14 (1), 2–11.

O'Brien, T. (ed.) (2001) *Enabling Inclusion: Blue Skies . . . Dark Clouds?* London: The Stationery Office.

O'Brien, T. and Garner, P. (2001) *Untold Stories: Learning Support Assistants and their Work*. Stoke-on-Trent: Trentham Books.

Rogers, C. (1974) *On Becoming a Person*. London: Constable.

Rose, R. (1998) 'Including pupils: developing a partnership in learning', in C. Tilstone, L, Florian and R. Rose *Promoting Inclusive Practice*. London: Routledge.

Schon, D. A. (1991) *The Reflective Practitioner: How Professionals Think in Action*. Aldershot: Ashgate-Arena.

Scruggs, T. E. and Mastropieri, M. A. (1996) 'Teacher perceptions of mainstreaming/inclusion, 1958–1995: A research synthesis'. *Exceptional Children*, 63 (1), 59–74.

Stout, M. (2000) *The Feel-good Curriculum: The Dumbing-down of America's Kids in the Name of Self-esteem.* Cambridge, Mass: Perseus.

Tharpe, R. and Gallimore, R. (1991) 'A theory of teaching as assisted performance', in P. Light, S. Sheldon and M. Woodhead (eds) *Learning to Think.* London: Routledge.

UNICEF (1996) *The State of the World's Children.* Oxford: Oxford University Press.

Vaughn, S., Bos, C. and Schumm, J. (2000) *Teaching Exceptional, Diverse, and At-risk Students in the General Education Classroom.* Boston, Mass: Allyn & Bacon.

Vygotsky, L. S. (1978). *Mind in Society: The Development of Higher Psychological Processes.* Cambridge, Mass: Harvard University Press.

# Index

action research 75, 79
actual level of development 116, 118,
    124, 130, 148
African-Caribbean males 80
articulating models 109
attachment theory 136
automatic learning 126, 128
autonomy 54–5

bipolar constructs 78, 81–2
Bowlby, J. 136–7
brittle bones 152
broadcasting 41, 42, 44–6, 50, 67,
    103, 167

case studies 156–8
challenging behaviour 33, 59, 93,
    114, 139
clown 58–9
coffee-cup-counselling 150–1
cognitive aspects of learning 122–8
cognitive factors in learning 52, 63–5
cognitive model of learning 130
collaborative reflection 57
common needs 14–17
connective thinking 90, 92, 94
constructs 29, 62, 77
    of learners 83–7
    of teachers 80–2, 161, 167
    triadic method 78–80
construing 26, 76
critical reflection 57, 156
crying 108
curriculum topography 150–1

da Vinci, L. 87–9
de-automization of learning 126
defence mechanisms 137
definitions of learning 6, 9–10
definitions of teaching 6
demographic factors 12
developmental levels 41
didactic practice 2
distant teaching and learning 5
distinct needs 14–17
Down Syndrome 16, 34

ecosystems of individuals 143
educational psychologist 33
ego 137
elements 77
emotional and behavioural difficulties
    33, 80–2, 93, 102, 154
emotional factors 52, 58–63
emotional management 148–52
emotional responses to change 18
energy, teacher and learner 108
energy transformation 108–10, 124,
    148, 162, 167
Eureka principle 125
existential terror 149
expectation 67
eyeballing 19, 76, 81, 134, 168

facilitation 2
fairness 158
feedback 37, 92
feedback discrepancy 136
fight-flight response 149
fixed questioning 74

fixed responses 100–1, 104–5
fixed solutions 97
fixed thinking 63, 90, 92, 95, 107, 113, 150
fluid questioning 74
fluid responses 101–2, 105–7
fluid thinking 63, 90, 92, 95, 107forced change 169
forms of teacher learner outcomes 40–51
Freud, S. 137–8

Garner, P. 55
gifted children 98
grounded learning 4, 6, 13, 69, 113, 118–19, 124, 139
grounded questions 131
Guiney, D. 17

hierarchy of needs 139

id 137
inclusion 65–7, 102, 116, 158, 169
independence 54
individual education plans 16
individual needs 14–17
insecure attachment 137
intimate learning 5, 69, 99, 111, 124, 144

jigsawing 66

Kelly, G. 29, 76, 78
Klein, M. 26

learner energy 110
learner value 36, 47
learner value continuum 39
learning biography 62
learning models 115
learning needs 14–17
learning outcomes 24, 164, 167
learning pathways 116
learning potential 116
learning support assistants 55, 102–4, 141

mapping self esteems 143–4
marginalization 68
Maslow, A. H. 139
mediation 2, 90, 117–18, 124, 137
mental maps 119–21
metacognition 64, 70
modalities of learning 64
model for complex learning 123–7
motivation 96
movement within systems 169
multisensory processing 20

negative attributions 96
negative self-image 133
negotiated agreement 49
Norman, D. 123
Norwich, B. 14
notional value of teaching and learning 38–41, 43
nurturing 27, 28

O'Brien, T. 11, 14, 52, 55, 80, 139
observation 75
optimum teaching and learning 37–41
optimum value 36–7, 47
organism 136

pedagogical attitude 116
pedagogical factors 52, 53–7, 157
penny dropping moments 99, 125
personal construct psychology 29, 75–80, 82–5, 145
personal meanings 78
personal qualities of teachers 8
physiological reactions to stresses 149–50
planned differentiation 91
potential level of development 116, 118, 124, 130, 168
power, positive and negative 68, 144–8, 169
pragmatics 23
praise 13
precocious puberty 153
principles for differentiation 11–13

problematic intervention 92
problematic situations 55, 92–8
  four questions 95–7, 100–2, 104–7
professional competence of teachers
  51
professional skills of teachers 7–8
psychoanalytic theory 26–8, 73, 124

questioning and differentiation 25,
  88, 145
questioning inappropriately 61
questioning relationships 24

reflective practitioner 56–7, 91
refugees 68
reincarnation 98
renaissance man 86
restructuring learning 124–5, 128,
  156, 167
revving up teaching 112, 113, 115
Rogers, C. 136

scale, sense of 144
scaling change 170
secure attachment 137
self 4, 135–8
self-esteem 132–5, 138–9
self-esteems 73, 133–5, 139–42, 152
  mapping 143–4
sensory impairments 11
Shakespeare, W. 71
snowballing 66
social class 68
social context of learning 116–19
social factors in learning 52, 65–9
social inclusion 65–7
social interactionism 129
social model of learning 130

soul 98, 132
special educational needs 50
staged model of learning 123–7
staged process of learning 119–21
stereotypes 28, 32–5, 57, 68
stereotypical thinking 29–32
stresses 92, 148–51
subject teachers 146
subjective reality 59
superego 137
susceptibility when learning 60–1

Taoism 19
teacher energy 110
teacher learner outcomes 38–41
teacher value 36, 47
teacher value continuum 39
teachers under the spotlight 99, 104
thinking on your feet 91
topography of esteems 143
tourist approach to differentiation
  111–13
transference 20
travellers 68
triadic method (in personal constructs)
  78–80

unified model of learning 129

value of teaching 84–6
Vygotsky, L. 90, 116–21

war poets 163
wisdom 171

zone of proximal development (ZPD)
  90, 117–21, 124, 129, 133, 161,
  167, 168

# CORMIER

# we all fall down

PUFFIN BOOKS

PUFFIN BOOKS

Published by the Penguin Group
Penguin Books Ltd, 27 Wrights Lane, London w8 5tz, England
Penguin Putnam Inc., 375 Hudson Street, New York, New York 10014, USA
Penguin Books Australia Ltd, Ringwood, Victoria, Australia
Penguin Books Canada Ltd, 10 Alcorn Avenue, Toronto, Ontario, Canada m4v 3b2
Penguin Books India (P) Ltd, 11 Community Centre,
Panchsheel Park, New Delhi 110 017, India
Penguin Books (NZ) Ltd, Cnr Rosedale and Airborne Roads,
Albany, Auckland, New Zealand
Penguin Books (South Africa) (Pty) Ltd, 5 Watkins Street, Denver Ext 4,
Johannesburg 2094, South Africa

On the World Wide Web at: www.penguin.com

Penguin Books Ltd, Registered Offices: Harmondsworth, Middlesex, England

First published in the USA by Delacorte Press 1991
First published in Great Britain by Victor Gollancz 1992
Published by Hamish Hamilton 1997
Published in Puffin Books 2001
1

Set in 11/13pt New Caledonia
Typeset by Rowland Phototypesetting Ltd, Bury St Edmunds, Suffolk
Made and printed in England by Clays Ltd, St Ives plc

British Library Cataloguing in Publication Data
A CIP catalogue record for this book is available from the British Library

ISBN 0-141-31223-8

*To Sam and Rosalie Chillemi*
*for all the years of friendship*

# Part 1

THEY entered the house at 9:02 p.m. on the evening of April Fools' Day. In the next forty-nine minutes, they shit on the floors and pissed on the walls and trashed their way through the seven-room Cape Cod cottage. They overturned furniture, smashed the picture tubes in three television sets, tore two VCRs from their sockets and crashed them to the floor. They spray-painted the walls orange. They flooded the bathrooms, both upstairs and down, and flushed face towels down the toilet bowls. They broke every mirror in the place and toppled a magnificent hutch to the floor, sending china cups and saucers and plates and assorted crystal through the air. In the first-floor bedrooms, they pulled out dresser drawers, spilled their contents on the floor, yanked clothing from the closets and slashed the mattresses. In the downstairs den, they performed a special job on the piano, smashing the keys with a hammer, the noise like a crazy soundtrack to the scenes of plunder.

There were four of them and although their vandalism was scattered and spontaneous, they managed to invade every room in the house, damaging everything they touched.

At 9:48 p.m., fourteen-year-old Karen Jerome made the mistake of arriving home early from a friend's house. She was surprised to find the front door ajar and most of the lights on. The sounds of yelling and whooping greeted her as she stepped into the foyer.

One of them, still holding the hammer that had demolished the piano, greeted her.

"Well, hello . . ." he said.

No one had ever looked at her like that before.

At 9:51 p.m., the invaders left the house, abandoning the place as suddenly as they had arrived, slamming the doors, rattling the windows, sending shudders along the walls and ceilings. They left behind twenty-three beer cans, two empty vodka bottles, and damage later estimated at twenty thousand dollars, and, worst of all, Karen Jerome, bruised and broken where she lay sprawled on the cellar floor.

The Avenger watched it all.

From his hiding place.

He watched in horror as they trashed the house he had come to love, ransacking and rampaging, the sound of carnage making him wince as if his own body were being ravaged.

Tears stung his eyes, blurring his vision until he blinked them away. This house was his territory. He had staked it out and claimed it for his own. He had become a part of the place and the Jeromes who lived in it, like a son and brother to them all. He had observed the family's comings and goings, had shared their daily routines, their good times and bad times.

Leaving his hiding place, The Avenger scurried from window to window, flitting in and out of the shadows, protected by the trees and shrubbery that surrounded the house. But these same trees and shrubs also prevented anyone in the other houses on the street from seeing what was going on inside. What was going on horrified The

Avenger. "Animals," he muttered as he watched the trashers running from room to room, screaming and yelling, tearing the place apart.

He did not know their names, had never seen them before, but he knew who they were. They were regular kids, not sleazies from Rock Point or the rough guys and dropouts who hung out at Bryant Bridge. They were nicely dressed. No leather jackets or black boots. They looked like high school baseball players or baggers at the supermarket or clerks at McDonald's.

The Avenger did not see Karen Jerome enter the house but he saw her being dragged across the front hallway. A moment later, the lights went out.

A small moan escaped his mouth, a sound that came from a place deep and dark inside of him because he could not help her. That was the most terrible thing of all, knowing that he could do nothing at this moment. He was out-numbered, unable to charge into the house and rescue her.

So, he waited. He was good at waiting. He closed his eyes and opened them again. The house was still dark. And quiet. Were they gone? Had they slipped out quietly while his eyes were closed?

Suddenly, they were there again, flitting in and out of the shadows, running through the rooms, not yelling this time but silent, hurrying, tripping over themselves. The Avenger shrank back from the window. He could not afford to be seen. It was important to remain hidden. To bide his time. To wait.

Wait for what?

To wait for his revenge.

I am The Avenger, he whispered to the night. And I will avenge this house and what has happened in it.

He knew he would have to be patient. He would have to find out their names and track them down, one by one.

3

He would have to plan a course of action. But he was expert at that kind of thing, had spent long hours observing, spying, witnessing. He was skilled at making plans and then carrying them out methodically, one step at a time. Like with Vaughn Masterson, knowing the right time and the right place to strike.

By the time the trashers had left the house, the tears on the cheeks of The Avenger were cold and hard, like tiny pieces of glass.

Jane Jerome was still numb two hours after returning from the hospital where her sister Karen lay in intensive care, hooked up to all kinds of machines, beeping sounds like small squeals of anguish. Karen's face and hands were the only parts of her body that had been visible. Her face, like a stranger's face, shrouded in white, seemed to be floating in all that whiteness. Her hands were tiny, helpless, fingers curled slightly inward.

Jane wanted to hold those hands, press them to her cheek, ask her pardon and forgiveness. Earlier on the evening of the assault, she and Karen had argued. The usual stupid argument. Karen was a borrower, took Jane's things all the time without asking permission, used her cologne, wore her blouses and sweaters. All of this was kind of humiliating because Jane was two years older and Karen should have been the small kid sister but there she was, fully developed, Jane's size but more style-conscious, improvising, taking one of Jane's sweaters, blending it with one of her own scarves, and, tra la, a smashing outfit.

Guilt assailed Jane as she scrunched herself into her father's big leather chair in the den, listening to him talk to the detective in the living room. A lot of guilt particularly because Jane had shouted at her: *Will you please go have an accident?*, one of the favourite phrases at Burnside High

School this year. What had happened to Karen was much worse than an accident, of course, worse than being struck by a car. It was savage, brutal, personal. Made the damage to the house seem minor by comparison. Not really minor, though. Both attacks were devastating and she knew that life in this house would never be the same.

Funny. At first, when her father had been transferred from Monument, she had hated this house along with Burnside High, hated leaving her old friends and classmates at Monument High, some of whom she had known since kindergarten. But in the months since, she had made friends at school — Patti Amarelli and Leslie Cairns, in particular — and they had shown her the sights, especially the shopping mall in downtown Wickburg, with its splashing fountain and stores like Filene's and Brooks, and the wild store on the second level where she bought the posters that covered the walls of her room and the Pizza Palace where the guys and girls gathered to eat and hang out.

The ConCentre was located across from the mall and all the big stars appeared there — New Kids on the Block and Billy Joel and Madonna — and although she didn't often attend performances, it was neat to be around early in the evening, watching the limos pull up, disgorging people from Boston and Worcester, but most of all knowing that the stars were staying at the Wickburg Hilton around the corner. She had caught a glimpse of Billy Joel one night as he emerged from the Hilton and that brief look was more intimate, more *personal* than seeing him onstage from a distance.

All of this meant nothing now. Not with Karen in the hospital, in a coma, and the house in ruins, her mother so stunned and heartbroken that Jane could barely stand to look at her. And her father simmering. That was the word. Not raging mad but simmering, anger swirling around inside of him, building to a boil.

5

As he spoke now to the detective, her father was barely controlling that anger. Making herself small in the big chair, she listened, hardly daring to breathe.

"Ever since we moved here, almost a year ago, it's been happening. Small stuff, ridiculous in a way but . . ." His voice trailed off, muffled a bit.

"What kind of small stuff?" The detective did not resemble a movie and TV detective. He was short and fat and had a squeaky voice, as if somebody were squeezing his Adam's apple. Two cops in uniform had spent hours here yesterday, and today the detective in regular clothes had shown up.

"Phone rings, nobody on the line. A stone tossed through the window last month. Marie, my wife, planted tomatoes last year and they got all torn up, scattered around the back yard. A dead squirrel in the mailbox."

"You never reported those incidents?"

"No," he said, biting off the word. Jane could picture his face getting red. She knew the symptoms, that tight voice, his words like firecrackers. He was getting ready to blow up, something that happened probably only once a year. But when he finally lost his temper, watch out. Yesterday, he had answered these questions patiently but today he was ready to explode.

"Call the police?" he asked, his voice rising a bit. "About tomato plants, phone calls, a dead squirrel?"

Then the detective asked a new question:

"Do you have any enemies, Mr Jerome?"

Yipes, her father, enemies. The thought was ludicrous. He was Mister Good Guy. Business manager of the telephone company in Wickburg. Wore white shirts, striped ties, smiled a lot, played golf on Saturday afternoons, went to church with his family on Sundays, served on the United Way committee every year. Who could possibly be his enemy? Although she would never admit it aloud to anyone, her father was a sweetheart. He never gave her a hard time or any grief at all. Never grounded her, never ran out of patience with her or Karen or their younger brother, Artie, who was at the peak of brat-hood. As a result, Jane tried to do things to please her father, to merit not being grounded.

"Do I have any enemies?" Her father's voice was suddenly like a little kid's voice, uncertain, puzzled.

She had to get out of there, didn't want to listen any more, hated hearing her father being questioned, hated the way he sounded vulnerable, a little scared. It made her feel vulnerable and scared too.

Out on the back porch, in the freshness of the April morning, she flung herself into the old wicker rocking chair. Ordinarily, she would have fled to her room, where she could always find comfort and consolation. But her room, too, had been ruined. She had loved that room, the predominance of blue, her favourite colour. And all her favourite things. Her special glass menagerie of frogs and puppies and kittens. The posters on the wall — New Kids and Bruce and messages like AFTER THE RAIN, THE RAINBOW; so many posters that her father said he could have saved the price of wallpaper if he'd known about her poster madness. The room was her turf, her refuge, her hiding place. Where she could close the door and shut out the world, the C-minus in maths — the worst mark of her life — the zits popping out all over her face, the agony of Timmy Kearns ignoring her completely after that first date. Her place of retreat to which she only admitted Patti and Leslie, with standing orders for everyone else to stay out.

Standing at the door in the first moment of discovery, seeing the torn mattress, her precious animals spilled on the floor, the posters hanging in shreds, yellow veins on the wall which she did not immediately recognize as pee, the puddle of vomit on the floor, she had grown weak, watery, felt as if she herself had been assaulted. She wanted to flee Burnside, get out of there, back to safe and sane Monument, deadly dull but peaceful, where her father played golf with the chief of police and everybody knew everybody else, even the names of the dogs and cats. A few minutes later, Karen had been discovered in the cellar, and the anger she had felt in her room paled beside the horror of what had happened to Karen.

"Damn it, damn it," she muttered now, rocking furiously in the chair, filled with anger and guilt and — what? She stopped rocking suddenly, sat still in the chair as she caught a movement down near the hedges, past the cherry tree. Somebody or something moving furtively, a blurred image, not quite seen, and then gone. She shivered, drew her arms around herself, wondering if the trashers might be lurking in the vicinity, had returned to the scene of the crime like they said criminals did.


When Buddy Walker broke the mirror in the girl's bedroom, using the Statue of Liberty, a splinter of glass struck him in the cheek and he saw blood oozing on his face in the mirror's jagged reflection. He stared at it drunkenly, dropping the statue to the floor.

Actually, he did not know whether he was drunk or not. He was dizzy, yes, and giddy, and felt like he was floating, his feet barely touching the floor. The lights hurt his eyes, bruising his eyeballs, but otherwise he felt pleasantly willy-nilly, letting himself go, carried along by this terrific feeling of drift, thinking: the hell with everything and everybody. Especially home.

The cut was minor, despite the blood. In the middle of all the carnage, the screaming and the shrieks of laughter and the sounds of destruction from the floor below, he made his way carefully to the bathroom and found a box of plasters in the cabinet above the sink. He removed two of them, slipped one into his shirt pocket for later use and, after wiping away the smear of blood with a towel, calmly applied the other plaster to his cheek. His hand was steady despite a sudden swirl of dizziness. The dizziness was pleasant, in fact, as he manoeuvred himself back to the bedroom where he leaned against the doorjamb, scrutinizing the damage: the posters hanging in tatters, the collection of small animals scattered on the rug, the torn blankets and sheets, the yellow stains of piss on the wall.

Suddenly, his earlier exhilaration vanished, replaced by a sense of despair, emptiness. He felt isolated from the others, separate from the howls of jubilation and the sounds of crashing and bashing below. *I'm going to be sick*. He dropped to his knees, almost in slow motion, as vomit rushed up his throat and streamed out of his mouth on to the soft blue carpet. The smell, acid and foul, invaded his nostrils. He retched, once, twice, kneeling in the doorway, retched again and again, until nothing came up. His stomach hurt, his chest hurt, his throat hurt.

He became aware of a sudden silence from downstairs, as if Harry and his stooges were listening to him being sick. Rising to one knee, he began to gather his strength, his arms and legs trembling. He averted his eyes from the puddle of vomit on the floor.

Why so quiet down below?

Pressing his hands against his stomach, he lurched towards the stairs, steadying himself against the wall. He wanted a drink. Was desperate for one, although he did not know how he would manage to swallow the booze with the taste of vomit still like acid in his mouth and throat.

On the landing halfway down the stairs, he spotted a half-full bottle of vodka and giggled. He never giggled when

9

he was sober, so he must be drunk. He placed his hand over his mouth to stifle further giggles and picked up the bottle. Still quiet downstairs. The lights out, too. He took a big swig from the bottle, grimacing as the vodka bombed down his throat, bracing himself for the lurch of sickness in his stomach. Instead, warmth spread throughout his body as if he were bathing in the glow of something beautifully soft and fuzzy.

He heard a sound, a moan. Or a gasp. Not sure which. Cradling the bottle in his hand, he went down the remaining stairs, hesitating in the foyer, squinting, and saw, finally, what was going on in the front hallway.

Harry Flowers had a girl against the wall. She was pinned there by Marty Sanders and Randy Pierce. They were holding her arms to the wall while Harry screwed her. Or was he screwing her? Buddy didn't know if you could screw somebody standing up like that. But he was doing something. His trousers and striped boxer shorts were halfway down his legs, his ass gleaming in the light spilling in from the front porch. The girl's face was partly hidden in shadows but he saw her frantic eyes, wide with horror. Randy's right hand was like a suction cup on her breast.

"Jesus," Buddy said, the word exploding from his mouth like the vomit a few minutes ago upstairs.

"Me next," Marty said, grinning at Buddy. He was small and wiry and did not weigh much over one hundred pounds but had this big foghorn voice. "Wait your turn, Buddy."

The girl looked directly at him now, her eyes agonized, pleading, and Buddy drew back into the shadows. He wasn't sick any more. Wasn't anything. As if he had stumbled out of his own life into another, a new existence altogether. He blinked, hugging the bottle as he would a new-born baby.

"Jesus," he said again, his voice a whisper.

Suddenly, Randy howled with pain, and the girl was loose. One moment pinned to the wall, the next moment free. Not really free but pulling away from her captors while Randy danced around, holding his hand to his mouth, sucking at it. "She bit me," he cried in disbelief.

"You bitch," Harry yelled as he fell backwards, tripping over his trousers and shorts, which were now down around his ankles. "Get her," he ordered in a tight, deadly voice.

Nobody moved, not even the girl, as if they were caught in the flash of a camera's naked bulb like a picture on the front page of a newspaper. Then: movement, swift, like fast-forward on a VCR, Randy sucking at his hand, Harry now doing his own dance as he pulled up his trousers, Marty grabbing at the girl. The girl tore herself away from Marty's grasp, gathering her torn blouse around her breasts. But she had nowhere to go, really, and ran blindly into the wall while Harry, trousers pulled up at last, threw himself towards her, yelling, "Bitch."

Buddy saw that the girl had not run into a wall but against a door. She tried to open the door as Harry grappled towards her. Crazy: she was trying to escape into a closet. When she pulled the door open, he saw that it was not a closet but the doorway to the cellar. As the door swung open, Harry leaped towards her, grabbing at her body, his fingers raking her back. She swivelled to avoid his grasp and the movement gave Harry enough time to fling himself forwards. But he did not grab her. Instead, he pushed. With both hands. Pushed at her shoulders, once, twice. The girl screamed as she fell forwards down the stairs.

Buddy closed his eyes against the sound of her falling. A long time ago, when he was a little kid, he had been in his father's car when it struck an old man crossing the street. He had never forgotten that sound. Like no other sound in the world. Not like a bat hitting a ball, or a hammer hitting a nail or a firecracker exploding or a door slamming. The sound had a hollowness in it and in this hollow place was the smaller sound that had haunted his dreams for weeks. That small sound was the sound of something human being struck. And that was the sound Buddy heard as the girl tumbled down the stairs, a series of terrible bouncings, while Harry managed to pull up his trousers and zip his fly as if he had just finished peeing in the bathroom.

"Let's go, bloods," he said.

Harry was talking black this week.

Later, in the car, driving from Burnside to Wickburg, Marty and Randy discussed the merits of ketchup and mustard on hamburgers and hot dogs. Marty insisted that ketchup should never be used on hot dogs while Randy said that ketchup could be used on anything because it had an American taste.

"What do you mean — American taste?" Marty asked, disgusted, voice deep, like an old-time radio announcer's.

"I mean ketchup is American. Like the Fourth of July, Thanksgiving. Can you imagine a Frenchman or Italian in Europe using ketchup?"

"How do you know? Have you ever been to Europe?"

The argument went on and on as Buddy stared out of the window at nothing in particular. He found it hard to believe that Marty and Randy were engaged in a conversation about ketchup and hamburgers and hot dogs so soon after what had happened back in that house, while Harry hummed softly as he drove the car, carefully, slowly. Harry always drove slowly, loved to frustrate drivers behind him, holding his speed down to ridiculous levels, until they tried to pass and then he'd speed up gradually, until the other driver realized he was being baited.

"All right, how about mustard?" Randy said. "Mustard

12

works better on hot dogs. I hate it at McDonald's when I find mustard in the hamburger."

"McDonald's doesn't put mustard in its hamburgers," Marty said. "They put a slice of pickle in the hamburger and ketchup but no mustard."

"Of course they put in mustard," Marty boomed. "Next time you're at McDonald's, look at the hamburger. Lift up the bun and take a look. You'll see the hamburger and the pickle and the ketchup but look real close and you'll see the mustard."

Buddy touched the plaster on his cheek. The cut didn't hurt and was not bleeding any more. He concentrated on the street, letting the stupid argument in the back seat flow around him. At least it kept him from thinking. Thinking of that house, how he had stood there, doing nothing, while Harry raped a girl. A kid, for crying out loud.

Silence came from the back seat now: argument over, the debate of mustard versus ketchup concluded.

"We relax now, bloods," Harry said suddenly, quietly. "We out of their jurisdiction now. We safe and sound."

Buddy pressed his lips together to keep himself from yelling: Stop calling us bloods, for crissakes. Harry's black talk was ridiculous because it was not black at all but Harry's version of black. He liked to pretend he was a street kid, from some mythical inner city, instead of the son of a prominent architect. Harry was probably the whitest kid Buddy knew. Blond, wore white painter's trousers, white socks, white Nikes.

"You did good, real fine, bloods," Harry said. "Followed orders nice." The only order Harry had given: Don't break any windows. "Nice, nice." Still talking his version of black. Last week, he had affected a British accent after seeing an old movie on cable about British soldiers in India. He had pronounced it "Injia".

13

No one had mentioned the house and the rape since they fled the place. When they stopped at Shelton Park where they cleaned up at the fountain, Buddy had studied the faces of the others, glancing at them cautiously. Their actions were calm and deliberate as they splashed their faces with water. Marty brushed an invisible spot of dirt from his suede flight jacket. The jacket looked old but was new, three hundred dollars' worth of new. Buddy knew how much the jacket cost because Marty put price tags on everything. Randy's jeans also looked old but were new. We pay a lot of money to make things look old, Buddy thought. Harry Flowers was meticulous as usual. Spotlessly clean. Blond hair so neat that it seemed like a wig. Handsome face unblemished, serene as he washed his hands.

Back in the car, Marty and Randy had begun their ridiculous conversation about hamburgers and hot dogs and then fallen into silence. Nobody in the car seemed to mind the silence except Buddy.

Finally he asked: "Why'd you pick that particular house, Harry?" He had other, more important questions to ask but had to begin somewhere.

"Dumb luck, blood."

*Blood* again.

"Not dumb, smart," Randy called from the back seat.

Randy Pierce followed Harry around school like a big overgrown pet, an invisible tail wagging every time Harry paid him the least attention. Marty Sanders was a smaller version of Harry Flowers, thin and wiry, trying always to be cool but betrayed by a sharp tongue, the tendency to come up with a wisecrack to fit any situation. The first time he saw Randy and Marty together, Buddy flashed back to an old movie on television: *Abbott and Costello Meet Frankenstein*. Marty was clearly Abbott, the sharp guy, the agitator, while Randy was Costello, the buffoon, overweight,

14

often looking bewildered. Glancing at Harry now as he turned on to North Boulevard, he decided that Harry was Frankenstein, the doctor who created the monster.

Who is the monster then? Buddy wondered. Remembering his part in the vandalism and his inability to stop what they had done to the girl, he thought: Maybe it's me. *But I am not a monster.* Or is that what all the monsters said?

"We shouldn't have left the girl like that," Buddy heard himself saying.

"What did you say?" Harry's voice crackled as he brought the car slowly to a halt under a streetlight, the kind of light that casts a ghastly glow on people's faces. Harry's face was stark and purple as he turned to Buddy.

"Listen carefully, Buddy," he said, all traces of black gone from his voice. "You wanted fun, we had some fun . . ."

"That wasn't fun," Buddy said. "Raping a girl, for crissakes." How he could use a drink, wishing now he had not abandoned that vodka bottle at the girl's house.

"You jealous?" Marty piped up from the back seat.

"She wasn't raped," Harry said. "We didn't have time to rape her. Didn't even get her nice little white panties off."

"But you pushed her down the stairs," Buddy said, hearing Harry's intake of breath, wondering if he had gone too far.

"Maybe I was trying to grab her and save her from falling," Harry said, his voice suddenly mild and reasonable. "Maybe it only looked like I pushed her. What do they say, Buddy? Looks are deceiving."

Although his voice was mild, it contained an undertone Buddy could not pin down. His eyes were dark and piercing as he looked at Buddy. All of which made Buddy shiver inside, realizing that Harry somehow was giving him a message, telling him what to believe.

15

"Maybe we weren't even going to rape the poor girl," Harry continued. "Just having a little fun with her. She shouldn't have been there in the first place . . ."

*But it was her house*, Buddy wanted to say. *We were the ones who shouldn't have been there in the first place*. He didn't say anything, held by Harry's eyes. Hated himself for not saying anything but still said nothing.

"Accidents happen," Harry said, leaning towards Buddy, his breath heavy with stale booze. "Understand, Buddy?"

Buddy nodded, eager to end the conversation, eager for Harry to turn away, eager to get away from him.

"Say you understand, Buddy."

Buddy was conscious of the silence in the back seat, as if Marty and Randy were holding their breaths. Or waiting to take action if Harry gave a signal.

"I understand," Buddy said, his need for a drink so overwhelming that his hands trembled and he dropped them out of sight of the streetlight.

Harry smiled, turned away and grabbed the steering wheel, his foot depressing the accelerator. The tyres sprayed gravel behind him. More silence from the back seat. After a while, Harry looked over at Buddy. And smiled. A forgiving smile. He hit Buddy playfully on the shoulder.

"You did good tonight, blood," he said. Black again.

Christ, Buddy thought, how did I get mixed up in all this?

Although he knew, of course, the answer to that question.

The problem with being an eleven-year-old Avenger was just that: being eleven years old and an Avenger. It would have been easier if he were older, like fifteen or sixteen, or old enough to have a driver's licence so that he could zoom around easier. He had to depend on his bike, a rickety three-speeder his mother bought him secondhand. He also had to depend on his ingenuity and, of course, his patience. Patience was the watchword, his mother always said, and she should know, she was the most patient person in the world. Washing, scrubbing, dusting. She kept missing her favourite TV shows because there was always something else for her to do around the house. Sewing, cooking, ironing, scrubbing, dusting.

The Avenger had other problems. His shyness, for instance. He was not shy when he was The Avenger, carrying out his acts of revenge. But in the classroom or in the schoolyard, he found it difficult to make friends, to be at ease with the other students. When called upon to recite in class, he blushed furiously, his throat tightening and his voice emerging in a ridiculous squeak. Which made Vaughn Masterson snicker. Vaughn Masterson spent the day snickering. When kids answered questions or went to the blackboard, or received good marks in a test. The Avenger realized finally that Vaughn snickered because he was jealous. And dumb. D-U-M-B. In capital letters. Cheated when he could. Tried to sneak glances at The Avenger's test papers because The Avenger always received good marks, A's most of the time. Vaughn Masterson sat behind him and poked him in the back. That was mild compared to what he did to the other kids. Took their lunch bags and squished the sandwiches in his hands and threw them to the ground. He would have had some respect for Vaughn Masterson if, for instance, he had eaten the stolen lunches instead of destroying them and humiliating the kids he took them from. Like little Danny Davis, whom Vaughn enjoyed tormenting, day after day. Tripping him, pulling his shirt out of his trousers, tweaking his cheeks. Especially in front of the girls. Making fun of Danny Davis while everybody giggled and those who didn't giggle turned away in embarrassment, feeling guilty because they didn't stand up to him. Why didn't they stand up to him? Vaughn wasn't *that* much bigger than anyone else in the fifth grade. But he carried a powerful air with him as he strutted through the schoolyard, a faint smile on his face as if he found the world an amusing place to be.

After observing Vaughn Masterson doing his dirty work for several weeks, The Avenger knew that *something* had to be done. He planned his course of action. He was good at planning. His mother called it daydreaming — you'll dream your life away, she'd say. In those daydreams, he was brave and daring, reckless and adventurous. He dreamed about what he would do to Vaughn Masterson. And how he would do it. He had to be patient, of course, had to wait for the proper conditions, one of the conditions being that it was necessary to obtain the means. And, after obtaining the means, he would have to wait a while — patience again — to let things cool down.

Finally, all the conditions were right and he carried out his scheme. On that particular day, he followed Vaughn home from school. Did not ride his bike, but walked. Did not really walk but scampered behind Vaughn, hiding behind bushes and trees, thrilling, like the movies. When Vaughn arrived home, The Avenger waited across the street, concealing himself in a gazebo on the front lawn. He had noticed the gazebo on an earlier expedition to Vaughn's street. He had observed several other things. That Vaughn Masterson was alone in the afternoon, his parents off working somewhere. The house with the gazebo also was unoccupied in the afternoon. Vaughn would stay in his house for a half-hour or so, changing his clothes, having a bite to eat in the kitchen. The Avenger had employed his skills at spying to learn Vaughn's routine.

Finally, Vaughn came out of the house, chewing the last remnants of his peanut butter and jelly sandwich. He had changed into jeans and a faded yellow shirt, his stomach bulging slightly at his belt. Made his way lazily down the steps to the back of the house where, if he followed his usual routine, he would open the garage door and fool around inside for a while. That's exactly what he did now.

The Avenger crossed the street, looking this way and that, to see if anyone was watching. Except for a stray dog sniffing at a car down at the corner, the street was deserted.

Standing a few feet in front of the garage, The Avenger called out: "Hey, Vaughn, how're you doing?"

Vaughn emerged from the garage, squinting into the sun, looking annoyed.

"What do *you* want?" he said, sneering, that *you* snapping with contempt.

"This," The Avenger said, smiling.

From his book bag he removed the revolver he had stolen from his grandfather. Kneeling, he held the revolver with both hands and pressed the trigger. The lower half of Vaughn's face exploded in bone and blood as the bullet struck. The noise of the shot was deafening and the recoil of the gun sent The Avenger sprawling backwards. He fell on his behind, on the hard pavement, pain shooting along his spinal column.

As the echo of the shot faded in the afternoon, The Avenger scrambled to his feet. The smell of sulphur filled the air. His breath came in short gasps as he looked around, listening for neighbourhood sounds. All was quiet. Nobody in sight. The dog down the street was gone.

Ignoring the blood and the shattered face, and the pain in his spine, The Avenger went about his business as planned, heart hammering dangerously in his chest. He wiped the handle of the revolver with a piece of Kleenex. The hardest part was placing the revolver in Vaughn's left hand — The Avenger had noticed in school that he was left-handed — and curling Vaughn's index finger around the trigger. He then let the revolver fall out of Vaughn's hand and clatter to the pavement. Just as he had seen it done on television.

Squinting, he looked down at the bloody fallen figure. Vaughn Masterson lay there in a ghastly kind of stillness. A thing, suddenly. He would not bully anyone again, and the kids in the fifth grade of Lucy Peary Elementary School could now go about their business in peace.

The Avenger smiled his smile of vengeance as he picked up his book bag, slung it over his shoulder, and went home. He arrived in time to share with his mother their usual afternoon snack of ice-cold milk and molasses cookies.

Pink. Bright, cool like a Popsicle. That was the colour this year. The colour she and Patti and Leslie had chosen as their motif. They had also decided to be subtle about it, not going wild but using pink in their accessories, alternating between necklaces, bracelets, and earrings. Pink tank tops, a touch of pink in their attire. Also pink thoughts. Which meant not hot. To play it cool with guys. They also used *pink* as a code word. But the word changed to suit the situation. Like with Johnny Taylor. Leslie was *pink* about him. And Patti would giggle, she was a giggler, giggles like bubbles gurgling out of her at the least provocation, which drove some people crazy but not Jane and not Leslie. Best friends put up with such things.

Pink united them in a secret alliance, their use of the word puzzling to others but drawing them together. Leslie, for instance, was the lady of Burnside High, always dressed up like Sunday, fussy with her hair and make-up. Yet, she had this crazy side to her that only Patti and Jane knew about. "Pink him," Leslie would cry out when angry momentarily with some guy. And they all laughed and giggled, knowing the word that Leslie had used *pink* for as a substitute.

Although blue was Jane's favourite colour, she went along with the pink delirium, glad to do so because she loved Patti and Leslie, would do anything for them, anything at all, and they felt the same about her.

Until the trashing.

She thought of it as "the trashing" but it was more than that, of course. It was also what happened to Karen and the coma that held her in a strange kind of sleep in ICU at the hospital. Jane tried not to think about that. In her mind she placed it all within the context of one word: *trashing*. Which included her house and her home and everything in it. Karen had been trashed, ruined. Tossed aside, down the cellar stairs, like a rag doll when someone was through playing with it.

The effects of the trashing had spread beyond the house, however, and the ICU. Had changed things. Had changed Arbor Lane and also Patti and Leslie. Oh, they were sympathetic, of course. Stunned at what had happened. They visited the house the day after the trashing, and Jane had led them reluctantly through the rooms, sorry she had invited them to view the damage. Had not actually invited them but had responded to their curiosity as they sat on the back porch. "Is it really as bad as everybody says?" Patti had asked. Who is everybody? Jane wondered. Then, wanting to see the damage through their eyes, Jane ushered them through the house, growing uncomfortable at the sight of the damage and disarray. More than that. *Ashamed* suddenly, wanting to hide somewhere, as if *she* had done something wrong, not the culprits, not the invaders.

Leslie, always the lady, picked her way through the house, nose wrinkled a bit, her arms at awkward angles. What angles? Jane realized that Leslie was trying to avoid touching anything, as if she might somehow become contaminated. Patti, the giggler, did not giggle for once. Which was worse than if she had giggled. Instead, she kept saying: "Wow." Murmuring *wow* again and again, in a breathless whisper until Jane wanted to scream: Pink you!

Later, they sat on the back porch banister, balancing themselves delicately, legs swinging back and forth.

"Who would want to do such a thing?" Leslie said. "I mean, why pick on your house? Why pick on Karen?"

The choice of words offended Jane. *Pick on.*

"The police said Karen was unlucky enough to come home at the wrong moment," Jane said, her voice flat and crisp. "It could have been anybody." She felt as though Karen had been criticized.

"Picking your house was certainly bad luck, all right," Patti said.

*Picking.*

"What about the police?" Patti asked. "What do they think?"

"The police don't know what to think," Jane said, banging her heels against the banister posts. "No clues." *Clues*, a movie word. "No witnesses." Another movie word. Which made it all seem unreal. "That other stuff, the phone calls, the dead squirrel. The police don't think they're connected. They think the trashing was done by someone else, more than one person. Four or five."

"You mean, Karen and four or five guys . . ." Leslie began, horror growing in her eyes, her voice dying away in that horror.

"They don't know about that," Jane said, avoiding the word that Leslie avoided and then going ahead with it. "Look, she was not raped. She was . . . assaulted, attacked. But even that much is hard to tell. She fell down the stairs.

22

Or was pushed down the stairs. But definitely not raped." That hateful terrible word again.

No one spoke for a while. A stillness pervaded the neighbourhood except for the distant purring of a lawn mower. Jane wanted to change the subject but also needed to break the silence in which that terrible word seemed to echo.

"The police are puzzled about how they entered the house," Jane said. "There was what they called 'no signs of forced entry'." Seeing their puzzled expressions, she said: "Which means, they didn't break down the doors to get in. Or didn't pry them open." Then, almost to herself, because it was so puzzling: "Another thing, they didn't break any windows. Broke like a thousand glasses and all the mirrors in the house but no windows . . ."

"What does that mean?" Patti asked, perplexed.

"I don't know," Jane said, her voice sounding distant and meek.

Their shoes drummed against the banister. "I used to love it here," Jane said. "Arbor Lane." Her voice wistful as she whispered the name of the street. After the initial resentment over her father's transfer to Burnside had subsided, she had been fascinated by Arbor Lane and her new neighbourhood, realizing that it was a dream street, like something out of *Leave It to Beaver* in the old television reruns. Neat houses, with shutters and rose arbours, birdbaths on front lawns, and the lawns carefully manicured. People waving hello to each other, evening barbecues in back yards and the aroma of burning charcoal or wood smoke from chimneys. A neighbourhood of station wagons and vans, family cars. Kids of all ages and sizes. Typical kids, some regular, some nerds. But then all kids just before reaching puberty seemed to have undergone some kind of brat injection. Like her brother, Artie, and his addiction to video games, barricading himself in his room while he zipped and zapped at the television set, causing his father to issue ultimatums and limits on playing the games. Mikey Bryan from two houses down who specialized in riding his bike helter-skelter on the sidewalk, running people down unless they leaped out of the way. Little Kenny Crane whom everyone picked on. Every neighbourhood had a kid like that and Kenny Crane with his baby face and sissy walk filled the role on Arbor Lane. She once saw Artie, who wasn't exactly her idea of a hero, defend Kenny, telling the other kids to leave him alone, placing his arm around Kenny Crane's frail shoulders. Maybe there was hope for Artie, after all.

"Hi, Jane."

She looked up to see Amos Dalton trudging by, taking a shortcut through the back yard. Amos: an old man's name and the boy himself like a prematurely middle-aged man. Always a worried look on his face, always carrying one or two library books. Always sly glances at Jane's boobs. She was self-conscious about her breasts these days and boys staring at them all the time. She was both proud of them — they seemed to have appeared practically overnight — and embarrassed about them. Wanted them and didn't want them. Wished she could flaunt them the way Karen flaunted hers.

She crossed her arms in front of her chest now as Amos stopped below.

"Sorry about your house," he said in a croaking voice. "And your sister."

She nodded, hoping he'd just go away.

"If there's anything I can do, just let me know," he said, scuffing the grass with his foot. He didn't wear sneakers like other kids but laced shoes, middle-aged shoes.

"Who was *that*?" Leslie asked, face wrinkled in disgust as Amos trudged away.

"A kid from the neighbourhood," Jane replied. "He's kind of weird but nice." Trying to hide her irritation, wanting to defend Amos, the neighbourhood, herself.

"Oh, oh," Patti said. "Speaking of weird . . ."

They looked up to see Mickey Looney getting out of his old beat-up truck. Mickey was the neighbourhood handyman, performing odd jobs, mowing lawns, shovelling snow, raking leaves, all in season. His old truck wheezed and rattled as it gasped its way through the streets. Short and plump, ageless, he could have been thirty years old or fifty.

"Who is he?" Leslie asked, as if she were at a zoo enquiring about some strange species.

"His name is Mickey Stallings but everybody calls him Mickey Looney," she said. "Behind his back of course." Needing to explain: "Because he looks like that old movie star, Mickey Rooney? But, Looney because he is sort of odd."

She was sorry she had told them about Mickey's nickname as soon as the words were out of her mouth. In the neighbourhood, the nickname Mickey Looney was used affectionately for this gentle man who patted dogs, tousled the hair of small kids, nodded respectfully to the men and tipped his faded baseball cap to the ladies.

"He gives me the creeps," Leslie said.

"Me too," Patti agreed.

"He's very nice," Jane said, anger stirring inside her. Anger at Patti and Leslie and also at herself. "He's smart, too. Knows how to fix things, knows all about plants and stuff. My father says he could have been an engineer if he'd gone to college. But he likes fixing things, working for himself . . ."

Patti rolled her eyes. Jane knew that look. It meant: Are you kidding?

"I still think he's weird," Patti said.

Jane felt like a traitor. To her house, which she had exposed to Patti and Leslie. To Mickey Looney, who was not really Looney at all. She had betrayed Mickey, her house, the entire neighbourhood.

Now the silence again as they watched Mickey unloading his garden equipment, silence thick and heavy like an invisible fog enveloping them all. Jane sighed, softly but tremulously, hoping that Leslie and Patti did not notice. Loneliness invaded her. Here she was, sitting on the porch banister of her house with her two best friends in the whole wide world, and she had never felt so alone, so forlorn, in all her life.

Buddy placed the pint bottle on the top of his father's workbench in the garage and carefully studied the label, *Seagram's Gin, 80 Proof,* then took the bottle in his hands and caressed it tenderly, as if it contained something precious. Which it did, of course. Actually, he hated the taste of the stuff. Despite its perfumey taste, it burned his throat and spread sourness in his stomach. He much preferred Coke, Classic. But Classic Coke did not do to him what gin did. Even when he mixed the gin with the Coke it did not take away the harsh edges of things, did not blur, did not bring the haziness, did not soothe him with soft strokings, letting him float pleasantly away while just sitting there. Two or three gulps and he would give himself up to sweet lassitude, and the hate and the ache folded their tents like the Arabs and silently stole away.

That's what was happening now, all the rotten things stealing away — this terrible house that was his home and that other house where the girl had bounced sickeningly down the stairs — replaced by a glow spreading through his limbs, as if his body were a light bulb on low intensity.

He glanced around the garage which his father never

26

used for cars but for storing the paraphernalia of house maintenance — lawn mower, wheelbarrow, shovels and rakes, all kinds of tools spread haphazardly here and there, which made it easy to hide the bottles of booze Buddy sneaked into the place. Neatness was not one of his father's strong points. He always left a trail of disarray and debris behind him. Kept losing things. Didn't hang up his clothes. Ironic: in this house, the son was neater than the father. The mother would nag his father to put things away, holding the son up as a model.

*Notice the formality here: calling them Mother and Father, not Mom and Dad. No more Hi Mom, Hi Dad, how did things go today? What's on for dinner? Pork chops? Swell. We all love pork chops. And then telling jokes at the dinner table, like we always do. Dad's atrocious talking-animal jokes which were funny without being funny. Like the kangaroo who orders Scotch on the rocks at the bar and . . .*

Christ.

Not only didn't call them Mom or Dad any more. Did not call them anything at all. Not even *hey*. Amend that. Called his mother *Mom* sometimes because it slipped out from habit. She still lived here at least. He had a soft spot for her but was angry with her, too. But it wasn't her fault at all, Addy said. But what did Addy know? Addy Walker, fifteen years old. Little sister but not so little, slightly over-weight. Not particularly likeable, either. Pain in the ass, in fact. Little Miss Know-It-All. Sometimes he almost hated her, her smarty-pants attitude, high honour roll, smirking as they compared report cards, Buddy barely managing to keep a B average, always in danger of flunking at least one subject, never acing anything. Addy was starring in the sophomore play, a play she had written with her English teacher, for crissakes. While he had even flunked basketball,

27

a hairline fracture of his knee ending potential stardom. Stardom? Hell, he had been lucky they let him sit on the bench: too short at five foot nine in a game that called for giants, too uncoordinated, with a knee that gave way on occasion, sending him unceremoniously to the floor.

Have another drink, Buddy.

He lifted the bottle to his lips, then hesitated. The moment always came when one more swallow was too much, made him cross the border between being pleasantly high and deathly sick and he never knew when that moment would come, which swallow would change things around. Like at that girl's house the other night. One minute, beautiful. Next minute, sick on the floor. Vomiting on the rug of a perfect stranger.

He drank anyway, but a small, tentative swallow. Testing, testing. Testing the state of his stomach, the state of his life. As he swallowed he heard the back door open and then slam shut. Glancing hazily at his watch, he saw that it was two thirty-three. Addy home from school. Unexpected: she usually stayed late, involved in all kinds of extracurricular stuff. His mother worked at the office till five, never got home till almost six.

Buddy sat still. Gathered himself. Blinked, relaxed. Slipped the bottle of booze under the pile of stuff on the workbench. He rose slowly to his feet, pleased to see that he was only a bit dizzy. He had found out since he had started to drink that he was a superb actor, that he could have stolen the show even in Addy's stupid play. He was often a bit high, a bit drunk, but nobody noticed. Maybe Addy did. She often regarded him curiously, scrutinizing him as if he were a puzzle she could not solve.

"How much do you drink?" she had asked one night, meeting him in the hallway upstairs.

Her question stunned him for a moment, almost made

him lose his cool. Not *do you drink?* But *how much do you drink?*

"Not much," he managed to mutter as he brushed by her.

So, he was always extra careful in her presence, tried to avoid her most of the time, which was hard sometimes because she seemed to be trying to track him down.

It was different with other people, especially teachers. He found that if you were polite, didn't say very much, chewed peppermints or Life Savers or gum — all of which he actually hated — you could fake your way through any number of situations. The trick, too, was knowing when not to take that extra swallow: like now. He had stopped at the right moment, Addy arriving home unexpectedly.

The door between the garage and the back hall opened. Addy stuck her head in. Clown face, round, sprinkled with freckles. She would never win a beauty contest.

"What are you doing?" she enquired suspiciously, looking around the garage. "God, you're acting spooky lately."

"All of us are," he replied. The secret: short sentences.

"You're weirdest of all," she said. Frowning, she said: "Have you been drinking?" Sniffing the air.

He had failed to pop anything in his mouth, had not anticipated Addy searching him out in the garage. Now, he pressed his lips together, tried to breathe through his nostrils. Made himself busy at the bench, as if he was looking for something.

"Mind your own business," he said, enunciating each word separately to let her know he really meant for her to mind her own business.

Funny thing: most of the time, they each minded their own business. Days passed when they hardly communicated. The good old days, that is. Not lately, not in these bad new days. These days, Addy tracked him down, popped in the house early from school. Like today, this afternoon.

"I hope you're not drinking *and* driving," Addy said. "That would be the most stupid thing in the world."

"I don't drink and drive," Buddy said. Which was true. His licence had been issued only seven weeks ago and Buddy had vowed never to drive while liquor flowed through his veins. This took an effort of will because his mother kept offering him the use of the car. Guilt, on her part, probably, trying to compensate for the dismal thing their lives had become. Buddy was not very proud of himself these days but he was proud about keeping his vow even though the car, sitting day after day in the driveway, was a constant temptation.

Addy studied him closely now, eyes narrowed in appraisal. "I have a feeling you're drunk right this minute," she said.

"I'm not drunk," he declared, bringing himself to his full height, which wasn't much, really.

She looked at him for a terrible moment, her dark eyes flashing darker than ever, and then turned away, slamming the door behind her as she dashed out of the place.

Buddy grimaced, realized he'd been holding his breath. He let the breath out. That terrible look in her eyes. They had always shot dynamite glances at each other when they weren't being completely indifferent, Addy dismayed at his lackadaisical ways, his lack of ambition, the way he bumped into things. He could not abide her schedules, her snap-crackle-and-pop way of doing things, always on time, on the ball. He was far from stupid but Addy made him look stupid, feel stupid.

Leaning against the workbench, resisting another swallow of gin, he tried to bring back her expression, the way she had looked at him a moment before abandoning the garage. That look. Not only disgust at his drinking but something else.

30

In the downstairs bathroom, he brushed his teeth, gulped mouthwash, gargled, hoping that the smell of gin had been obliterated. He went upstairs, listened at the landing, heard nothing. In the second-floor hallway, he saw that her bedroom door was closed. Not unusual. Neither was the absence of sound. Addy hated the radio, couldn't stand rock music or anything resembling contemporary stuff while studying. Buddy could not face homework or a theme paper without Bruce Springsteen or somebody to help him along.

He knocked at her door, softly. *What am I doing?* Knocked again. *I should be glad she's in there and I'm out here.*

"What do you want?" she asked, voice muffled.

"I don't know," he said. Which was exactly right.

"Stupid," she called out. Her voice sounded funny. Not funny, but broken.

He stood there. Waited. What was he waiting for?

She opened the door, slowly, letting it swing wide open before appearing. Her face, when he finally saw it, was red and shining. Eyes wet. She sniffed, blew her nose with a Kleenex.

She'd been crying, for crissakes.

"You've been crying?" he said.

"You're so observant," she replied. Sarcastically, of course.

And suddenly he, too, felt like crying.

Because he saw himself and Addy for what they were: two kids whose parents were divorcing, living in a house where nobody loved anybody else any more.

While a bruised and battered girl lay in a hospital somewhere.

"Come in," she said.

But he could not go in. He stared at her for a long moment and then turned away, dashed down the stairs, through the front hallway and out of the house, not realizing he was running until he found himself a block away on Oak Avenue heading nowhere.

While Karen slept.

Deep in her dreams — or did she dream? Or even sleep? Jane wondered about the strange place Karen now occupied, between life and death: alive but not alive, sleeping but not sleeping.

Karen was seldom alone in that hospital room. Someone in the family remained with her almost all the time, except the late night-time hours. Jane's mother kept vigil in the morning and Jane often joined her in the afternoon after school. Her father and mother sat beside Karen's bed in the evenings, sometimes together, sometimes alternating with each other. Jane dropped in at the hospital at odd hours, not only after school but on her way home from the shopping mall or from a movie, and sometimes found her father, sometimes Artie, there. The family had no formal visiting plan. The ceaseless routine of visiting had developed naturally, became a habit around which the rest of their lives centered.

One day, Jane found herself alone in the hospital room and it seemed to her that Karen was sinking, deeper and deeper, into that strange terrible sleep, her body slight and slender under the sheet. Occasionally, she moved, twitched, sudden involuntary movements that, for one split second, brought a flash of hope. Then, nothing, the stillness again.

The doctor had encouraged the family to talk to Karen but Jane found it hard to do that. Just as she had found it hard to communicate with Karen at home. Although Karen was two years younger, Jane did not feel like her older sister. Karen glided easily through life, popular at school, adjusting quickly to Burnside, the telephone ringing constantly for her only a few days after the family had moved from Monument. Secretly, Jane regarded Karen as a snob, immersed in her social life at school, ignoring her parents as well as Artie and Jane herself, acknowledging Jane's existence only when she invaded her room to borrow, without asking, her clothes, her cologne, her jewellery. Which provided arguments and accusations.

"Why does she act like I don't even exist and then borrows my things?" Jane had asked her mother.

"Maybe she envies you."

"Me? She's the one with a million friends, has such a flair for style . . ."

"Yes, but you have taste, Jane," her mother said. "Remember, she's younger, she looks up to you. That's why she borrows your things . . ."

"Then why doesn't she just ask me? Instead of going behind my back . . ."

"She's shy . . ."

Karen shy?

"People are not always what they seem to be," her mother said, using one of those mysterious sayings parents rely on to end conversations at a convenient moment.

Regarding Karen in the bed, looking vulnerable and, yes, shy and unguarded, Jane said, "I'm sorry," her voice too loud in the quiet room where the small *beep* of the monitor was the only other sound.

"If you envied me, maybe I was jealous of you," Jane admitted, hoping that Karen *could* hear her words. "Please come out of this, Karen, so we can talk about it, do something about it . . ."

The echo of her voice died out, along with the odd but somehow comforting words she had spoken to her silent sister.

While Karen slept in that high hospital bed, the house

underwent repairs. A sophisticated alarm system, connected with police headquarters, was installed. New furniture was purchased plus three television sets, a CD set, and two VCRs. Her mother also bought new bedding — sheets and blankets to replace those that had been torn to shreds by the invaders. Her mother, in fact, went on a sad kind of shopping spree, replacing things that she thought the trashers had even *touched*. Particularly clothes. She and Jane went to the mall and bought tops and skirts — and she brought home new shirts and underwear for Jane's father. Meanwhile, the repairs were completed in record time as the workmen performed with urgency, working overtime willingly, as if they knew it was important to obliterate all evidence of mischief as soon as possible. *Mischief*. That was the word used by a man named Stoddard, a friend of Jane's father who was boss of the work crew. He kept muttering the word under his breath as he directed the repairs and performed along with the crew as they scrubbed and painted and replaced.

Within a week, the house was restored to what passed for normal. Everything bright and new. The old wallpaper had been removed from Jane's room and she decided to have the walls painted, choosing white instead of her favourite blue. Blue was spoiled for her for ever and so, in a way, was pink. She did not replace her posters but allowed the walls to remain uncluttered, untouched, pure. She wasn't quite sure that *pure* was the right word but it suited the room somehow.

The smell of paint lingered in the air after the workmen's departure, along with other smells Jane could not identify, probably turpentine or the liquid wax on the floors. But something else, too.

"The smell of newness," her mother said, sniffing the air, making her voice light and bright.

34

"That's right," Jane said, forcing brightness into her own voice, wondering if her mother also was play-acting, whether her mother could detect that other smell, the smell that persisted, rising to her nostrils on occasion, lurking under all the new smells. She was aware of the smell when she entered her bedroom, a soiled scent just barely there, making her pause and sniff tentatively, wrinkling her nose. The smell of something spoiled and decayed, an under-the-surface odour, hinting of vomit and things gone bad. Faint, yes, but unmistakable, not always there but coming and going, elusive sometimes, but other times strong, over-powering. She avoided looking at the spot near the door where she had encountered that puddle of vomit. To her surprise — and horror — she began to detect that elusive smell elsewhere, catching a drifting whiff when she was on the bus going to school, on the sidewalk in front of the mall, in the classroom once, the smell suddenly stronger than schoolroom chalk. She would sniff cautiously and sometimes the smell evaporated, disappeared at once or lingered for a while, tantalizing in a horrible way. She won-dered, a bit panicky, if the odour came from herself, if somehow it was being manufactured by her body, created out of her own horror at what had happened. She began to douse herself with cologne, applied creams and salves, sought out the strongest deodorants to rub into her armpits. She began to hold herself aloof from people, not letting anyone come too close, leaning over awkwardly when she kissed her mother and father goodnight. Sometimes, she caught her mother looking at her peculiarly and quickly turned away or left the room or began to jabber like a madwoman. And sometimes she caught her mother's own face lost in deep thought or sadness and wanted to reach out to her, cry out, touch her or fling herself in her arms. But could not, could not, always holding back.

35

And all the while Karen slept.

It wasn't only that foul odour, that terrible smell, but the house itself that began to bother Jane. She started fleeing the place, finding excuses not to be there. After visiting the hospital, she sometimes took the bus to downtown Wickburg and wandered the mall, killing time, going in and out of the stores, trying on jackets and skirts, drinking a 7-Up. She did not stay too long in the stores or linger on the plastic benches near the fountain, did not want to give the appearance of being a stray, homeless. At home, she quickly changed and roamed the neighbourhood or simply hung out in the back yard. She didn't seek out the company of the other girls on the street because she wasn't in a mood for polite conversation or talk about clothes or make-up or movies and television. She wished she were a writer or a painter or a musician so that she could lose herself in some form of creativity, express the emotions that stirred inside her. What emotions? She felt as though she were fooling herself because she felt no emotions, really. Felt dead inside. Empty. Like a vessel waiting to be filled. Filled with what? She didn't know.

Her father called a family meeting one night. He did not issue special invitations but somehow let them all know that they should gather in the living room after supper. He faced them, standing self-consciously at the fireplace, frowning. Jane wondered whether he had a headache because he kept rubbing his forehead.

"I'm going to make a speech," he said. "A short one. But your mother and I feel that certain things should be said."

If her mother was in on the plan, then that meant the speech was really being made to an audience of two, her and her brother, Artie.

"We can't pretend that the vandalism didn't take place," he said, voice strained as if he had been shouting against the wind all day. "But we have to go on living. Living here, in this house. We have to put it all behind us. Not as if it didn't happen but looking ahead instead of behind us. We also can't pretend that Karen isn't in the hospital. In a . . . ." His voice faltered and he skipped the word *coma*, after pausing for a minute. "So we have to be concerned about her, think about her, pray for her, and visit her. Which we've all been doing and which we must and will continue to do. But we also have to get on with our own lives. We can't afford to be bitter, to let what happened spoil our lives."

He took a deep breath and paused. "Now let me talk about something we've all avoided talking about. The trashers themselves.

"We don't know why they did what they did. Why they chose our house. Everybody, and that includes the police, thinks it was a random thing, that we shouldn't feel as though we were special targets, that it was a personal attack on us as a family. The world is filled with weird people, and some of those weird people came upon our house and did terrible things. We can't deny that it happened but we have to get over it. The trashers would be the big winners if we let what they did change us, spoil our lives. Yes, Karen is in the hospital. But she's alive and the doctors are optimistic about her chances of recovery. The police are convinced that she was what they call an unintended victim. That the trashers were attacking the house, not her, not us. We have to believe that and get on with our lives."

Such a brave speech, delivered with such determination and resolution that Jane wanted to rush to him and embrace him.

After that, she and her family settled into a kind of a routine, caught up in busy days and evenings. Her father left for work every day as usual, spent long hours at the

37

office and the rest of the time at the hospital. He did not play golf any more on weekends. Her mother acted as if someone had cranked her up in the morning and dispatched her on her daily rounds. She was a whirlwind of bustling activity, dashing between home and the hospital, meanwhile doing the housework, cleaning, dusting, knitting, seldom pausing to catch her breath. All of which made Jane wonder: Was all of this normal? What was normal, anyway?

She developed her own routine in the neighbourhood. Sometimes, she did not feel like taking the bus trip to Wickburg, and found the house lonely and forlorn. She'd put on her Nikes and shorts and jog the streets, dodging the bike brigade and the brats, ignoring them when they whistled and yelled or tried to sideswipe her. The kids were pests but she preferred them to that silent empty house.

"Hello, Jane."

She paused her jogging as Mickey Looney tipped his baseball hat.

Jane drew up, breathing heavily, glad for the respite. She was not the most athletic of persons, probably the least.

"Hi, Mickey," she said. He blushed when anyone looked directly at him, deep crimson sweeping his face.

"Almost time to plant tomatoes?" she asked.

"Thirtieth of May," Mickey said, seriously, suddenly the professional planter. "Any time before then is too early, New England being what it is."

He seemed to hesitate, then kicked at something invisible on the ground. "How's Karen?" he asked. "I've been meaning to enquire but don't like to intrude."

"She's still in the coma," Jane said. Observing how stricken he looked, she reassured him: "She's not suffering, Mickey, and she's not any worse."

"I hope she'll come out of it," he said, still kicking at nothing.

Weird Amos Dalton came along, his arms loaded with books as usual. He did not look up as he trudged by.

"Hey, Amos," Jane called on an impulse. "What're you reading?"

Amos looked up with a pained expression as if it hurt him to encounter someone face-to-face. "What do you want to know for?" he asked.

"Just curious."

Mickey said: "I don't read so much since we got television."

Weird, Jane thought. Television began thirty, forty years ago.

"Television is for morons," Amos said, a middle-aged scowl on his face.

Mickey recoiled, stepping backwards, *"Jeopardy*'s my favourite programme," he said, not looking at Jane. Or Amos.

"Hey, Amos," Jane said, "I watch television. Millions of people watch it. We're not all morons. I like *Jeopardy* too."

Amos hugged his books closer to his chest. Turned away, then turned back, grimacing. "I hope your sister's getting better," he said, his voice rusty, as if it hurt him to speak.

Still clutching his books, Amos marched away, a lonesome parade of one, while Mickey began to fuss with his tools at the back of the truck.

"Time to go to work," he said, tugging at his baseball cap.

Jane resumed jogging, not really jogging but a quickstep kind of walking. Going down the street and turning the corner, she felt somehow cheered up by the meeting with these odd people. Maybe because the man and the boy, both so very different, had mentioned Karen. Everyone else avoided speaking about her, as if she had ceased to exist, had passed out of people's lives.

She herself had passed out of people's lives. She seldom

saw Patti or Leslie any more. They nodded when they met in the corridors at school and sometimes endured awkward lunch hours at the same table, the conversation stilted and superficial, broken by prolonged silences. Jane did not blame them for not continuing the friendship they had enjoyed, if indeed it had been friendship. She was the one who had first withdrawn, avoiding them, sensing that she had become an embarrassment, a feeling that began that morning on the porch. Her separation from Patti and Leslie meant that she did not have to play-act any more, did not have to pretend that everything was fine, did not have to be on the defensive about her house and family and Karen. Yet, sometimes, when she saw the two girls walking down the corridor, easy with each other, laughing, casual, she was filled with a longing, a yearning for — she was not sure what — perhaps simply a friend to talk to.

But all of this was minor, of course, compared with what had happened to Karen, although sometimes she almost envied Karen as she slept on that high hospital bed.

The death of Vaughn Masterson was reported as an accident in the newspaper. The story noted that the weapon had been stolen from the apartment of retired police sergeant Louis Kendrick a month earlier. Allowing the victim the benefit of the doubt, police deduced that the boy probably found the weapon after it had been either lost or discarded by the thief. Vaughn Masterson evidently took the weapon home, hid it away somewhere in his house or in his father's garage, and had taken it out to play with on that fatal day, not realizing it was loaded. The boy died instantly when the weapon was discharged. The newspaper did not sensationalize the story, ran the boy's picture — one taken by a school photographer the year before — but did not go into great detail about the fatal shooting.

The Avenger read the story avidly, his heart pumping joyously, his eyes bright and his head warm as if he had a fever. But a nice fever. He studied Vaughn's face in the picture, his neatly combed hair, the big smile that revealed small sharp teeth.

Although he felt an immense satisfaction as he read the story, he did not make the mistake of cutting it out of the newspaper, to save as a souvenir. He had seen a movie in which the killer was apprehended when a yellowed newspaper clipping about the murder was found years later in his attic.

The entire fifth grade attended the funeral at the First Congregational church. The Avenger was amazed at the hypocrisy of his classmates, especially the girls who cried and sniffled and blew their noses. Even the guys — and Danny Davis in particular — looked sad. The Avenger arranged his face in what he considered a mournful expression. Although he hated doing this, he knew that he could not afford to stand out in the crowd, could not draw attention to himself.

Vaughn's parents walked down the aisle a moment before the coffin was wheeled in. The Avenger felt a tug of sympathy, picturing his own mother in church if he should die. In a way, The Avenger felt sorry for Vaughn's parents as they sat down in the pew. Mr Masterson's hand trembled as he placed his arm around Mrs Masterson's shoulder. Chances were they did not know what a terrible person their son had been. No wonder they were sad. The Avenger realized he had done them a favour by killing him before he grew up to disgrace them. The Avenger was convinced that Vaughn Masterson would have grown up to be a terrible person.

The minister began to speak. Like a teacher in school, speaking softly and slowly as if he was going to pass out a test at the end of the sermon. He spoke about eternity and goodness and living one's life in the glow of the Lord. He spoke of the tragedy of an early death but the glory of going to the Lord without a tarnished soul.

The Avenger barely listened as he kept his eye on the gleaming wood of Vaughn's coffin. The minister said we should be thankful for Vaughn's time with us on earth. The Avenger was also thankful for Vaughn Masterson. He had shown The Avenger how easy it was to get rid of someone who did not deserve to live. Easier than on television, where the murderers always got caught before the final commercial was shown. *Why had it been easy?* The Avenger frowned, seeking an answer as the minister droned on. Why hadn't the police caught him? Two policemen had visited the school and talked to everyone. Asking questions. Had Vaughn been acting strange recently? Had anyone seen him with the gun?

When his turn came, The Avenger had looked them straight in the eye and lied. No, he had not seen Vaughn Masterson after school on the day he died. He learned that it was easy to lie, easier than reciting lessons in class. In movies and TV, the guilty party always looked guilty, sweating, not looking anyone in the eye. But The Avenger answered their questions in his best helpful voice, like when he asked his mother if she wanted him to run an errand even when he did not feel like running an errand.

As he yawned with boredom, trying to tune out the minister, The Avenger made a startling discovery. The discovery came when the minister said: "No one knows why Vaughn had to die that afternoon." The words banged around in The Avenger's head. *No one knows why. Why.* In other words, neither the police nor anyone else knew the reason for the killing, the motive. He seized on that word *motive.* He had heard that word a million times in movies and television — *once we know the motive, we will find the killer* — but never realized its deep meaning until this moment. The motive is what links the killer with the victim. The motive is the arrow that points towards the killer. If the motive can't be found, then the killer can't be found. Simple. Terrific. That's why they couldn't connect anyone with Vaughn Masterson's murder and why they did not even know that it *was* a murder.

Remember that the next time, he told himself as the minister finally shut up and the organ boomed forth, the pews trembling with the vibrations.

The Avenger found it hard not to smile and had to cover his mouth with his hands as everyone stood up to watch Vaughn Masterson's coffin roll by.

Buddy dreaded dinnertimes. That's because his mother insisted that he and Addy show up at the table at six-fifteen on the dot: "The least we can do is get together once a day."

She was sleek and stylish, every hair in place, slim and elegant. When preparing meals in the kitchen or baking a cake, she never appeared dishevelled, never a dab of flour on her face. Even her aprons were stylish, not merely to protect her from spills or splashes. They matched whatever she was wearing.

The dinners were excruciating. The food was not exactly a thing of inspiration either. Because she worked five days a week in downtown Wickburg as an executive secretary, his mother prepared casseroles ahead of time and heated them in the microwave oven. Casseroles or frozen dinners, low-cholesterol, low-calorie meals. She made up for this on weekends when she prepared special dishes following exotic recipes from her collection of cookbooks. She was experimenting with ginger these days. All these crazy dishes,

Japanese especially, laced with ginger, which Buddy ate without enthusiasm or dislike, going through the motions like everything else in his life. Addy chewed away listlessly, food was never an exciting thing for her. "I live the life of the spirit," she was fond of saying, although Buddy found about a thousand candy bar wrappers when he went into her room one day looking for a dictionary for his homework.

Food aside, the dinners consisted of chitchat between his mother and Addy, nonstop, as if fines would be handed out if a silence fell. Chatter. About school and work and the weather and traffic conditions, for crissakes. Buddy tuned them out. Which was easy to do when you were in the glow of the gin.

He wondered what would happen if he disturbed the dinnertime routine. Like showing them the story Randy Pierce clipped from the newspaper.

### HOUSE VANDALIZED
### GIRL, 14, INJURED

See what your son has been doing, Mom, dear ol' Mom? Keeping busy, but not keeping out of mischief. Randy had made Xerox copies of the news story and spread them around the school, even thumbtacking them up on bulletin boards and on lockers until Harry, his voice withering in its fury, ordered him to take them down. "We don't call attention to ourselves." No more trashing, Buddy had finally said to Harry. Your wish is my command, Harry had replied, bowing low, like an actor on a stage. Harry, the actor, only pretending to give in, as Buddy learned later.

At the dinner table, Buddy was the actor and maybe his mother and Addy were also acting. Pretending that the chair across from their mother was occupied. The empty chair and the lack of plates and utensils. One afternoon, Buddy looked into the dining room as Addy was setting the table, saw her burst into tears and realized what she had done. Out of an old habit, she had laid out a plate, a knife, fork, and spoon at her father's place. Her face hideous with grief, she swivelled away from him.

"Stop it," Buddy said, voice harsher than he intended. "He isn't worth crying over."

Buddy hated the dining room because it was the place where his father announced that he was moving out of their lives. The announcement, while surprising as well as shocking, made something click inside Buddy and suddenly solved a lot of puzzling things going on in their lives. For weeks, his father had been abstracted, quiet at the table, not participating in the usual dinnertime talk. He was often late for meals, rushing in at the last minute, suddenly talking too loudly, making too many excuses. All of which had been only mildly puzzling to Buddy. Until his father made his big announcement. Apologetic, frowning, clearing his throat, hands moving everywhere, touching his plate, knife, fork, wineglass so that the chardonnay swirled inside and almost overflowed the rim.

"Your mother and I have decided that I should move out of the house for a while," he said in a strangled voice. Which Buddy learned later contained some untruths. First of all, it was his father's own decision: his mother had nothing to do with it. And it wasn't "for a while". He was not planning to come back.

"Are you going to move in with that woman?" Addy asked.

This was the real shock to Buddy, realizing that Addy had known about the woman all along. So shocking that he could not remember later what his father had replied or whether his father, too, had been shocked by Addy's words.

Those words later hung in his mind, like washing on a clothesline, whipped by the wind, the words lashing around, echoing: *that woman*. What woman?

"Look, I'm sorry, kids. I didn't want to tell you this way. But there was no good way to tell you." Looking down at his plate, avoiding their eyes. "Yes, there's a woman involved. But I'm not moving in with her. And this is not something I planned. It just happened."

Buddy shot a careful secret glance at his mother. How was she taking this? She was holding herself rigid as if posing for a picture. Her hands folded on the table in front of her, food untouched. Not looking at his father or at Addy or him. Staring off into space, trance-like, as if she were lending her body to the scene but she, herself, her essence, whatever she was, not there at all, absent, gone off somewhere because the words were too terrible to bear.

"Buddy, Addy — I love the two of you," his father continued. "You both know that, I shouldn't have to say it. But I'm saying it anyway. What has happened between your mother and me has nothing to do with you or my love for you."

Later, of course, Addy answered his arguments, refuted them all.

"Did you hear what he said? And how he said it?" Mimicking him: "*'Your mother and I have decided'*." Snorting: "*He* decided. Mom decided nothing. He wants this woman and he's moved out to be with her, no matter what Mom thinks, no matter what we think." Mimicking him again: "*'What has happened between your mother and me has nothing to do with you'*." Flinging herself on the bed. "Bullshit. Who does he think it has to do with? Other people? It took the two of them to bring us into the world, didn't it? And now, all of a sudden, what happens to them has nothing to do with *us*? It has everything to do with us. What happens to them, happens to us. Affects us. Changes our lives."

Buddy was still unprepared, felt stupid, didn't know what to say. "Who's this other woman, Addy?"

"First of all, she's not a woman. She's almost a girl. I mean, Mom is a woman. This . . . this person is maybe in her twenties. I don't know her name." She sat up in the bed, grimacing, face getting red. "Okay, I hate to admit this but I knew about this woman, girl, whatever, because I listened in, eavesdropped on Mom and Dad arguing one night. Felt like a creep standing outside their bedroom, my ear practically glued to the door. Her name is Fay. She's a secretary at his office. Know all those late nights he worked? That's when it started." Again, cruelly mimicking their father, "*'We didn't mean to fall in love'*. Imagine, telling that to Mom. Telling Mom he fell in love with someone else. The bastard . . .'" She pulled a blanket around her as if for protection.

Later, his mother knocked at his bedroom door.

"I'm sorry," she said, standing in the doorway, as if unsure of her welcome.

"It's not your fault, Mom," he said, although later he was not thoroughly convinced about whose fault it was.

"I'm also sorry for the way he told you and Addy. That *was* my fault. I wanted to be there when he told you. Wanted to hear him say it. Which was cruel of me, perhaps, but I did it anyway."

Buddy did not know what to say. Wanted to say a lot of things, ask a lot of questions, but said nothing. Saw the grief in his mother's face, more than grief, a stunned shocked expression as if she had just heard that the world would end in ten minutes and everybody would perish, all she held dear. Stricken by that look, his mother's shattered eyes, he turned away from her.

"Look, Buddy, I'm not going to make excuses for your father. I don't know what's going to happen. I don't know whether this is temporary or not. Whether he'll get over it. I don't even know if I want him to come back if he *does* get over it. Christ, I don't know anything . . ."

He had never heard his mother swear before. She was always fastidious, elegant, cool, precise. Or maybe she hadn't sworn. Maybe *Christ* had been the beginning of a prayer.

"He's your father, Buddy. Yours and Addy's. You belong to him as much as you belong to me, as much as either of you can belong to anybody. I want you and Addy to love him . . ."

But how are we supposed to love him after this? Buddy wondered. Thinking of his father with someone else, another woman, and shutting them out of his life, walking out on them this way, deserting them. And nothing he could do about it.

The next night he met Harry Flowers and his stooges at the shopping mall.

And got drunk for the first time in his life.

He had made his way to the mall through a series of bus transfers and hitches. The hitches were time-killers between buses, filling small gaps of space. He arrived downtown at dusk and entered the mall, where it was never dusk or dawn, afternoon or evening, but a world without seasons, without weather.

He sat on a yellow plastic bench, looking at the fountain that did not work any more but not really seeing it. Not seeing anything. Not wanting to see anything but unable, after a while, to ignore people coming and going, drifting by. Guys and girls holding hands or brushing against each other. Felt sad watching them and did not know why this sadness should be added to the other sadness that had brought him to this place.

A couple walked by, holding hands: the girl with long, flowing blonde hair and the guy tall, a basketball type. Stopped walking and embraced suddenly, as if they were alone on the planet. Would they someday marry, have kids, two kids maybe, and then separate and later get divorced?

"Somebody die?"

Buddy heard the words at the same time as he raised his head and saw Harry Flowers looking down at him. *Is he talking to me?* Buddy recognized him immediately. Harry Flowers — one of the popular guys at Wickburg Regional and also the subject of rumours: drugs, drinking, wild times.

"You *look* like somebody died," Harry said, speaking unmistakably now to Buddy. "I've been watching you a while — you're from school, right?"

Buddy nodded, getting to his feet. Harry Flowers was about Buddy's height but seemed taller because he stood almost at attention but at the same time managed to be completely at ease. His eyes were the colour of khaki, hooded sometimes but other times, like at this moment, sympathetic. Buddy had seen him strolling the corridors at school, always surrounded by his friends, laughing easily, never hurrying to class like other guys.

"You okay?" Harry asked.

"Nobody died," Buddy answered, realizing that Harry Flowers had not bothered to introduce himself, assuming Buddy would know who he was. Buddy said no more, shrugging, unwilling to share family secrets with Harry Flowers.

"You need action," Harry said, smiling his confident and confidential smile. "A bit of diversion. A bit of fun . . ." Waggling his fingers, eyebrows dancing. Astonishing: cool Harry Flowers doing a Groucho imitation.

Buddy did not discover booze that first night with Harry.

But he discovered the marvellous escape it provided. He had taken drinks before at parties or quick gulps from a pint bottle in a paper bag at football games. The excitement of drinking had intoxicated him more than the liquor itself. Or what he regarded as intoxication. But sitting in the front seat of the car with Harry while Randy Pierce and Marty Sanders carried on their Abbott and Costello routines in the back seat, Buddy discovered the marvellous methods of booze, the way it soothed and stroked, made hazy the harshness of things, made him — almost — happy. Languid, and feeling what the hell.

That first night, they only drank and talked and joked and Harry dropped him off in front of his house. Buddy made his way haphazardly up the front walk, stumbled going into the house, lucky his mother and Addy were asleep. Fell into bed, the splendid magic of the booze tumbling him into the bliss of sleep.

Later came "Funtime", Harry's label for the exploits, stupid when sober but exciting and daring when drunk. The evenings always began the same, drinking leisurely in the car while talking casually, joking, listening to Marty and Randy's conversational routines in the back seat. Buddy noticed after a while that Harry did not drink much, if at all, but encouraged Buddy and the others to do so, supplying an endless amount of booze. Including the gin that became Buddy's personal drink. He loved the beautiful exotic smell of the gin and what it did to him. Finally, Harry would cry out: "Funtime." And off they'd go.

To the movies where they caused disruptions, laughing too raucously at scenes that were not funny at all, spilling food, particularly popcorn, all over the place, tearing wrappers off candy bars and sending them flying through the air, guffawing, scuffling mildly, knowing that the ushers were high school kids, most of them easily intimidated, not eager to notify the theatre manager about the noise and distractions.

Other nights they merely cruised the streets, searching for mischief, Harry intimidating other drivers by driving too fast or too slow, cutting in, tailgating.

One weekend Harry obtained some fireworks in New Hampshire while on a trip there with his parents and showed off his display of lethal-looking bombs, an evil grin on his face. Off they went to the countryside, the outskirts of Wickburg, where they blew up mailboxes with the miniature bombs, delighting in the *whomp* of the explosion, giddy and laughing as they roared away. What made this especially exciting, Harry said, was that blowing up mailboxes was a federal offence.

Sometimes, their exploits were senseless, war-whooping their way through Shelton Park, disturbing couples making out in the dark, tossing debris into the decorative pots, pissing in fountains. The next morning, Buddy would shudder, recalling dimly the events of the night before. Those mornings presented him with his first hangovers — stomach in distress, eyes like raw wounds, head bulging with pain plus the knowledge that he had acted shamefully the night before. Looking at himself in the mirror, seeing the perspiring sallow flesh, the bloodshot eyes, the unkempt hair, he vowed that he would not allow Harry to lead him into further "Funtimes". But somehow by nightfall he would capitulate again, following Harry Flowers wherever he went.

More important than Harry, however, was the liquor that forgave everything. "Funtime" with Harry Flowers and the stooges gave him camaraderie, a sense of belonging to something. Drinking, however, gave him bliss in his loneliness. When he drank and began to drift, the lovely vagueness taking over his sensibilities, he did not need comrades or

51

companions. Needed nobody. Especially did not need his mother and father.

Artie's screaming began two weeks after the vandalism. The first time it happened, Jane vaulted from her sleep, unsure of the sound, unable to identify it immediately as screaming. There was silence for a moment, and she heard a door close and then a shriek, this time muffled. Instantly and completely awake, she checked the digital clock on the bedside table: 2:11.

When the screaming began again, she slid out of bed, went to the doorway and listened, shivering a bit in the chill of night. The sounds came from the bathroom across the hallway from her bedroom. More screaming, more shrieking, sheer terror in the sound, which set off a kind of terror in her own self.

The oak floor was cold beneath her feet as she paused near the bathroom. Silence within now. Then, whimpering, like a small animal trapped and crying. As she opened the door slightly, she recognized the soothing murmurs of her mother and father. Peeking in, she saw her father sitting on the edge of the bathtub holding Artie in his arms while her mother knelt on the floor, her arms encircling Artie, whose face was pressed into the folds of his father's pyjamas.

Artie began to scream again, lifting his face away from his father's protection, his eyes open in terror. Then became mute, silent, but holding himself rigid.

Her mother looked up and saw Jane.

"A nightmare," she said.

But it was not a nightmare. It was sheer terror that Artie could not remember when he finally woke up after a few minutes.

The terror happened three nights in succession, Artie screaming and sobbing, eyes wide with horror as if he were

52

witnessing acts so horrible and obscene that his mind refused to acknowledge them. His eyes were always wide open as if he were awake. Crying out inconsolably, he inhabited a private world nobody else could enter, beyond the borders of comfort or consolation.

On the fourth day, they took Artie to Dr Allison back in Monument, their old family doctor who had taken care of the family during all their illnesses.

Dr Allison ran all sorts of tests in the small clinic he operated. The tests were negative. He said that pre-adolescent boys sometimes experienced night terrors of this sort. They passed with time.

"Does he think it's connected with the vandalism?" Jane later asked her father.

"Possibly," her father said, weariness in his voice. "Dr Allison wants us to keep in touch. He said that it's easy to deal with what can be seen — fractures, sprains, cuts and bruises. Or symptoms — fever, high blood pressure and such. But it's difficult dealing with something that you can't see. He said that in other cases of this sort, time takes care of it."

Dr Allison had been right. A few days passed before Artie's next night-time terror. Then they stopped. "Let's hope for ever," her mother said. Jane and her parents remained tense each evening as bedtime approached and Jane, tossing in bed, felt that a part of them remained awake during the night, listening and waiting.

And Artie? He remained an enigma to Jane and maybe her parents, too.

He had always been the standard kid brother, similar to the brothers of all her friends. A tease, a pain in the neck sometimes, living in the private, mysterious world of boyhood, secretive, furtive, coming and going but barely touching her life except when he chose to torment her with his bathroom humour. His vocabulary was filled with words to describe bodily functions with which he plagued Jane when out of their parents' earshot. He also provided sound effects for those same functions, which drove Jane out of the house, hands over her ears.

"Is Artie okay?" Kenny Crane called to her one day from across the street while she was out half-jogging.

She pulled up. "I guess so," she said, puzzled at the concern on Kenny's thin face. She crossed over to him. "Why are you asking?"

Kenny lifted his thin shoulders in a kind of shrug. "I dunno," he said. "He doesn't hang out any more. We used to swap Nintendos but now he's not interested."

"I think Artie's going through a bad time," Jane said. "Like everybody does once in a while. But he'll be all right." Telling him nothing, actually, because she herself did not know what was wrong with Artie.

"Artie's my friend," Kenny declared, chin lifted, his words sounding like a challenge.

After that brief talk with Kenny Crane, Jane kept track of Artie's comings and goings and discovered that he did not play his crazy video games any more and, in fact, seldom went into his room except to change his clothes after school and go to bed. He wandered the neighbourhood and sometimes disappeared for hours on his bike.

"Where do you go?" Jane asked when he returned from one of his trips and was tightening the bike chain.

"No place," he said.

This had always been his standard answer, even before the vandalism.

"You had to go *someplace*," she declared.

He shrugged, concentrating on the chain.

"How come you don't play your Nintendos any more?" she asked. Then, deciding to use a bit of flattery, "I thought you were an ace with the games." *Ace*, one of his words.

He shrugged again, looking away. "I kind of lost interest. It's kids' stuff, anyway."

"Kids' stuff? I thought you had to be some kind of genius to play those games."

He looked directly at her, squinting: "How come you're so interested, all of a sudden?"

"It's not the games I'm interested in, it's you. And why you're not playing them any more . . ."

No answer, but at least he wasn't walking away from her. She took the big plunge. "Has it got something to do with what happened to Karen? The vandalism?"

No answer again, still fiddling around with the bike.

"I don't like our house any more," he said, speaking so low that she barely heard the words. "I hate Burnside, too."

"I'm not crazy about it either," she said. "But we've got to live here. We just can't move."

"Why not? We moved here from Monument. Why can't we move again?"

"You heard what Dad said. That would be giving in, Artie." She saw him suddenly not as a bratty kid but as a troubled boy for whom she had a lot of affection.

"Giving in?" he asked, looking up at last. "To who?"

"To whoever did that to us," she said. "I think maybe they'd like us to move, to show that they changed our lives." Discovering the thought for the first time as she spoke. "And damn it, Artie, we can't let them do that."

He grimaced, eyes narrowing.

"Can we?"

"I guess not," he said, looking directly at her.

She felt that for the first time they had somehow touched each other as human beings. She had to stifle a desire to embrace him, the way she would embrace a friend.

"Think about it, okay?" she asked.

He nodded, their eyes meeting again before he went back to working on his bike. We connected, she thought, pleased, as she went into the house.

But Artie still did not play his video games.

Three weeks after Vaughn Masterson's funeral The Avenger's grandfather had begun asking him questions about his stolen gun.

"Know what's funny about that gun?"

"What's funny, Gramps?" The Avenger asked, keeping his face blank.

"Here's what's funny," said Gramps, who always talked slow and easy, drawing out his words. "I wonder how anybody from outside could have stolen my piece."

He always called his gun his *piece* but the word that hung in the air now, menacing and threatening, was *outside*.

The Avenger did not say anything. His grandfather liked to talk. The Avenger always let him ramble on. Most times, he was a good talker and told stories about his days on the police force, especially the old days when he walked the beat in the Bryant Bridge section of town, the tough section.

"I mean," his grandfather went on as if answering a question The Avenger had asked, "I always keep the doors locked. How did the thief get into the place? No visible signs of entry."

The Avenger swallowed. "Maybe he had a key."

"A key?" His grandfather turned and fastened his dark brown eyes on him, his policeman's eyes.

"Maybe one of those skeleton keys you told me about, the kind that fits all doors?" The Avenger said, gulping.

"Not this door, not this lock," his grandfather said. "This is a special police bolt. Nope, we have to rule out a key. What does that leave?"

His grandfather was still looking at him and The Avenger

tried not to blink. "The windows?" he enquired. "You keep them open sometimes to catch a breeze."

"In two words: im-possible," his grandfather said. He was always quoting a man by the name of Sam Goldwyn, an old-time movie producer who said crazy things. Like: include me out. "How could anybody reach a fifth-floor window?"

"A ladder?" The Avenger ventured.

His grandfather did not bother to dignify the suggestion but snorted and looked out at the park, suddenly very interested in the joggers passing by. They were sitting on a bench in Cannon Park, across from the high school, basking in the September sun. Resting my bones, his grandfather called it. He had been a policeman for forty-five years, most of them standing on his dogs. He always called his feet *dogs*. He never drove a cruiser, always walked a beat. That's what's wrong with the world, he said, not enough cops on the sidewalks. Should take them out of the cruisers and put them on the sidewalks.

"If I didn't know any better, I would say it was an inside job," his grandfather said now, stretching his legs before him, folding his hands over his small round belly and closing his eyes.

The Avenger hoped he was about to take a nap, something his grandfather did at all hours of the day and night, slipping into sleep without any warning at all.

"What do you mean, inside job?" He was sorry he asked, the minute the words were out of his mouth, because he had a good idea of what an *inside job* was.

"Means somebody inside the place stole the piece," his grandfather said. "Which is again im-possible. I'm the only one living here."

"A visitor maybe?" The Avenger said, grimacing. Why couldn't he keep his mouth shut?

"Not likely," he said, voice faint. He seemed to be drifting off, into his nap maybe. "I only got four rooms. The piece was hidden away in the closet. Bullets in a separate box. No way a visitor could sneak *two* boxes out. Unless . . ."

His voice grew even fainter and a moment later a soft snore came from his mouth, fluttering the ends of his moustache. The Avenger sighed "Whew . . ." softly, glad that the conversation was over. But he frowned as he stretched his own legs in front of him, although they barely touched the ground.

"Of course, my memory isn't what it used to be," his grandfather said, startling The Avenger, who thought he was sound asleep. His grandfather spoke without opening his eyes, his hands folded on his round stomach. "Maybe I *did* leave the door unlocked by mistake. Maybe somebody *did* get into the place." Silence for a while. "Can't trust anybody these days. Anybody . . ." His eyes were still closed.

Anybody.

The word echoed in his mind, the way *inside job* had echoed earlier.

He tried to finish the sentence that began with that word: Anybody . . . anybody in the world. Anybody . . . even you!

The Avenger leaped with alarm, as if his grandfather had actually said the words, had flung the accusation at him. But the old man was still napping, eyes closed, breath rattling through his partly opened mouth.

The Avenger closed his own eyes and made himself sit still on the bench, even though his nose immediately began to itch. He did not scratch it. He did not move at all, not even his eyelids. He sat there thinking *anybody* until his grandfather woke up, snorting and coughing. They walked out of the park in silence.

The silence lasted all the way home and was worse even than that word *anybody*. His grandfather did not tousle his hair and pat his head as he usually did when he said goodbye to The Avenger at the corner of Spruce and Elm.

The telephone rang as Buddy came into the house from school. Dumping his books on the couch in the family room, he picked up the receiver. Then was sorry he'd answered. Harry was on the line.

"Want some fun tonight, Buddee?"

That cool insinuating voice, this time a French accent.

"Not tonight," Buddy answered, clearing his throat first to make his voice steady. Feeling guilty about the house they vandalized, he had promised himself that he wouldn't take part in any more of Harry's adventures. Drinking was one thing, the exploits were another.

"Bizzee? Beeg plans? Too beeg for your friends?" Maybe he was trying a Mexican accent.

"No, it's not that," Buddy said, mind racing to find an excuse and coming up blank. Except for: "I've got a lot of homework tonight." Frowning, knowing how lame this sounded.

Silence from Harry's end of the line. A silence filled with disbelief, Buddy knew. Then: "Conscience bothering you, Buddy?" In his normal voice.

That was Harry, always capable of coming at you from your blind side. "Not really," Buddy said, grimacing. "I'm just not in the mood." Then, loading his voice with sincerity: "And I do have an awful lot of homework." Somebody once said that if you can learn to fake sincerity, you'll be a success in life.

"Plan on drinking alone?"

"What?"

"That's a sure sign, Buddy."

"Sure sign of what?" Buddy, helpless, asked. Not wanting to ask, not wanting to continue this conversation but helpless to end it.

"Alcoholism. Drinking alone is one of the sure signs."

"I'm not going to drink," Buddy replied. "Alone or otherwise." But he was going to do exactly that.

That was one of the reasons why he disliked Harry Flowers so much: He always spoiled things. What was wrong with a drink now and then? Or whether he drank alone or not? Harry delighted in finding the rotten side of anything. Always lifting a lid to reveal something terrible underneath. Like the other day in the park.

He and Harry had been sitting in the car, trying to figure out what to do for "Funtime" that night, although Buddy hoped that they wouldn't do anything, still recoiling from the events at the house they'd wrecked.

Children frolicked in the park, soaring high on the swings, swooping down the slides, the air filled with happy squeals and laughter. Some little girls held hands as they walked around in a circle singing:

"Ring-a-ring o' roses . . . a pocket full of posies . . . A-tishoo! A-tishoo! . . . we all fall down . . ."

"Stupid," Harry said.

"What's stupid?" Buddy asked, annoyed that Harry would find something stupid about a bunch of kids playing in a park.

"Those little girls don't know what they're doing," Harry said, pointing with his chin. "Potter in English Lit. last week told us all about this nursery rhyme. It's what kids sang back in the olden days when the Black Plague was killing millions of people. People would get a rosy kind of rash and rub themselves with herbs and posies. Then they fell down and died . . ."

Buddy scowled, kept his eyes on the little girls, who had

scrambled to their feet again, preparing to form another circle.

"Know what you are, Harry?" he asked. "You're a spoiler. I always thought Ring-A-Ring o' Roses was kind of a nice thing for kids to do. But now you've gone and spoiled it all."

"I'm sorry, Buddy, but I didn't make up that story," Harry said. He did not sound sorry. "I aced the test Potter gave and that's why I remember it at all. I usually don't go in for that nursery rhyme kind of crap."

"It's not crap," Buddy said as the little girls began to circle, singing the song again, their small voices rising in the air.

"A-tishoo! A-tishoo!"

One little girl with long blonde hair tripped and stumbled.

"We all fall down . . ."

Down they went on the grass, in a tumble of arms and legs, the blonde girl crying, her cheeks shiny with tears.

"Maybe it isn't crap, after all," Harry said. "Because we all fall down, don't we?" His voice dry, sharp as ice cubes clinking.

And on the telephone now, his voice was dry and icy again as he said: "Of course you're not going to drink alone."

Then snapping words like whips: "Remember this, Buddy. What happened the other night, you enjoyed it. You got your kicks. You're probably having conscience trouble now, but you had fun that night."

Buddy didn't answer. And didn't try to deny it. Because Harry was right, damn it. Buddy *had* enjoyed himself, found great satisfaction smashing and trashing that house, like striking back at his mother and father and the whole goddam world. Or was that only an excuse? But an excuse for what?

"Right, Buddy?" That cool persistent voice.

"Right, Harry," Buddy said, capitulating. *But I didn't pee against the wall. And I didn't attack the girl.*

"Good, Buddy. Which means you're one of us."

*But I didn't help the girl, either, did I? Did not come to her rescue like a hero. Some hero, Buddy.*

"See, Buddy? You're not alone. You don't have to drink alone."

Buddy let a sigh escape his lips. Then tried to inject his voice with more of the old sincerity.

"I know that, Harry, and I appreciate it. But, actually, I *do* have all this stupid homework and I don't feel that great. Maybe it's the flu bug or something . . ."

"Sure, Buddy. I was just checking in, anyway." Brief pause. "Take it easy, Buddee." French again. "Zee you around . . ."

And hung up before Buddy could answer.

Jane's visits to the hospital had become as much a routine part of her life as going to school. Although Karen did not respond during Jane's visits, she felt a closeness to her she had never known before. Sometimes she held her hand, placed her finger on Karen's wrist and was gratified to feel the pulse throbbing regularly, strong and vital. She pretended the pulse was a kind of Morse code by which Karen was telling her that she would come back, don't worry, all will turn out fine.

Occasionally, when nurses had to attend to Karen's needs, Jane wandered the hospital corridors, trying not to look into the rooms she passed, not wanting to observe other people's misery or to invade their privacy. One afternoon, she discovered the hospital chapel. Barely a chapel, nondenominational, pews without kneelers, subdued lighting, a faked stained-glass window, back lit, set into the inner wall. Sitting in the pew, removed from all the activity outside the door, she discovered a kind of serenity. She even prayed, sort of, altering the old prayers of her childhood for Karen ... "God is great, God is good, please help Karen to get better ..." and "Now I sit me down to rest, I pray for God to help my sister." ... Should have felt silly doing such a thing, silly and irreverent, but didn't.

She realized that she had not really prayed for a very long time. Although she and her family attended Sunday services regularly, Karen had simply gone through the motions. Sunday mornings at the old Methodist church back in Monument had been more of a social act than religious. She liked to see the families gathering in the churchyard after services. Pastor William Smith had been old and holy and devout but also immensely boring. Here in Burnside, her parents had enrolled the family in the local Methodist church, a building so modern it resembled a recreation centre, and the pews arranged in the round, like in a theatre. The pastor here was not old or boring but he tried too hard, preached too long, and Jane's mind wandered. Why do we go to church, anyway? she wondered. Somehow she believed — and did not know where that belief came from — that if you were kind and patient and did not hurt anyone intentionally, you would go to heaven someday. *Someday* seemed so far away that she did not think about it often. But she thought about it now in the chapel. I must make myself a better person, she vowed. Ran through the Ten Commandments, those she could remember, shocked to find she could only think of two or three — thou shalt not steal, thou shalt not kill, thou shalt not covet. She did not steal or kill or covet, dimly aware that *covet* meant being envious. But what was that to brag about? Honour thy father and mother. I must do better by my mother and father, she thought. Must be kinder to them, help them get over this. But didn't know how.

63

In the hospital chapel, she realized she had not been aware of that terrible smell for a few days. Had it gone for ever?

Returning from the chapel one day, she heard her mother talking to Karen as she turned to enter the room. Hoping that Karen could hear them, the family kept her up-to-date on what was going on at home, and in the neighbourhood. Her friends from school reported almost daily, hesitant at first, but quickly losing their self-consciousness as they told her what was happening at Burnside High.

Arrested by the anguish in her mother's voice, Jane found herself shamelessly eavesdropping.

"I don't know what to do. I shouldn't be saying this to you but I've got to talk to someone. I have this crazy thought, Karen, that something is holding you back from regaining consciousness. Because you're afraid. Of something. Don't be. Don't be afraid. We all love you. We'll protect you. That terrible vandalism won't happen again. We've had a real good alarm system installed. We'll take care of you . . ."

Silence now in the room. No response from Karen, of course. Peering in, she saw Karen, eyes closed, silent in the bed. The anguish — more like desperation — in her mother's voice caused Jane to draw back. She did not want to confront her mother at this moment. Her mother had been putting on such a show of bravery as she cheerfully went about her housework, her daily errands. All of it a sham. Pretending for the sake of the family.

"You've got to come back, Karen. Until you do, nothing will be right. We all live in the same house but we are separate. We aren't a family any more."

Which was true, Jane admitted with a kind of horror. They were all so polite with each other. *Pass the salt, please. That's a pretty blouse, Jane. Wonderful report card, Artie.* Not like the old days of family arguments about staying out late, mediocre report cards, who's wearing whose sweater. Now they treated each other as if they were made of glass, would shatter if a cross word was uttered.

Jane did not finally enter the room, left her mother to carry on that sad one-sided conversation, and returned to the chapel instead.

Buddy opened the letter which wasn't really a letter at all, not tearing the envelope but slitting it open carefully with a kitchen knife. Doing it slowly, which allowed him time to ponder the possible contents. He knew what the *actual* contents would be — the weekly cheque his father sent him. Twenty-five dollars. Which was almost twice as much as his previous allowance when his father was still living at home. There was never anything else in the envelope and Buddy always pretended he wasn't disappointed. Screw it, he would mutter, crumpling the envelope and tossing it away. *Screw it all, Buddy, and cash the cheque.*

What he hoped for every week was a note from his father accompanying the cheque. He'd have been satisfied with a few words scrawled hastily on a scrap of paper. But the envelope always contained only the money. The twenty-five dollars was terrific, of course. That's what kept him supplied with booze. But — but what? He wasn't sure what.

His father had made no promises the day he left the house. He'd been in a hurry, hastily packing his clothes, frowning, scratching himself as if the clothes he wore were too tight for his body. He kept saying: *Sorry. Really sorry to be doing this to you, Buddy.* Throwing shirts every which way into his suitcase, sloppy to the end. *Tell Addy how sorry I am.* Addy had refused to speak to him, wouldn't open her bedroom door to him. *I'll send you your allowance every week — sorry it has to be by mail.* Sorry, sorry, sorry.

"Can't we get together sometime?" Buddy had asked.

"Sure, sure," his father replied, concentrating on the packing. That didn't sound at all convincing, sounded more like *no, no*. Watching his father struggling to close the bulging suitcase, Buddy realized that you could live all your life in the same house with a person and not really know him. His father had always been his Father. With a capital *F*. Did all the things a father was supposed to do. Went off to work and came home. Threw a baseball to Buddy in the back yard. Took him and Addy to the circus, to fireworks on the Fourth of July. Famous for naps, could drop off to sleep at the blink of an eye. Hated driving, let their mother drive on long trips while he dozed. My sleepytime guy, Buddy's mother called him affectionately, tenderly.

No more tenderness these days. His mother abandoned and the twenty-five-dollar cheque in the mail. That's what his father had become.

Twice he had called his father at the office. More *sorrys*. *Too busy. Maybe next week. I'll call you*. He didn't call Buddy but the cheques still came. The cheques which bought the booze and the booze which made it easier not to have his father get in touch.

Now, he looked at another cheque, looked at the signature he had seen on report cards until recently. His mother had signed his report card last week. In a sudden fury, he thought: I should send this cheque back, show him that he can't buy me off with money.

He found an envelope in his mother's desk in the den, along with a ballpoint pen. Wrote his father's name on the envelope, his address at the office. Tore a sheet of paper from the pad his mother kept on hand for making notes. Pondered what he should say. Decided he would not say anything. Let the returned cheque speak for him. He found a small book of stamps in the drawer, detached one and placed it on the envelope. Slipped the cheque, folded over once, inside. Licked the flap, sealed the envelope, sighed with relief. *It was better to do something than do nothing.* Some writer had once said that.

He checked his wallet — three lonely one-dollar bills. Buying liquor at his age was not only illegal but also expensive. Harry had introduced him to a homeless downtown wanderer called Crumbs, unshaven, bleary-eyed, pushing a grocery cart filled with rags and paper bags whose contents Buddy could only guess at. Despite his name and his slovenly appearance, Crumbs was a shrewd businessman. He charged a flat rate of five dollars a bottle for his services, which did not include the price of the booze itself. Even if Buddy ordered only a pint, which carried a price tag of less than four dollars, the service charge did not change. This often forced Buddy to order a quart bottle.

As a result, he had come to rely on his father's extra twenty-five-dollar allowance. With the addition of the fifteen-dollar allowance from his mother, the total should have been more than sufficient. But wasn't. He also had to pay for everyday expenses out of that sum, plus lunches at school and the extra money spent when he was out with Harry and the stooges.

For the next two days, he carried the envelope with the cheque inside his jacket pocket. Approached several mailboxes, checked the pick-up times on the inside of the cover as he balanced the envelope in his hand. Finally, he did not mail the cheque. Why should his father get away without paying for his freedom? Why shouldn't he pay, even a little bit, for what he had done? Twenty-five dollars was cheap enough. A bargain.

The Avenger was amazed to find out how easy it was to commit murder twice and get away with it. He learned something new each time. First, he had learned about the importance of motive — or lack of it — when he killed Vaughn Masterson. What he learned the second time was that you did not need a weapon, like a gun or a knife, to kill someone. Of course, you needed opportunity. And sometimes you had to wait for the opportunity. Or, as in the case of the second time, the opportunity presented itself when you weren't even sure you wanted to commit murder. That was another lesson he learned: be on your toes, be alert all the time, ready to take advantage of any opportunity that might come up.

The way it had happened with his grandfather.

He had not planned to kill his grandfather that Saturday afternoon. He had, in fact, been avoiding him, afraid to hear more questions about the gun. His grandfather visited The Avenger and his mother once or twice a week because he knew she was often lonesome. The Avenger's father had left town a long time ago, without saying goodbye or leaving a note. His mother did not believe that he had abandoned them or met with foul play or had been killed in an accident. She believed he had somehow lost his memory.

She pictured him — and so did The Avenger — roaming the world, trying to find his way home. His picture sat on the television set and his father's face was burned into The Avenger's mind. He searched every day for his father, studying the faces of all the men he met on the street. He hadn't found him yet.

When his grandfather visited, he brought good stuff to eat and sometimes flowers for his mother. He called The Avenger's mother "daughter", although she was not his daughter. They sat and watched television, all the soap operas, and later they shut off the set and his grandfather would talk about the old days, his days on the beat or about when "Donnie", The Avenger's father, was a boy.

"Don't see much of you these days, keed," his grandfather said the last time he visited. He often called him "keed".

"I've been busy," The Avenger said, his face growing warm. "School, helping out Mom." Which was true. The Avenger always helped out his mother. Did the daily chores without being told. Ran the errands. These days, when his grandfather visited, he made himself scarce, sometimes left the house before the old man arrived or got out of the place as soon as possible.

"You make me feel bad, keed," his grandfather said, "running off all the time." And for an instant he felt bad for the old man, realized that he looked *really* old these days, frail and skinny.

"Sorry, Gramps," he said. And he *was* sorry. Sorry for the circumstances that made his grandfather an enemy, somebody to be suspicious of.

"He's such a good boy," his mother said, in her wispy voice. "He takes such good care of me . . ."

"I know, Ella, I know," his grandfather said, his voice soft and gentle. But his eyes weren't gentle. When The Avenger looked up at the old man's eyes, they were shrewd and glittering. They studied him, bore down into him. The Avenger always looked away.

The next week when he answered the telephone, his grandfather's voice greeted him: "Hi, keed, how's tricks?"

What did he mean by *tricks*?

"Fine, Gramps," he said, keeping his voice bright, determined to be natural.

"Listen, this is an invitation to go out with your old Gramps. You're so busy these days I figure I got to make a formal invitation. So — how about next Saturday afternoon?"

The Avenger swallowed hard, felt his Adam's apple bouncing up and down. "Well . . ." His mind raced, looking for an excuse. Trying at the same time to gauge his grand-father's voice, looking for secret things in the voice.

"I figure we can go to the movies. There's a good cop movie coming up next week." They both liked cop movies with gunfire and car chases and explosions. "Then we can grab some grub." He always called the hamburgers at McDonald's "grub". "What say?"

What could he say? He had to say yes. He did not want to spend any time at all with Gramps, but the movie theatre was the best place of all if he had to do it.

As it turned out, they had a good time at the movies. Loaded up with popcorn and M&Ms and Cokes and enjoyed all the action on the screen, especially the long chase across streets and bridges between a car and a *man*, a policeman.

They were both too full of candy and junk to grab some grub at McDonald's but instead walked leisurely along to his grandfather's apartment. "For a good talk," his grand-father said, which made the day turn cloudy although the sun was warm on his cheeks.

His grandfather's apartment was small and cramped. The Avenger found himself out of breath, as if the walls were closing in on him. The apartment was in a high-rise for the elderly. What they called a four-room living area, although it was actually three rooms, the dining room and kitchen combined in one room. The only thing The Avenger liked about the apartment was the balcony, with iron railings, five storeys high, looking out over the town. You could see across the smaller buildings to the hills in the distance. Sometimes, his grandfather brought out his binoculars and The Avenger studied the windows of the other buildings or looked down at the people walking below.

"Want some Coke?" his grandfather asked.

The Avenger shook his head. "No thanks, Gramps."

"Cookies? Piece of cake?"

"Still full, Gramps."

What he wanted was to go home. His eyes ached a bit and his head hurt.

"Feeling all right?" his grandfather asked, eyes narrowed as he studied The Avenger.

"Ate too much," The Avenger said. He was afraid he was going to be sick. He felt hot all over, not warm but hot.

"Let's get some fresh air," his grandfather said, heading for the small balcony. "We can talk better out there. We can sit and talk."

But his grandfather did not sit. He told The Avenger to sit down in the black wrought-iron chair but he himself leaned against the railing, his back to the town, his eyes on The Avenger. He began to ask questions. About school. How were his marks? Was his spelling improving? What did he do after school besides the chores? Stuff like that. The Avenger answered the questions willingly, talking fast, going into details, simply to hold off more questions. He had a feeling his grandfather was not really listening to the answers, his eyes kind of glazed now, as if he was seeing things far away or thinking of something else altogether.

Finally, the old man turned his back on The Avenger. Leaned against the balcony railing, looked out over the city. "I've got to ask you something important, keed," he said, his voice muffled a bit.

*Important*. The word made The Avenger's insides shrivel.

He knew the question: Did you kill Vaughn Masterson?

That's why his grandfather could not face him. He was like the district attorney in the TV movies who turned away from the killer in the witness stand and faced the jury to ask his questions. Like the whole city out there was now the jury and he, The Avenger, was on the witness stand.

71

The Avenger had to say something. So he said: "What do you want to ask me, Gramps?" Keeping his voice bright as usual.

Then the moment arrived.

As if it had been planned that way.

"Hey, what's that?" his grandfather asked, distracted, leaning forwards over the railing, checking something down below.

The Avenger began to get up from his chair and suddenly everything was in slow motion, which was crazy because he was moving very fast, his arms and legs working perfectly, beautifully, as he leaped up, but also slow, slow as possible, moving across the balcony, as if he were off somewhere watching himself running now, fast, hands raised in front of him, as his grandfather began to turn almost as if he had heard an alarm going off and was half turned when The Avenger, no longer watching now but *doing it*, crashed into him. Crashed into him low, not slow motion either but fast, fast, and low, just below his behind, the thin hard bones there, and lifting at the same time, finding somehow the strength, the determination, the *means* to do it, and desperate, too, because he knew that he could not fail, it would be the end of everything if he failed. Without warning, his grandfather seemed to lift himself up, his hands flung out, and he was propelled upward as if he were about to fly, his long thin arms like the wings of an aeroplane or a wounded bird and he wailed, a terrible sound coming out of him, as he was caught and held for one moment in the air, arms flailing, grabbing nothing. Then he fell. Like a puppet whose strings were cut, like a tree branch taken by the wind. Down he went, all arms and legs thrashing the air.

At the last moment, The Avenger took his eyes away from his grandfather's downward flight. Did not want to see him land on the pavement below. Like in the movie

72

when the camera turned away at the last minute and you gave a big sigh of relief because you did not want to see the smashing, the splatter, all of that.

He withdrew from the railings and sat in the chair for a moment. Waited to hear something. But did not hear anything. Did not hear screams or sirens or anything. As if he had gone deaf. He counted to ten. Slowly. Then he went into the apartment and picked up the telephone, paused a moment, and remembering the instructions about emergencies he had learned at school, he punched 911 and told whoever answered to please send an ambulance, his poor old Gramps had fallen off his balcony.

Jane woke up with a start, having heard *something* — a footstep in the hallway? a door closing? — and wondered if somehow the trashers had come back, had broken into the house in the middle of the night. Then calmed down as she recognized her father's footsteps as he padded down the hallway in his slippers on his way to the bathroom.

Unable to go back to sleep, she fought the blankets that seemed too heavy for this mild night. When she threw them off, her shoulders in the thin nylon nightgown grew cold. She thought of Karen in the hospital who slept night and day, did not know heat or cold. Realizing finally that her father had not returned from the bathroom, she sat up in bed, saw the time in the glowing red figures of the digital clock: 2:57.

She slipped out of bed, went down the hallway, saw, at the head of the stairs, a spill of light below. She found her father in the kitchen, leaning against the sink, a glass of milk in his hand.

"What's the matter, Dad?"

"Couldn't sleep," he said, yawning, but a fake yawn, rubbing his hand across his faint stubble of beard.

73

"You always sleep like the proverbial log," she said, quoting his own words.

He smiled, a small wan smile. "Things change," he said. "Somebody said your body changes completely every seven years. Maybe I'm going into a new cycle."

Which she did not for a minute believe.

Studying him surreptitiously, she realized that people do not often look at each other. Not even fathers. Her father had grown a moustache a few years ago, wore it for a few months and then shaved it off one morning before breakfast. No one at the breakfast table noticed his clean-shaven upper lip. When he was leaving the house to go to work, Artie, whose sharp eyes missed very little, said: "Hey, Dad, something wrong with your face?" But even Artie had not realized the moustache was gone, only that their father's face looked different that day. Her mother finally noticed the missing moustache at the dinner table that night.

No missing moustache now, only her father looking forlorn and lonely at three in the morning. Hair dishevelled, eyes dull, listless. Needing a shave. A faintly familiar tone to his voice when he spoke, disturbing to her. Where had she heard that voice before? Then remembered. The voice in which he answered the detective who had asked if he had any enemies. A small boy's voice. Not really her father. Jane got the shivers again as she had that day but worse now. Middle-of-the-night worse. She shivered, not from the cold, but from a sense of dread. She remembered a poem from school: "Things fall apart, the centre cannot hold." Her family falling apart and her father at the centre. Could he hold them together? If he couldn't, who could?

"How about you, Jane? What are you doing up at this crazy hour?"

"I heard you come downstairs and wondered if you were okay, not sick or anything."

"I'm okay," he said. "Just restless."

Her father startled her with his next words.

"Actually, I had a bad dream," he said. "I've been having bad dreams lately. At least, I think they're bad dreams. They wake me up and I'm in a sweat but I can't remember the dreams, only the feeling of them, their aura. Like a black cloud, although the dreams aren't about black clouds. Just a feeling of something dark and menacing . . ."

*Oh, Dad, don't say that.* Fathers aren't supposed to have dreams like that. Kids run to their fathers in the middle of the night when the *kids* have bad dreams. Fathers are supposed to soothe them and say: It's only a dream, only a dream.

"Do you think the dream is about Karen? Because she's in kind of a black cloud?"

He glanced at her sharply.

"You think so?"

She shrugged. Tried to appear calm although panic whistled through her veins. He was supposed to know the answers.

"I worry about her, of course," he said. "We all do. I guess what's especially bad is the sense of helplessness. We can't do anything to help her . . ."

"Maybe she knows, Dad," Jane offered. "Maybe she *does* hear us when we visit and talk to her, like the doctor says. Knows we're there." She wasn't sure she believed this but needed to offer him comfort of some kind.

Silence for a while. Night-time silence different from morning or afternoon. No cars passing, no shouts from kids outside. No lawn mowers. Not even the sounds of nature, birds, dogs or cats.

Her father's jaw tightened, a pulse throbbing at his temples, lips pressed tight. "Another thing," he said, and the simmering anger again. "Helpless against who did this

75

thing to her, to us. If I could get my hands on them . . ." He looked up at her sheepishly. "Sorry," he said. "This is middle-of-the-night talk, that's all." Rousing himself, pushing himself up from the table. "Let's go to bed, Jane. Sleep, the best medicine . . ."

Jane did not fall asleep for a long time. Tossed and turned. Got all mixed up between sheet and blankets. Punched the pillow. Could not get comfortable. Remembering that look on her father's face. The anger below the surface. The helplessness as he clenched his jaw. *If I could get my hands on them.*

She was suddenly afraid *for* her father.

And almost hoped that the trashers would never be found.


Buddy reached into the pile of rags, probing for the familiar touch of the paper bag and the bottle it contained. Felt – nothing. He groped further, to the left and right, mildly puzzled but not really concerned. Frowning, he cleared the shelf of the accumulation of rags, tools, old paint cans, placing them on the floor next to the workbench. Still not there. He looked under the shelf, scanned the floor. Even checked the old tin wastebasket next to the bench and the hanging shelf above the bench. No bag and no bottle.

Breathing a bit heavily, perspiration bubbling on his forehead, he leaned against the wall, eyes closed. He had heard that one of the bad effects of drinking was blackout. Had he somehow blacked out and couldn't remember where he'd placed the bottle? Ridiculous. His memory was sometimes hazy the day after a wild night but he had never drawn a blank.

"This what you're looking for?"

Turning, he saw Addy in the doorway, holding the bottle, her nose wrinkled as if a foul odour came from it.

"What the hell do you think you're doing?" Buddy asked, holding back an impulse to grab the bottle out of her hands.

"I'm trying to save your life."

"Save your own life," he said, walking towards her, reaching out for the bottle.

She stepped back, moving the bottle away from him.

"*My* life's not in danger," she said. "I'm not in danger of becoming an alcoholic."

Buddy shook his head in disgust. "Look, there are plenty of other bottles I can put my hands on," he said. "Keep the goddam thing. Have a drink or two yourself. Maybe it'll make you more human."

"Is that what you think it does? Make you more human? Let me tell you something, Buddy. It does just the opposite. Makes you a monster. A silly-looking monster. Ever look into the mirror when you're so stupidly drunk? You ought to see yourself. That silly look on your face, like a moron. And you ought to see yourself at the dinner table. That stupid grin of yours. Mom won't admit it. She's so wrapped up in her own worries that she doesn't see *anything*, not even how stupid you look and act."

*Silly, stupid. Didn't she know any other words?*

"So you think you can stop me from being stupid and silly by taking my bottles?"

"Now you're being stupid and silly when you're sober. Bad enough when you're drunk but absolutely ridiculous when you're sober. I assume you're sober, anyway. So, no, I don't think taking this bottle will stop you from drinking."

"So what's this all about?"

"I'm simply trying to get your attention."

"Why do you need my attention? I don't need yours. Don't want yours."

"Because . . ." Now she faltered and the bottle in her hand seemed ludicrous.

"Because why?" Challenging her. *Okay, here I am, you have my attention. Now tell me why you need it.*

"Because we have to talk. I can't stand this any longer. Mom going around in a permanent daze, like she's sleepwalking. You drunk most of the time. Your father out there with that woman, that *girl*."

"Well, what are we supposed to do?" he asked, but not really interested because there was nothing they could do. Which, he decided, he ought to tell her: "There is nothing we can do."

She heaved the bottle as if throwing a football and it struck the stucco wall, breaking into a thousand pieces, the neck flying away while the rest of the bottle and the precious liquid dropped to the floor.

"Christ," he said.

"See? There's always something that can be done."

"And you think you've been acting like a sane person?"

Which made it a draw, as he turned to look at the soggy mess on the floor.

"Look," she said, conciliatory. "All I want to do is talk. Is that asking too much? And I've got a present for you. In my room." She took a step towards the hallway. "Please," she said, her voice cracking forlornly.

Reluctant but curious, he followed as she led him upstairs to her room, opened the door and gestured him inside. She pointed to the bureau where a gleaming bottle of gin stood, a glass beside it.

"Help yourself," she said. "From me to you."

His first reaction was to think that Addy was a boozer too, with her own secrets, but a moment later he realized that this was not possible. Not Addy, of all people.

"No, the bottle's not mine," she said. "I wouldn't drink this stuff for anything in the world. And never mind how I got it. It involved bribes, from the friend of a friend. But

I got it for you and this is another bribe. So that we'd talk. If you have to drink, then do it with me. Not alone. I can't stand being alone in this house any more."

Suddenly, he did not want a drink. His eyes became ridiculously wet and he fumbled in his pocket for a stray piece of Kleenex. Saw how pathetic they'd become, brother and sister: the brother a drunk, the sister abandoned, tracking down a bottle of gin in order to make contact.

"We've got to do something, Buddy," she said. "We can't keep on like this. Remember the sins of omission?"

Buddy shook his head, didn't remember. He remembered only vaguely those religious classes on Monday nights in the basement of St Dymphna's church. Old Father O'Brien conducted the classes, explaining the Bible and the Ten Commandments and other stuff. Buddy had paid scant attention. Monday nights were ridiculous nights for religious classes. Kids were already loaded up with regular homework. His mother insisted that he and Addy attend the classes. "Her conscience bothering her," Addy surmised. Their mother was Catholic and their father a Presbyterian if he was anything at all. He seldom bothered going to church. Their mother herded them to Sunday masses and Christian Doctrine classes on Monday evenings. Until the last two or three years when she seemed to give up on the classes although she made Buddy and Addy sit through interminable services on Sunday morning, or sometimes Saturday evenings. Saturday evenings were even worse than Sunday mornings.

"The sins of omission are the sins of doing nothing," Addy said now in her smart-alecky way. "Like, I think wars get declared because somebody somewhere does nothing to stop them. And we're doing nothing to stop what's going on with Mom and Dad."

"But what can we do?" he asked, still not looking at her,

his eyes remaining moist, concentrating on the window and the yellow plastic butterfly she'd installed to cover a hole in the screen.

"I don't know. But let's talk about it. About the possibilities."

Which made him realize that Addy dreamed of possibilities when she was sober and he only indulged in them when he was on the booze. "Okay, let's talk . . ."

"Do you need a drink first?" she asked.

The word *need* stung him, made him flinch. Was she being sarcastic? Saw her face and decided she was sincere.

"No," he said, glad to be saying no. "Let's hear about these possibilities."

Addy flung herself on the bed, cupped hands holding her chin, while Buddy went to the window, stared at the back yard where the old picnic table needed paint and the barbecue grill rusted away. The family suppers out there were only dim memories now.

"Maybe," Addy said, "we ought to have plans."

"What kind of plans?" Speaking almost absently, still staring into the yard.

"Plans to end this crazy stuff between Mom and Dad. Maybe we can do something to get them together again. At least, to talk . . ." She launched into a series of plots — arranging a meeting between them on "neutral ground", like in a restaurant. Approaching that woman, *that girl*, as Addy always described her scornfully, and trying to reason with her. "If she sees us, his son and daughter, she probably will *see him* in a different light."

All of it impossible, of course. Which he tried to tell her without hurting her feelings or fracturing this sudden intimacy. "Addy, this is dream stuff. Sounds beautiful but I don't think it can work. That woman, that girl — you can bet your life she's already seen us, she knows who we are.

80

And getting Mom and Dad together — do you think that can really work out? This thing just didn't happen overnight. Who knows when it began? Maybe Mom and Dad began falling apart long before that woman came along . . ."

"Maybe we could sue them," she said, brightly, the kind of brightness that flashes just before tears.

They both laughed, brittle laughter ringing hollowly in the bedroom, and as they looked at each other Buddy saw that they had accomplished something at least, a sort of bond, not exactly friendship but a kind of alliance.

"Know what we are, Buddy?" Addy asked, voice rueful.

"What?" Buddy replied warily, a bit unsure of himself with this new Addy.

"Victims. Victims of child abuse."

"Wait a minute," he said. "Mom and Dad never laid a hand on us." Frowning, suddenly aghast: "Did something happen to you? Did Dad ever . . ."

"That's not what I mean," she scoffed, and for a moment she was the old Addy again, the pain-in-the-ass kid sister. "Not sexual abuse or even physical abuse. But just as bad in its own way. Divorce. A family breaking up. Mothers and fathers too selfish about themselves and ignoring their children . . ."

"They haven't ignored us," Buddy said, not certain why he was defending them. "Mom's here. Dad keeps in touch." That twenty-five-dollar cheque each week.

"That's not what I mean by ignoring. I mean, ignoring the hurt, the invisible stuff that happens to kids. What's happening to us."

Buddy hated arguments, confrontations, did not like to articulate feelings, as if feelings would go away or would not have any existence at all if they were not put into words. He did not comment. In fact, he wanted to end this conversation, get out of here.

"Listen, Buddy, when I fell out of the tree that time I was nine years old and broke my arm, I didn't cry. It hurt like hell but I didn't cry. But I've cried three times since Dad left. Middle-of-the-night crying."

Tears gathered now in her eyes and she turned away, smacking her hands together the way a pitcher does before throwing the ball to a batter. His little sister in this pathetic parody of a ball player simply because she was trying to hide her tears.

"I hate them, I hate them," she muttered, still turned away, still smacking her hands together.

He looked at the bottle on the bureau, the glass beside it. Reached out to touch her shoulder but unable, again, to do it. Reached out towards the bottle but stayed his hand.

"Don't hate them, Addy," he said. "Anyway, Mom's still here. Dad was the one who left."

"But he wouldn't have left, wouldn't have been attracted to someone else if everything had been fine with them." Turning to him again: "Why doesn't she fight back?"

That's the difference between us, Buddy thought. Addy was a fighter, his mother wasn't. Neither was he. He drifted, let others do the leading. Like with Harry Flowers. Following him in his exploits, into that house and the terrible things they did. "I don't know," he said, feeling useless.

"Poor Buddy." Almost whispering, her voice sad and wistful.

He went to the door, unable to say any more. He did not want her pity. Did not want her bottle. Did not completely trust her yet. Maybe later. All he knew now was that he wanted to get out of the house, wanted to get downtown where Crumbs would supply him with the stuff that would take away all the lousy things in his life.

❖

82

The Avenger hated the shopping mall.

He hated the crowds and the white lights and the music coming from the loudspeakers. He felt lost and alone, not like an Avenger at all, his head aching from all the sights and sounds, his eyes sore from all the searching and looking. He was surprised to find so many old people in the mall, looking sad and abandoned, lingering on the benches, some of them staring into space, others napping, eyes closed, mouths open.

The teenagers were everywhere. Moving, always on the go. Alone and in groups. Laughing and calling to each other. The guys pushing and shoving sometimes. Flirting with the girls and the girls flirting back, sidelong glances, secret smiles. Eating hot dogs and pizzas and big crazy sandwiches. Gulping Coke, 7-Up, other stuff.

Although he hated the mall, he went there every day when the schools let out, having decided, through a process of elimination, that the mall was the most likely place to find the trashers. He had reached this conclusion one day in his shed, where he had put his thinking cap on. Whenever he came across a tough problem, his mother always said: Put your thinking cap on. So that's what he did. In his mind, he made out a list. He was good at picturing things in his mind. On one side, he saw the questions. On the other side, the answers. Like: What do you know about the trashers? Answer: They are young guys, all dressed up, teenagers. To find them you have to go where teenagers hang out, right? Right. And where do teenagers hang out? At the schools, high schools. Do teenagers really hang out at schools? Don't they get out of the schools as fast as possible when the last bell rings? Right. Where do they go? Home, to part-time jobs at places like McDonald's, the stores downtown or at the mall.

The mall. Right.

Sooner or later, everybody went to the mall. To work in the stores or to hang out.

The Avenger sighed, dreading the prospect of going to the mall every day but knowing that he had no other choice.

For the next three weeks, he went to the mall almost every afternoon that his chores permitted him to go. He stationed himself for periods of time at the entrance, then walked through the place, looking, always looking, but acting as if he was not looking, trying not to act suspicious. But how do you do that? He figured that it was best to look natural, not to lurk behind the fake birches or the huge ferns placed here and there in the mall. He did not stay in one spot too long, either, and whistled softly, looking at his watch occasionally, as if he was waiting for someone. Meanwhile, his eyes were like secret cameras, taking pictures of the guys going by or standing around in groups, his eyes darting here, there, and everywhere.

He learned to avoid the security guards, although they were not a problem. Even though they wore impressive uniforms, they were old, weary-looking, retired police officers, maybe. But The Avenger still avoided them, moving on if one of them approached. Meanwhile, he kept looking, searching, ignoring his aching head, his sore eyes.

Once in a while, his heart leaped in his chest as he spotted a face that looked familiar. This happened a few times. He would follow the guy, squinting, trying to get a clear look at him, trying to superimpose the face of a trasher on the suspicious face. He was always disappointed it was never a trasher. Then a terrible thought: Suppose he had already seen one of the trashers but had not recognized him? Suppose his memory was faulty? Impossible, he told himself. He was The Avenger. Whenever he closed his eyes, even in the turmoil of the mall, he could bring forth the faces of the trashers, the way they had walked and talked and yelled, the way they had looked, without any doubt at all.

But where were they?

He went into the stores, looking at the clerks, and learned that most of the clerks were girls, especially in the department stores. He spotted boys carrying boxes or pushing carts piled high with merchandise. Guys worked in the food places — McDonald's, Papa Gino's, Friendly's. The Avenger got sick of eating pizzas and hamburgers, although he would not have thought that possible before his vigils at the mall.

One day he saw Jane Jerome. His heart swelled up, seemed too big for his chest. Then began to pound. She was beautiful. She did not see him. He could not take his eyes from her. Like those nights when he used to watch her in her bedroom. She'd pull down the window shade but not all the way, leaving an inch or so at the bottom. The Avenger watched her through that inch. Saw her doing her homework, the pencil tip between her lips. Full lips, pink. Saw her undressing. Taking off her blouse, revealing her white lacy bra. Dropping her skirt to the floor. She never picked up her clothes, left them draped over a chair, or flung on the bed or simply to the floor, a puddle of skirt, blouses, or sweaters. She sometimes walked around in her bra and panties. He felt his eyes bulging. Felt hot and cold at the same time. Like chills and fever. Could hear his breath going in and out. He wondered if she knew he was watching at the window. Was performing for him, walking around almost naked. He blinked, confused. What if she took off her bra and panties? He had never seen a naked woman before. Did not know what he would do if she took off everything. But it was impossible for Jane Jerome to do something like that. Not his Jane. She was not like other girls. Not like her sister who did not even say hello to him when she walked by, always in a hurry, never stopped to speak to him. He would not bother looking into *her* window. But at Jane's window, he always felt strange — shivering and warm at the same time, hoping she would take off her bra and panties and yet not wanting her to do that. Only a bad girl would parade herself around knowing that someone was watching at the window. And Jane was not bad. As she tugged at the top of her panties, pulling them tight around her behind, he wondered: Was she bad, after all?

One night, he found the shade pulled all the way down. Still down the next night. And all the other nights afterwards. He was sad at first, as if he had lost something precious, and then he was relieved. You must resist temptation, his mother always said. He knew that Jane must be temptation, especially with the shade open.

Seeing her now in the mall, he faded into the shadows under the escalator, watching her pass, eating her up with his eyes. Everything bright and shining about her. The way her body moved when she walked. Her hair bouncing. She had tied it at the back of her head in a ponytail and it bounced gently as she walked. He liked the back of her neck, the white skin peeking out of the wisps of hair. Why does she make me feel feverish? he wondered. She's only a girl. She entered a store, out of sight, and he was both relieved and sad.

The Avenger began to dream of the mall at night. Dreamed of himself walking through the place like it was a museum, all black and white and the kids standing around like statues. Statues with big eyes staring at him. Following him as he walked by. He woke up sweating. And discouraged. Which was unusual because The Avenger never allowed himself to be discouraged. But all those afternoons at the mall had been without success. Maybe the trashers were not from around the Wickburg area. Maybe they came from places like Boston or Providence. Too far away. He groaned, tossing in the bed. How could he track them down in Boston? Or, wait, maybe they were just lying low. Keeping out of sight. Maybe they suspected that The Avenger had seen them that night and were staying away from public places. That could be the answer. Which meant that he would have to be patient again. Watch and wait. Bide his time. Wait for the means and the opportunity. It had worked before. With Vaughn Masterson and his grandfather. It would work again. He was The Avenger and The Avenger never failed.

He fell asleep and his dreams were sweet this time, although he could not remember them when he woke up in the morning.

"They've caught him," her father announced, coming into the house, dropping his briefcase on the small table next to the front door.

Jane and her mother were descending the stairs from the first-floor bedrooms and said simultaneously: "Caught who?" Like a comedy act on television.

But it wasn't comedy at all as they immediately realized who had been caught.

"One of the trashers," her father said. "The ringleader, in fact."

"Who was he?" Jane asked, strangely reluctant to hear the answer. She was afraid that it might be someone she knew, someone who was supposed to be a friend or a classmate at Burnside. Which would be worse than a stranger.

"Kid by the name of Harry Flowers. Lives in Wickburg. He's a senior at Wickburg Regional."

As her father talked Jane realized that something was wrong. But what? The words were right. The way he spoke, fast as usual, was also right. But something else was not right at all.

"How did they catch him?" her mother asked.

"Jack Kelcey who lives around the corner on Vista Drive? He just came back from a business trip to the West Coast. He'd been gone almost a month and didn't know about the trashing. When his wife told him about it, he remembered seeing a car on the street that night. He'd been suspicious and actually wrote down the plate number. Just in case. He's a methodical guy, keeps a small notebook, records everything. He didn't think any more about the car until he came home and heard about Karen and the house . . ."

Still something wrong, Jane thought.

"They traced the plate number to Wickburg. To a big-name architect. Winston Flowers, who's involved in designing condos. This kid is his son . . ." Her father loosened his tie. "The boy admits doing the damage. But he denies touching Karen. Said she fell down the stairs. He also says he was alone in the house, that nobody else was with him."

"But the police said there must have been at least three or four of them," her mother said, sinking to the bottom step of the stairs.

Finally, Jane knew what was wrong.

"He claims he was alone although he's obviously lying," her father said. "He's probably also lying about not touching Karen." Her father hesitated, still fumbling with his tie. "Thing is — the police don't have much to go on."

"Much to go on?" her mother said, rising to her feet again, voice shrill with anger. "Karen in a coma, what he did to this house, Mr Kelcey who saw his car and he admits being here. What else do they need?"

Her father frowned, perspiration glistening on his forehead, face flushed. He patted his pockets as if searching for cigarettes, although he had not smoked in years.

"The police have to go according to the evidence," her father explained. "There is no direct evidence that he

88

touched Karen. The boy denies it and Karen can't testify. There is no evidence that he was *not* alone. There is no evidence that he broke into the house so they couldn't arrest him for breaking and entering . . ."

This is what was wrong: her father had not looked at her since he had entered the house. Had looked only at her mother, as if Jane weren't there, did not exist.

"Dad . . ." Jane began, chilly suddenly as if someone had left a window open and a cold wind was blowing across her flesh, causing goosepimples.

But her mother interrupted, still indignant, face flushed: "Why can't they arrest him for breaking into this place? He was in here, wasn't he? He admitted doing the damage, didn't he?"

"There were no signs of forced entry," her father said slowly, pacing the words, emphasizing each word separately, as if he were writing on a blackboard.

"What does *that* mean?" Jane's mother asked.

While a shadow crossed Jane's mind.

"It means," her father said, still not looking at Jane, "that he didn't have to break into this house. Didn't have to break a window or break down a door."

"Then how did he get in?"

Look at me, Jane wanted to shout, why won't you look at me? But stood there, silent, in dread, a stranger in her own home.

"Because he simply walked in," her father said, voice harsh and dry, as if his throat hurt. "He had a key to the house. He put the key in the lock, opened the door and walked in."

"A key to this house, *our* house? In heaven's name, how would he get a key?"

For the first time since he arrived home, Jane's father looked at her. Looked directly into her eyes, his own eyes flashing with — what? — anger? More than anger. She groped for the word and, to her horror, found it. Accusation. That's what she saw in his eyes.

"He said that Jane gave him the key." His voice flat, the voice of a stranger.

Standing in the hallway of her home with her mother and father, while a lawn mower whirred away someplace in the neighbourhood, Jane Jerome suddenly knew what the end of the world would be like.

# Part 2

**M**ARTY Sanders was waiting for Buddy when he stepped off the bus in front of Wickburg Regional the next morning. A dull ache in his head and his eyes stinging from the morning sun, Buddy grimaced as Marty's foghorn voice greeted him:

"Hung over?" Fake concern in his eyes.

Buddy did not bother to answer. He saw Randy Pierce lurking near the school's entrance, bland as usual, as if waiting for someone to draw an expression on his face.

Marty drew Buddy aside and spoke out of the corner of his mouth like a gangster in some cheap old movie. "Bad news, Buddy."

The other students streamed by them, one guy jostling Buddy with his elbow. The bus emitted stenches of exhaust.

Trying to figure the categories of bad news, he came up with a name: Harry Flowers. The dull ache in his head intensified into a sharp pain that embraced his entire skull. The sun made him blink. He looked towards Randy, whose face was a sunspot.

"Harry was picked up yesterday by the cops," Marty said. "Rang the bell at his house about four o'clock and hauled him off to the police station. Arrested him for vandalism — that house in Burnside we hit . . ."

Buddy moaned, a strange alien sound he barely recognized as his own as he watched the bus lumbering away. *We Are Sunk. The End.*

"Don't worry," Marty said, confidential, face so close to Buddy's that a pimple near his nose looked like a crater on the moon. "Harry won't tell. He's not a squealer."

*Tell, squeal*. Fifth-grade words.

"Everybody squeals," Buddy said, but what he meant was: *I would squeal. I wouldn't want to squeal but I'd do it. I would break down and admit everything*.

"Look, Buddy," Marty said, voice deeper than ever, if that was possible. "I've known Harry all my life. We were in preschool together. Harry never double-crosses his friends."

*But I am not his friend. I could never be his friend*.

"Have you talked to him?" Buddy asked.

"Just a quick talk. He called last night, about eight when he got home. He said to not worry, he was taking the blame. He won't be in school today — has to go back to the police station today. With his father. He said his father's going to make restitution for the damage, doesn't want to make waves, doesn't want publicity. Which lets us off the hook. Harry said he'd call me tonight with the details."

In the distance Randy nodded his head, as if he could hear what Marty was saying.

*I could use a drink*. Even at eight-ten in the morning. Even though a drink this early would make him sick to his stomach.

"How did the police find out about him?" Buddy asked, barely aware that the first warning bell had sounded, usually the loudest bell in the world that jolted most students into an instant run for the front door.

"Harry said a witness saw his car that night."

"What witness?" Buddy asked. "And why did he wait so long? It's been more than three weeks." Three weeks plus

92

five days — Buddy knew exactly when the trashing had occurred.

"I don't know," Marty said, leading Buddy towards the school's entrance, where Randy greeted them, a sickly smile on his face now, the smile like a bandage covering a wound. "All I know is that Harry said not to worry. And he's a man of his word."

*In the first place, he's not a man. He's a high school senior. And what do I know about his word?* Buddy looked over his shoulder, as if expecting to see a police cruiser streak towards the school, turning on the siren the instant the cops spotted them.

"If the witness saw Harry, he probably saw us," Buddy said.

Randy finally spoke: "We don't know if the witness is a *he* or a *she*."

"Stop splitting hairs, for crissakes," Marty said to Randy. "Who cares if the witness is a he or a she?" The kind of stupid argument Marty and Randy usually carried on. "The witness, *he* or *she*," emphasizing the words for Randy's benefit, "saw the car. Got the licence plate number. The cops traced it to Harry's house." Still talking sarcastically to Randy, as if speaking to a little kid. "They didn't think his father had done the damage. Middle-aged guys don't ordinarily get their kicks trashing houses. So they arrested Harry." Snorting with contempt as he shook his head.

The second warning bell sounded, clanging inside Buddy's head. Two minutes remaining to get inside the place and to their lockers. Then to their homerooms for attendance.

"Relax, Buddy," Marty croaked, his voice more like a bullfrog's now than a foghorn. "Harry won't let us down."

Famous last words, Buddy thought, as they pushed their way into the school. His locker contained a hidden half-pint of gin that he kept for emergencies. He wondered whether he had enough time to sneak a couple of gulps. He felt in his jacket pocket for Life Savers. Despite his throbbing head and queasy stomach, he needed the easing of tension and dread the gin would supply while waiting for the cops to come and take him off to jail.

That evening, he leaped with alarm when a knock came at his bedroom door. The cops, he thought. His mother, grim-faced, greeted him as he reluctantly opened the door. "Could I have a word with you, Buddy?" She knows, he thought, as his face grew warm, like shame made visible. "Addy's in my bedroom, waiting . . ."

He followed her there and found Addy sitting on the dainty delicate chair in front of his mother's dressing table. Addy shot him a look of curiosity, as if saying: I don't know what this is all about, either.

Hands on hips, shoulders stiff, as if standing at attention, his mother drew a deep breath and said: "I'm thinking of going away for a few days . . ."

Buddy sagged against the wall, a surge of relief flowing through him, as if he'd had a fever that had suddenly stopped. Then wondered in a panic: Is she leaving us, too? He looked at Addy but found no answer in her eyes.

As if reading his mind, his mother said: "No, I'm not moving out or anything like that. And I'm not taking a vacation, either. I'm thinking of going on a retreat . . ."

The word echoed vaguely in Buddy's mind, something to do with religion and prayer. But he asked the question anyway: "What's a retreat?" And immediately felt stupid as usual when involved in a conversation with his mother and Addy.

"It's a place to go for meditation and prayer," Addy explained, but not in a wise-guy voice, trying to be helpful.

"Exactly," his mother said. "It's a five-day retreat, a long weekend, Friday through Tuesday at a kind of monastery, south of Worcester." She sank down on the bed. "I've got to get myself together. I mean, I've only been going through the motions, at work, here at home with the two of you. During the retreat, I'll have a chance to think. To meditate, pray. There's a counsellor. I'll be going with a group of women from all walks of life."

"That's just great, Mom," Addy said heartily.

And Buddy echoed the word: "Great." Trying to inject it with enthusiasm.

"We'll get along fine," Addy said. "We'll load up on frozen stuff, order Chinese goop, and I can make my specialities . . ."

"Meat loaf and shake-and-bake chicken," Buddy said, chiding her pleasantly, wanting to be a part of her cheerfulness and his mother's decision. At the same time, he looked searchingly at his mother, trying to see her not as his mother but as a woman. A troubled, unhappy woman. Saw the small network of lines at the corners of her eyes, the thin, downturned lips. Had her lips always been so thin? Had she always looked this way? Sadness made him take his eyes away from her. Since his father's departure, his mother had been only a presence in the house, as insubstantial as a shadow. He had awakened each day thinking, today somehow we'll talk, I'll ask her how she's doing, how she's *really* doing, we'll get past all that polite table talk and get things out in the open. But as each day wore on, and the booze took hold, his morning vow dissolved. His mother remained preoccupied, distant at the table although she talked — how she talked — but mechanical talk, about work, enquiring about school, but not absorbing the answers, distracted.

"Look, kids," she said now. "Maybe I haven't been the best wife and mother and I've also been a lousy Catholic. Your father did his best for you. He went along with all the demands of the Church when we married. Agreed that our children would be brought up Catholic, although I decided at one point that you both should make your own decisions about religion and what to be."

When did that happen? Buddy wondered. All he knew was that at some point in his life, his mother had stopped going to mass and they had stopped too. And she did not insist on those boring religious classes any more. Was that one of Addy's sins of omission?

"I have to do something," she continued, sitting straight on the bed, her hands stroking the spread. "And I have to start somewhere. The other day I realized it was either a psychiatrist or a retreat. Maybe it'll be both in the end." She closed her eyes. "All I want is a little peace." Tears oozed through her closed eyelids.

"Oh, Mom," Addy cried, and flung herself at her mother, kneeling on the floor, her arms around her mother's waist. Buddy envied them, together like that. Envied his mother, who might find that peace she wanted on retreat. Envied Addy, who could embrace her mother passionately, live passionately, writing plays, doing things. While he waited for the cops to show up, which would bring disgrace to them all.

But the cops never came.

Three days later, just before supper, Harry called, telling Buddy — not asking but *telling* him — that he would pick him up at eight o'clock.

"Time to have a talk," Harry said, voice dry and crisp with no sign of an accent.

Buddy's hand stayed on the phone for a long time after he hung up.

The Avenger was angry, almost in tears — not childish tears but tears of anger and frustration — as he sat on the bus on the way home from the shopping mall. He knew that he would not go to the mall any more in his search for the trashers. He was tired of looking, looking, but never seeing them. A few minutes ago, a security guard had approached him as he stood across from the escalators trying not to act suspicious, acting as if he was waiting for his mother to show up. The guard was old with red blemishes like small flowers on his cheeks, but his eyes were dark and watchful. He did not speak to The Avenger but stood close to him. Too close. When The Avenger moved on, the guard moved with him. The Avenger did not know whether this was a coincidence or whether the guard did not want him hanging around the mall. The Avenger finally slipped through the revolving doors with the knowledge that he would not return to the mall any more. Three weeks of looking had failed to turn up any of the trashers.

As the bus lumbered down Main Street, The Avenger pondered his next move. Maybe he should start visiting the high schools, although he knew that this was almost impossible to undertake. A lot of schools in the area. Too many. Why hadn't the trashers shown up at the mall the way hundreds of other guys did? He beat his fist against the window until his knuckles hurt and an old woman in the seat in front of him turned and frowned at him. She wore thick glasses that magnified her eyes. He looked bleakly out of the window at the stores passing by. Felt helpless, unable to proceed with his plans for revenge. Anger stirred inside him, his heel drummed the floor, and the old woman shuffled her shoulders and half glanced back at him again. He realized he had been hitting the back of her seat with his knee.

Making an effort to keep his knee from moving, his foot from tapping the floor, his knuckles from hitting the window, he put on his thinking cap. The cap was tight on his head, like a real cap, too small for his skull. He closed his eyes, carried along by the bumping and thumping of the bus. He dreaded to wonder what Jane would think if she knew he had failed her, had failed to find the trashers.

Sadness replaced his anger. Sadness, because he could not spy on the Jeromes any more even though he did not consider himself a spy. He had been an observer. By observing them, he had become part of the family. But with the shrubbery all gone now and the branches of the old oak trees trimmed back, the house looked naked, exposed to the world. No more hiding places for him to look at the family.

In his months of observation, he had come to love them. That's why he had done the things he had done. Because of that love. *You always hurt the one you love.* That was a song his mother always sang. An old song. Her theme song, sort of. When she lost her patience and punished him, those words echoed in his mind. This is for your own good, she would say. And he would think: You always hurt the one you love. So when he began to love the Jeromes, he knew that he had to hurt them, to show them his love. Even though it made him feel bad to do things. Things like yanking Mrs Jerome's tomato plants out of the garden, which hurt not only her but *him* as well, because he loved to see the brave and pretty plants sunning themselves. Plus putting the dead squirrel in the mailbox. The Avenger had not killed the squirrel — he had found it by the side of the road, hit by a car, no doubt. He would never kill a helpless animal, especially a small one.

Now the anger was gone and so was the sorrow as the bus left downtown Wickburg and made its way to the outskirts where Burnside awaited him. He had nothing but a vast emptiness inside of him. Like hunger, although it had nothing to do with eating food. Hunger for — what? Action.

To do something. The old woman had got off the bus —
he had not noticed her departure — and now a young lady
sat in the seat in front of him. She had a small baby in her
arms. The baby began to fuss a bit and the young lady
hoisted the baby up to her shoulder and the baby looked
at him. The baby started to cry, face all scrunched up in
its bonnet. Was the baby a boy or a girl? He couldn't tell.
But he wished the baby would stop crying and stop staring
at him.

He looked away, out of the window, at the houses with
their lawns and cars parked in driveways and the baby
stopped crying. But when he looked again, the baby was
looking at him. Did babies have some kind of special power
when they looked at people? Ridiculous, of course. But who
could tell what babies were thinking? This baby had dark
eyes like the security guard at the mall. The baby looked
at him with those dark eyes, face all wrinkled like a paper
bag that had been crushed in somebody's hand. He did not
like the way the baby was staring at him and looked out of
the window again. He also began to get angry again. Angry
at the mall which he had always hated and hated even more
now because the trashers had not gone there. Angry, too,
at this baby staring at him. And the baby's mother paying
no attention at all. He wondered if the mother would pay
attention if he did something to the baby.

The bus lurched again, hitting a bump in the road and
came to a stop. The doors hissed open and closed and the
young lady got up. She did not get off the bus but took
another seat in the front of the bus near the door. The
Avenger told himself to take it easy, not to get angry again.
But why did she change her seat? Did the baby's mother
have powers of her own? Did she read The Avenger's mind
as he sat behind her? He looked out of the window again,
hitting the glass with his knuckles, not caring whether he

was making noise or not. He told himself to get rid of these thoughts. How could that lady read his mind anyway? And what special powers could a little baby have? Ridiculous. And yet . . .

He was relieved when the bus arrived at downtown Burnside. He got off the bus without looking at the young lady and the baby. He should focus on the trashers and not strangers. He shivered as he considered what he might have done to that baby. He was in a hurry now to get to the shed and map out new plans. What kind of new plans? He wasn't sure. He glanced in the window of a hardware store and looked at the tools. Hammers and saws — like weapons waiting for his use. Maybe he should start a collection while waiting for the trashers. Round up all the weapons he could find. Excitement rose in him and he almost bumped into a man who was standing in front of a drugstore reading a newspaper. The newspaper fluttered in the air like a soiled flag.

"Excuse me," The Avenger said in his polite way, excitement making his blood race now. Knives and guns and axes and pliers in his thoughts.

Because The Avenger seldom read a newspaper he would never know that the newspaper the man had been holding carried a story with the headline:

### ARCHITECT'S SON
### ADMITS VANDALISM

"Harry's glad you're here," Harry Flowers said as they sat in his car, two streets away from Buddy's house. Buddy preferred this spot rather than some public place. He did not want to be seen by anyone, particularly the police, in the company of Harry Flowers.

"Harry thought you might have better things to do." That same phoney voice. Buddy hated people, like ball players and politicians, who referred to themselves in the third person. He shrugged, did not feel particularly like talking. Let Harry Flowers carry the ball. This meeting was his idea, anyway.

Silence gathered in the car as dusk deepened into the first stages of night, the streetlights brightening in the gathering darkness.

"Have a drink," Harry said, offering a half-pint of gin he had pulled out of the glove compartment.

Buddy wanted to refuse, wished desperately that he could refuse, but he needed all the defences possible when talking to Harry Flowers and he accepted the bottle, took a tentative gulp, then a good healthy swallow, grimacing as usual at the taste, the burning in his throat.

He handed the bottle back to Harry and noticed dimly that Harry did not take a drink.

"Tell me something, Buddy, why don't you trust Harry?"

The question surprised Buddy. But Harry always was capable of the surprise, the verbal ambush.

"What makes you think I don't trust you?" Buddy asked, hoping the gin would do its work quickly, relaxing him so that he would be able to hold his own with Harry Flowers in what promised to be a delicate conversation.

Harry handed him the bottle again. Buddy hesitated, still wanting to refuse it but giving in. Christ, he always gave in. As he raised the bottle to his lips, he stalled before drinking, studying Harry's face.

Buddy could not deny the fact that Harry had kept his word, had shouldered the blame for the trashing without naming anyone else. His father had paid for the damages. Sat down and wrote a big cheque without quibbling, according to Marty. Throughout the week, Buddy had waited for the phone to ring, a knock on the door, a summons to police headquarters. None of that had happened. A three-paragraph story on the inside page of the newspaper ran under a modest headline in small type:

ARCHITECT'S SON
ADMITS VANDALISM

The brief story gave no details, only the names of Harry and his father, and reported that restitution had been made, Harry placed on probation. Did not mention the name of the family whose home was vandalized and omitted any reference to the girl who had been pushed down the stairs.

"Admit it, Buddy. You thought Harry would blow the whistle on you and Marty and Randy," Harry said.

Swallowing the booze, eyes watering a bit, Buddy knew he could not deny the truth of Harry's statement.

"Of course, I don't blame you for that," Harry continued. He had dropped the third-person Harry: "The kind of world we're living in, nobody expects you to do the right thing . . ."

"Okay, Harry," Buddy heard himself saying. "I appreciate what you did. I really do. I think it's great . . ." Buddy groped for more words and could not find them.

"Big statement," Harry said. "But you ran out of steam there, Buddy. Know why? Because you were about to add *but, Hell, I think it's a great thing you did, Harry, but . . .* What the *but* means, Buddy, is you're looking for the angle. You're figuring that I must have an ulterior motive for what I did. Right?"

"But *why* did you do it, Harry?" Buddy asked, giving in to his curiosity. "Why did you take all the blame? How did you get your father to pay the entire bill? We did as much damage as you did. Maybe more." The booze was beginning to work and he thought of the girl's room, the exhilaration of ripping her posters from the wall, sweeping her knick-knacks from the shelf, tearing her bed apart.

"Is it so hard to understand?" Harry asked. "Am I supposed to be a bad guy or something? Sure, I like to raise a little hell, have a good time, smoke a little pot, drink a little booze. Does that make me a prize heel? Hey, Buddy, I'm good to my mother and don't hassle my father. I make the honour roll. My folks appreciate all that. And when I got into trouble, my father helped out. My father loves me. He wrote the cheque and asked no questions."

Buddy glanced again at Harry. Harry Flowers, good student, good son, good guy. *What's wrong with this picture? Or was there anything wrong?*

"I'm sorry," he said, the booze making it easy to say the words again.

"You don't have to be sorry. Just accept what I did for what it was. I wasn't trying to be a hero. I just did what I thought was best for all of us. Why drag my friends into a mess when it wasn't necessary?"

*But I'm not your friend.* Didn't that make Harry's gesture even more noble then? Buddy had always thought in terms of good and evil, that you were either good or bad. And he automatically placed himself in the category of good guys. Which made Harry a bad guy, automatically. Now he wasn't certain, not certain about anything about himself. A good guy didn't do rotten things. And he, Buddy Walker, good guy, had helped wreck a family's house. He also drank in secret, went to school drunk sometimes. Missed the honour roll. Harry made the honour roll. Buddy's father had left home, abandoned his family, while Harry's father loved him, *My father loves me*, and was willing to pay the damages for Harry's vandalism.

"What's the matter?" Harry asked.

"Nothing," Buddy answered. But, yes, there was something.

"I know what's bothering you," Harry said.

Buddy turned to him, alarmed. Could Harry read his thoughts? Harry had always been capable of surprises — was this another one?

"You're wondering how I got away with it, right? Why the judge gave me probation, why there was so little publicity, why the charge against me was so minor? Is that what's bothering you?"

The gin spoke for Buddy: "Right, yes, that's exactly what I was wondering." But thinking: no, I wasn't wondering about that at all, relieved that Harry, after all, was not a mind-reader.

"You see, Buddy, they *had* to believe me and go along with what I said." Harry's customary coolness had vanished and he actually seemed excited as he talked. "They had no choice."

"Why did they have no choice?" Buddy asked, sensing that he was playing into Harry's hands like a straight man in a comedy act.

"Well, actually, they *thought* they had a choice. Thought they could throw the book at me. Breaking and entering. Malicious damage to property. Assaulting the girl. But as it turned out, they had to forget most of the charges. No breaking and entering, no assaulting the girl. That left them only with damage to property. Also, I'm only eighteen, from a respectable family, no previous arrests."

"But the girl is in the hospital, Harry. In a coma. How could they overlook that?"

"They didn't overlook it. They just didn't blame me. I told them that she fell down the stairs. Came rushing in the house in the dark and opened the wrong door. When she comes out of the coma — *if* she comes out of the coma" — a distinction that gave Buddy the shivers — "it's her word against mine. Besides, there were mitigating circumstances. Know what mitigating circumstances are, Buddy?" Harry handed him the bottle again.

Buddy sipped, floating with the booze now, but somehow his mind sharp and clear. "Tell me, Harry." Fascinated, despite the revulsion he felt.

"Mitigating circumstances means that I came up with the clincher. And the clincher made all the difference in the world. You must always have a clincher, Buddy, and I had the clincher even before we went into that house."

Buddy knew that Harry was waiting for the next question and Buddy supplied it, speaking slowly and carefully: "What was the clincher, Harry?"

"The key, Buddy," Harry proclaimed, triumph in his voice. "I had a key to the house. The key opened the front door. As a result, no charge of breaking and entering. Remember the order I gave: Don't break any windows. That's why, Buddy. So that they couldn't say we broke into the place . . ."

Buddy flashed back to that night, remembering how Harry had parked the car on a quiet neighbourhood street, whispered, "Wait here," and disappeared around the corner. Reappearing a few minutes later, he beckoned Buddy, Marty and Randy from the corner, maybe a hundred feet away. Befuddled by the booze, Buddy had been only mildly curious about the ease with which Harry ushered them to the Jerome house, the front door open, lights on inside. He had quickly forgotten his curiosity as the vandalism began.

"That's why it went so easy in court, Buddy. That's why, when my father agreed to restitution, everybody went along, the judge and the cops. I pleaded nolo contendere. Know what nolo means? It means I admitted to the facts of the case without admitting guilt. Neat, right? A bit of legal sleight-of-hand, my father's lawyer said. The judge placed me on probation and my father paid up . . ."

Something was wrong here, something was missing. "How about the other family, Harry? Why did they go along? Didn't they want to see justice done? Their house wrecked? Their daughter in the hospital?"

"Her father was there all the time, Buddy. And he was ready to blow his top. Or bust a gut. I thought at one point that he was going to jump over the guardrail and attack me. But he didn't. He couldn't. He had no choice . . ."

"Because you had a key to the house," Buddy said, still a bit puzzled. Suddenly, he knew what had been missing. "How did you get the key, Harry?"

Harry smiled expansively, leaning back. "I told them the girl gave it to me. The man's daughter." A chortle of triumph in his voice.

Buddy recoiled as if Harry had struck him. "That girl, the one who . . ."

"Not the girl in the hospital," Harry said. "Two girls live in that house. The other one. Her name is Jane. Jane Jerome . . ."

"She gave you the key to her house?" Buddy asked, unable to keep the disbelief from his voice.

"You're not paying attention, Buddy. I said I told them she gave me the key. Notice the difference?"

Buddy nodded, sober suddenly, all wooziness gone, the pleasant drifting over, and a headache asserting itself, throbbing dully above his eyes.

"How did you get the key?"

"Simple," he said. "Picture this: I'm in the mall one afternoon and I see a girl pull her wallet out of her pocket. A key falls to the floor. She doesn't see it fall. Because I'm such a gentleman" — and he leered at Buddy with such an evil grin that Buddy flinched — "I went over and picked up the key. Was going to give it to her. But she was walking away, into the Pizza Palace. I watched her go, holding the key in my hand. Looked at it. What kind of key was this? Didn't look like a car key. What other key would a girl her age have? Locker key at school? Most lockers have combinations. No. Must be — *voilà* — her house key, the key to her home." Harry paused and his voice grew dreamy. "Funny thing happened, Buddy. I thought: Here I hold the key to her house in my hand. This key can open the door to her house, to her family, to her private life. Christ, what a feeling. So I followed her into the Pizza Palace, made a few enquiries about her. And found out that her name was Jane Jerome and she lived in Burnside . . ." He waved his hand in the air. "The rest is history . . ."

Then, turning to him, serious again: "Listen, how I got the key is not important. What's important is the *effect* the key had on everybody at the police station. One minute everybody is ready to make all kinds of charges. Next minute, they say: Whoa, let's take another look at this case. Her father pulls the cops aside. His face is the colour of ashes in a barbecue pit. I know what her father is saying, know what he's thinking. He's thinking headlines. Like: GIRL AIDS IN VANDALISM OF HER OWN HOME. Her picture in the paper, on television maybe. See, Buddy? See why they had to believe me, why her father agreed to the lesser charges, accepted the restitution without making waves? Why the cops decided to believe I was alone? Everybody was suddenly glad to have it all over with . . ."

It wasn't until later, long after Harry had driven off and Buddy was crawling into bed, hoping the Alka-Seltzer would ease his nausea, that he thought:

But how about the girl?

Hey, Harry, how about the girl?

Seven hours and twenty minutes (she did not keep track of the seconds). The longest seven hours of her life. She spent them all in her room. Did not open the door when her mother knocked and called her name. Did not respond when her father rattled the doorknob and pleaded with her to come out.

"Please, Jane," he said, his voice strangled. "Please come out. Let's talk about this."

She did not answer, merely sat on her legs, knees crossed in front of her — like a wistful Buddha. "Hey, Jane," Artie called once, after rapping his knuckles on the door, their secret signal to each other: three short raps, two long, when they used to try to outwit baby-sitters in the olden days when they were young. "Don't be a sap, Jane. Come on out."

She did not answer Artie, either. *Don't be a sap, Jane.* Where did he get that word, *sap*, anyway? Stupid word.

She did not like her room any more. Missed her posters. Most of her small glass animals had been spared damage but she refused to put them on display again. They were tucked away in tissue paper in a box on the closet shelf. She always carefully stepped over that spot near the door where the vomit had lain in a terrible puddle.

She sniffed, wrinkling her nose, seeking that foul odour under the surface of things. No odour now but she knew it lurked there, threatening to emerge when she least expected it.

"The key," she muttered. "The damn key."

She went to the window, looked out, surprised to find that rain was falling. She'd heard no raindrops on the windowpane. Soft, gentle spring rain, a melancholy rain, the street deserted, no children playing, no dogs in sight. Were trashers lingering in the woods?

She should have told her parents about the key immediately. As soon as she realized she had lost it. But she'd been losing things around that time. Her red leather wallet, a Christmas gift, that she'd somehow lost with twenty dollars in Christmas money inside. Lost it at the movies. Two days later, the theatre called, reporting that the wallet had been found. It was damaged, torn, and money gone, of course. Next, she had lost a pearl earring, another gift from her favourite aunt, Aunt Cassie, back in Monument. Didn't mention it to anyone. Her mother had found it in a corner of the kitchen floor. Which made it worse. "Didn't you know it was missing?" her mother had asked. "Why didn't you tell us?" Then to Jane's father: "Know what's happening, Jerry? Our kids are keeping secrets from us."

All of which surprised Jane. Didn't her parents know that all kids kept secrets from their parents? Hadn't her mother and father done the same thing when they were kids? Or did growing up cause a kind of amnesia about stuff like that?

When she lost the key, she kept quiet about it. Did not mention it to anyone even though Karen and Artie probably would have helped her look for it. Actually, there did not seem to be any serious need for a key. Most of the time, somebody was home when Jane arrived. The key was a pain in the neck. She had no other keys. No car key — she was taking Driver's Ed at school, did not drive her father's car yet. Combination lock on her school locker: she kept her house key either in her pocket or in one of the slots of her wallet. Half the time she couldn't find it. Sometimes it slipped out of her jeans pocket into the chair. When she discovered it was missing, she wasn't sure when or where she had lost it. That was another reason for her delay in reporting the loss: she couldn't have supplied any details. In time, she completely forgot about the key. Even when the trashing occurred, she did not connect it with her missing key.

"Jane."

Her mother.

What Jane could not forget: the way her father had

refused to look at her, had kept ignoring her, as if she had been barred from the family. When finally he *did* look at her, his eyes were the eyes of a stranger. An accusing stranger. Until that moment, she had not realized how the eyes contain the secret of who you are and what you are. Looking into her father's eyes, she had seen a stranger, the man other people met on the street or at the office, because the man in the front hallway was certainly not, for that blazing moment, repeat, *not* her father. *Her* father could never look at her that way, as if he, too, were seeing a stranger and not his daughter. A moment later, when he had uttered those terrible words, had asked that terrible question — *Did you give him the key?* — her mother had regarded her in the same way, her eyes like her father's but with surprise and befuddlement mixed in with the accusation.

Or was she being fair?

She had turned away, so quickly, so eager to get away from those accusing eyes, scurrying up the stairs, a sob escaping her lips, that she thought maybe she hadn't waited long enough for her father to offer an explanation for his behaviour.

She looked at the clock. She had been in her room now for seven hours and thirty-two minutes. Had had no dinner — had not turned on her television set. Had not opened a book or placed a record on the CD. She had lived these past few hours like a hermit or a monk, fasting, keeping silent. In the first two or three hours, there had been no sounds from downstairs, not even a door closing or the muffled voices on television. The telephone did not even ring. Then, first her mother knocking and then her father. Taking turns.

Now her mother again:

"Know what you're doing, Jane?"

She did not answer but her silence asked: What *am* I doing?

"You're punishing us. For something you did."

They were still accusing her.

"Jane."

Her father's turn, his voice:

"You didn't give us enough time. I didn't say I *believed* that boy. I was only asking you, to hear you say it in your own words."

He hadn't asked. He had told her what the boy had said — that she gave him the key. She would never forget those words or his eyes or the way his voice had sounded.

"We know you didn't give him the key. We know you wouldn't do a thing like that."

And her mother: "You lost the key, didn't you? And you were afraid to tell us because you're always losing things. Right?"

She knew, of course, that her mother and father had been discussing the situation all this time, downstairs, in the kitchen, the living room, the way she had been agonizing here in her bedroom.

What she hated most of all was:

The trashing. The thing that had led her to this situation. Her friends Patti and Leslie gone, now her father a stranger and her mother his conspirator against her. How she hated them, those faceless trashers and that fellow, Harry Something-or-other, who had lied and tried to implicate her in the trashing.

They were the enemy, not her father or mother. They were the reason she was a prisoner here in her own room. The reason her mother and father were in such agony.

She went to the door, turned the key, opened it. Saw her mother and father, their faces filled with apprehension and concern as they peered tentatively at her. In a moment, they were embracing, arms tangled around each other, cheeks damp, her mother whispering softly, *Jane, Jane*, like a prayer, as if she had returned from a long trip, her father pressing her close to him, as if he had to feel the contours of her body to be sure she was there.

She gave in to their ministrations, letting herself go, basking in the circle of their love and their warmth and their comfort, but in a small distant part of herself wondering if things would ever be the same again.


"I'm sorry."

A whisper of a voice, soft, distant, as if coming from a faraway country, another planet.

"Who is this?" she asked, puzzled, wary, wondering if she had misunderstood what the voice had said. *I'm sorry*. For what? "What did you say?"

She was alone in the house. After school. When the phone rang she'd picked it up automatically, without any thought about who might be calling. Nobody called her these days. That's why the ringing of the phone didn't excite her as it did when she had that stupid crush on Timmy Kearns and the days when Patti and Leslie had been her friends.

"Is this Jane Jerome?" the voice asked. A boy's voice, kind of breathless as if he had been running a long distance.

"Yes," she said. "Who is this?" A slight quiver of fear now in her voice. *I should hang up*. Ever since the vandalism, fear had crouched under the surface of everyday events, whether it was the ringing of the doorbell or an unfamiliar face on the street or someone who seemed to be staring at her at the supermarket checkout line. Now this unknown voice on the phone.

She was about to hang up when a soft sigh came over the line, the kind of sigh a child makes at the end of a long weary day. And after the sigh, the same voice, tender now, saying: "I'm sorry about what happened."

Big pause.

Caught by surprise, she looked at the phone as if the instrument could provide the answer to who was calling. Then pressed it against her ear in time to hear the line go dead, followed by the blurting of the dialling tone.

Her hand trembled as she replaced the receiver on its cradle. She stood there a moment, indecisive, trying to straighten out her thoughts. Her thoughts were all jumbled these days, as if her brain had short-circuited. Silly thought, of course, but she did not know how to express what had happened to her, what *was* happening to her.

She went to the window, blinked at the streams of sunshine against her eyeballs. Rain should be falling to suit her mood. Her black mood. She turned back from the window, hugged her arms around her chest, staring bleakly at each piece of furniture in the room. She found it hard these days to stay in the house at all. For a while, she found it difficult to be *alone* in the house and had fled the place. Now, she found it was almost impossible for her to be in the house even when her family was around. When her father glanced her way, she shrivelled a bit. When he touched her shoulder and gave her a good-night peck on the cheek, she could not respond even though she knew this was wrong. But what he had done, doubting her, was also wrong. I've got to get over this, she told herself. But found it hard to do. She kept telling herself that her father was not the villain. The guy whose name was Harry Flowers had lied, had made her father doubt her.

Harry Flowers. She wondered about him. What did he look like? Was he tall or short? Fat or thin? What kind of person was he? What kind of person would do such terrible, sick things? She tried to picture him in her mind but he was a terrifying blank. Terrifying because she might have already met him, on the street, at a dance at school, at the mall, and did not know it. When she strolled the mall, she looked curiously at the various fellows she met, wondering: Is this him? She decided at one point to stay away from the mall and then said: no. She would not let Harry Flowers control her life. He had already damaged her — her house, her feelings for her mother and father, her life.

And now that phone call. That soft and gentle voice full of sorrow and regret. Someone out there who felt bad for her, who had tried to communicate how he felt. But why was he so mysterious? Why didn't he identify himself, tell her his name? Was he — impossible — Harry Flowers? Calling to say he was sorry?

Harry Flowers seemed to have invaded her life, her thoughts. The caller couldn't be him. He could not have faked such an apology. Not the Harry Flowers who had wreaked such havoc. Harry Flowers, Harry Flowers, Harry Flowers, she thought as she headed upstairs for a jacket and then to be out of here, out of this house. To where? Anywhere except here. Harry Flowers, Harry Flowers, Harry Flowers, the name filling her mind. Harry Flowers, Harry Flowers, Harry Flowers. Opening drawers, the closet, unbuttoning, buttoning. Harry Flowers, Harry Flowers, Harry Flowers. Combing her hair, hand shaking, shoulders shaking, body shaking. HarryFlowersHarryFlowersHarry Flowers. Maybe if she said his name long enough, fast enough, it would not be a name any more, would lose all meaning, all power to threaten her. HarryFlowersHarry FlowersHarryFlowersHarryFlowersHarryFlowersHarry Flowers . . . as she bounded down the steps and out of the door into the outside world with HarryFlowersHarry FlowersHarryFlowersHarryFlowers . . . stop it stop it but could not could not HarryFlowersHarryFlowersHarry

FlowersHarryFlowers until his name passed out of existence and became only syllables, a dim sound in her mind, then, thank God, nothing.

The instant he heard her voice he remembered her face. Everything happened at once — the sound of her voice on the phone, then the flash of her features and the instant knowledge of where he had seen that face: in the picture on the bureau in that bedroom he had destroyed almost a month ago. He had completely forgotten about the picture in its chrome frame. He had been about to dash it against the wall when he paused, looked at the portrait of the girl for a long moment — dark hair falling to her shoulders, eyes slightly slanted, the hint of a smile on her lips but not quite a smile, as if she was trying to decide whether to smile or not and the camera caught that hesitation. For some reason, he replaced the picture, undamaged, on the bureau before continuing his frenzied assault on the room.

He had not given the picture another thought until: *Hello*. And then: *Who is this?*

He had winced at the hesitancy in her voice, more than that, her apprehension or maybe even fear, as if she was afraid of whoever was on the other end of the line. Did she answer all phone calls that way? *Is this what we did to her?*

Ever since Harry told him about the key, Buddy couldn't stop thinking about the girl. Even though she had been a cipher, a zero, blank, like a connect-the-dots face in a comic-page puzzle. Then, he began to wonder about her. How she must have felt walking into her bedroom and seeing all that damage. *But I didn't pee against the wall, somebody else did that*. He was surprised to find that he had a girl on his mind whom he had never met. He had known a lot of girls, but had never *had* a girl. Agonized over crushes — although he was convinced they were not crushes at the time but anguished love that would never end — Alice Currier in the sixth grade with her hair like melting caramel and Cindy Dennedy with whom he had his first dance in the ninth grade and Debbie Howington, the love of his life sophomore year, Debbie of the full tight sweaters and pouting lips who smiled at him one day and ignored him the next, who deigned to accept his invitation to the movies one night and then called the next day to cancel, all of which caused him to shun the female sex, made him think of becoming a monk in a monastery somewhere. And here he was, all involved — in his thoughts, anyway — with a girl he did not know, a girl he had never met but a girl he knew collected small glass animals, had had a poster of Billy Joel on her wall (which he had torn to shreds), a girl Harry Flowers had used as a victim to protect himself as well as Marty and Randy. And Buddy, too.

That's why he found himself at the telephone that afternoon, woozy with the booze, filled with compassion for that poor poor girl, dialling the phone as if he were performing some tragic ritual, then astonished and shocked when he heard her voice.

As usual, when it came to the opposite sex, he had failed abysmally in what he had set out to do. Yet, he hadn't been quite sure what he had set out to do. Apologize? Not sure. But what else? He did not know.

After hanging up dismally, a failure at whatever he had planned to do, blaming the booze — he should have called when he was cold sober, icy (but then he wouldn't have had the nerve, would he?) — and weary now with his thinking and drinking and his usual ineptitude, there was only one thing left to do:

Have another drink.

Which he did, of course, although it failed to erase the

girl's face from the terrible thing his memory had become.

He began to follow her. Breaking his own rule and disregarding Addy's questioning glances, he drove his mother's car to school. Then, grateful that Wickburg Regional dismissed classes thirty minutes earlier than Burnside High, he drove to Burnside and waited for Jane Jerome to emerge. He followed slowly, almost stalling the car, as she walked to nearby Burnside Hospital where, he surmised, she visited her sister. He sat rigidly behind the wheel, waiting for her to reappear, trying not to think of Karen Jerome in her hospital bed. Once or twice, he had telephoned the hospital to enquire about her condition. The answer invariably was an impersonal "Stable — no change".

Jane Jerome remained in the hospital for different periods of time — sometimes a few minutes, sometimes an hour or so, sometimes the remainder of the afternoon. On those days when she left the hospital after only a brief visit, she waited for the Wickburg mall bus. Buddy then drove ahead, parked in the garage adjacent to the shopping mall, and was waiting for the bus when it disgorged passengers, Jane among them, at the mall's entrance.

Following her from store to store, he tried to act casual, bought magazines which he pretended to read when she walked by only a few feet from him. She browsed leisurely, not buying anything, lingering at certain counters, pausing to rifle dresses hanging from the racks. He learned to be careful, to keep a certain distance, discovering in Filene's the danger of multiple mirrors. He came upon his reflection unexpectedly, startled to see himself reproduced in a dozen different angles, and almost panicked, wondering whether she had spotted him in one of the mirrors and was leading him on a merry chase.

Fleeing the store, he sat on a plastic yellow bench near

the dry fountain, chipped and peeling, as if it were diseased. When she emerged from Filene's a few minutes later, she wandered towards the escalator. He watched her ascend to the second level, saw her moving along the second-floor guardrail, her head barely visible. After a minute or two, he stepped on the escalator and, as he alighted, spotted her going into a bookstore at the far end of the corridor.

In the bookstore, he discovered the merits of peripheral vision: how you could see things without looking directly at them. He was able to open a book at the *Best Seller* — *20% Off* display and still see her in profile as she leafed through magazines ten feet away. When she closed a magazine with finality, he guessed that she was about to leave the store and he closed the book — he had no idea of its title or what it was about — and left the store before she did. That should convince her, if she had become suspicious, that he was not following her.

In front of the New Age Clothing store, he knelt on one knee as if checking the shoelaces of his Nikes and saw the flash of her legs as she passed by. He remained on his knee as she went beyond the escalator and continued to Marsh's, disappearing into the doorway. He waited a while, counting to five hundred slowly, and then made his way into the store, walked warily through Housewares and Home Furnishings. She wasn't in sight. He checked out Women's Clothing and Summer Fun and even drifted through Men's Clothing before going to the down escalator. Halfway down, he spotted her below at the perfume counter, sampling the spray from a blue bottle. As he stepped off the escalator, she had drifted to the counter containing scarves and draped a red scarf across her chest before letting it settle back on the counter like a small collapsing tent.

Inhaling the remnants of perfume as he went by the counter, he looked for her without trying to look as if he was looking for her. Sighed impatiently at the sudden absurdity of what he was doing. Spying, for crissakes, on a girl he didn't know. Didn't see her anywhere — was she hiding behind a display case watching his befuddlement? He felt stupid, realizing the futility of what he had been doing. His legs were restless as he stood there, indecisive, glancing at his watch, a frown on his face, acting as if he was waiting for someone who was late. Where was she? This pointless chase of his. But it wasn't pointless. He had found out a lot about her. Found out that she was bored and restless and kind of sad, too. She had not smiled at all, had never looked amused or entertained by anything she had encountered. Seemed to be sleepwalking, killing time, hating to go home, maybe, the way he hated to go home.

He spotted her again as she pushed through a revolving door leading to the outside world. Hurrying, he side-stepped two elderly women, one of them with a cane, as he headed for the door. Pausing at a window next to the door, he saw her standing at the kerb beneath the bus stop sign. For the first time, he *really* looked at her. Her blue plaid skirt fell in pleats and her pale blue sweater was fuzzy. She lifted her face as a gust of wind tousled her hair. Her hair was long enough to touch her shoulders, so black and shining that he thought it might squeak if he grabbed a bunch of it. Her features were delicate: small nose, high cheekbones, lips bare of lipstick. At that moment, she took a deep breath and her breasts rose in the sweater, straining against the fuzzy material. Looking away quickly, he felt dirty, like some kind of pervert. Yet aroused at the same time. When he looked at her again, the bus was pulling up and she stepped towards it. A moment later, she had boarded the bus, the door closing behind her with a sigh. Watching the bus lurch away, he began to miss her. Which was ridiculous, of course, because he did not even know the girl.

The next day, she followed the same routine — hospital visit, then the bus to the mall — and he trailed her from store to store as she drifted again, aimlessly. Because he was able to anticipate her movements, he didn't stay close to her, although he enjoyed being in her vicinity. Growing careless, he strolled by one of those multiple mirrors in Filene's and was stunned to see her reflection along with his own. Swivelling away, he almost collided with her, his right hand and her left hand touched briefly as they turned towards each other, so close that he smelled her perfume or cologne, something light and airy and spring-like. The scent compounded his confusion and embarrassment. "Sorry," he muttered, aware of her mouth slightly open in surprise, her eyes startlingly blue, the blue of a child's crayon. Flustered, he stumbled away, cheeks flaming, disgusted with himself, swearing silently, damn it, damn it. Was his cover blown? His face known, his anonymity gone for ever? He wondered as he left the store whether he should risk following her again. If he didn't, how would he ever meet her? The question surprised him. Why should he want to meet her? Shrugging the thought away, he headed for the parking garage, eager to get home, to seek the solace of the bottle.

Vowing to be extra careful, hoping she would not remember him, he followed her for the rest of the week. He refused to speculate about why he continued to observe her. Did not want to figure out his motives or reasons. All he knew was that she gave a purpose to his afternoons. He was pleased by the sight of her, the way she moved, her habit of touching her hair lightly now and then, her head tilted slightly.

On Friday, he knew that he would not see her again until the following Monday and he took more chances, shortening the distances between them. Then drew away, afraid of another encounter. Yet wanting an encounter.

Standing on the first level, he saw her come out of Miss Emily's Styles below. From this distance, she seemed forlorn, lonely, abandoned. An immense pity welled in him. *I told them she gave me the key*, Harry Flowers had said.

Getting on the escalator, he floated pleasantly downwards. He glanced up as he prepared to step off the bottom step, saw the girl across the lobby looking hesitant, as if she was wondering what to do next. More than hesitant, sad.

That's when he tripped and fell. Did not really trip. The trick knee that had kept him out of basketball suddenly gave way as he stepped off the escalator, went all hollow on him, and he was propelled forwards by the moving step, falling finally as if from a vast height, his nose brushing the tile floor, his elbow singing with pain as it struck the floor. Humiliated as he lay on the floor, wondering if his nose was broken, his arm aching as he raised his fingers to touch his nose — was it broken, bleeding? — he was relieved at the absence of blood. Disgusted, however, he did not raise his head, did not want to look up and see anybody, especially the girl, as he felt a crowd gathering, feet scuffling, heard murmurs and a clear child's voice saying: *He faw down*. No blood, nose intact. He opened his eyes and saw the small forest of legs around him and began to protest, as he muttered, "I'm all right, I'm all right, my trick knee," rising slowly by degrees, his nose numb, checking it with his hand, still no blood, his elbow still ringing with pain. Shamefaced, cheeks pounding, trying to ignore the faces around him, some sympathetic, others amused, old people, young people. He was surprised at the size of the crowd and looked to where he had seen the girl standing. She was gone. He breathed a sigh of thanks. Maybe she had not seen him fall so ingloriously, maybe had turned away before he went crashing to the floor.

"You okay?" A security guard in cop's uniform frowned as she regarded him, waving off the small crowd at the same time.

"Sure," Buddy said. "My trick knee." The words echoed in his mind as if he had said them a million times in the last few minutes. Maybe he had. "I'm fine," he assured the guard, wanting to get away. Walking away, in fact, even as he said the words, but carefully, not wanting to fall down again, second time in three minutes.

Responding to a sudden urgency for fresh air, grateful that his knee had righted itself and that he was barely limping, he headed for the nearest exit, aware of the eyes of the gathering at the escalator following him.

The air on the sidewalk was pleasantly bracing and he inhaled sharply, rubbing his elbow as if the pain could be eradicated that way. His nose was still numb but did not seem broken. He touched it tentatively.

"Does it hurt badly?"

He turned at the voice and saw the girl standing there, Jane Jerome, frowning, face tender with concern.

More blushing, more blood bouncing around in his cheeks. "It's okay," he said. "My trick knee." Damn it: *my trick knee* again. Shame suffused him once more as he realized she had seen him fall down so stupidly, after all.

"I fell down once, too," she offered. "My first day at Burnside after we moved there?" The curl of a question mark at the end of the sentence touched her words with beauty. "My heel broke and here I am, in a new school, right, and I start off by falling down in front of everybody . . ."

Rubbing his elbow, listening to her voice, looking at the

122

lips speaking those words, Buddy Walker fell instantly and irrevocably in love with Jane Jerome. At exactly 2:46 p.m. on a Friday afternoon in May at the mall in downtown Wickburg.

She had had her crushes, her tragic loves, her worshippings from afar, but never anything like this. There had been unattainable Jeremy Madison, who played the lead in the school's abbreviated version of *Grease*, and made her feel weak when he passed her in the corridor and sent her heart into scary palpitations when his bare arm brushed her bare arm once in the cafeteria. He was one of the unattainables among many: for instance, the entire Burnside High School football team, with whom she fell impossibly in love one glorious Saturday afternoon as they headed for the huddle, mysterious and glamorous in their helmets, their faces glistening with sweat, a love that lasted no more than the length of the game but inducing in her body small sweet longings and strange intimate warmths. Then Timmy Kearns. Her first and only date. The agony and the ecstasy, like the title of that old movie. Both terrible and beautiful. She had adored him at a distance for weeks and he finally asked her to the movies. Sweet ecstasy, head in a whirl, breathless, could not concentrate on homework, got that awful C in maths. Timmy Kearns had turned out to be barely articulate, not shy or bashful but, frankly, kind of stupid. He kept scratching one particular spot on his head. Scratched and scratched and scratched. Practically ignored her, too, although they sat together on the bus, stood in line at the movies, sat next to each other in the theatre. He never looked her in the eyes. Not even once. He never called her again, either. Which crushed her beyond belief. Not because she had any *desire* to go out with him again but because not being asked out on a *second* date was worse than no date at all, as if somehow you had failed miserably. Patti and Leslie sympathized with her — this was before the vandalism had changed everything — but she still felt ashamed, especially when Timmy Kearns who had been shooting her admiring glances for weeks suddenly began to ignore her altogether, even when they once met face-to-face carrying their trays of food in the cafeteria, with practically the entire school watching.

So this thing — she had not yet given it a name — with Buddy Walker was not like any of the other times she had lost her heart. In fact, she did not feel as though she had lost her heart but had found it at last. As if, until now, she did not know she had a heart, not that kind of heart anyway. It began with empathy — she had shared his embarrassment when he fell down at the bottom of the escalator and she saw the stricken look on his face even at that distance. She had left the scene because he looked familiar — she had seen him somewhere before, maybe at Burnside High — and it's always more embarrassing when you fall or do something like that in front of people you know, rather than strangers.

Then observing him outside as he rubbed his elbow, looking so dismal, as if he had been abandoned by his family and friends, good-looking but something sad and wistful about him, she had spoken to him spontaneously, surprising herself even as the words came out of her mouth. She had then made up that crazy story about her heel breaking. To make him feel better. Why should she have wanted to make this boy, this stranger, feel better? She did not know, but a small curling inside her body responded to him, a leap in her veins when he looked at her, a look on his face that she could not interpret. The nearest she could come to describing that look was this: as if he was listening not only to her voice but to some sweet music coming from somewhere. And the somewhere was her.

She did not fall in love with him for another twenty minutes — it happened while they were chewing pizza with pepperoni at the Pizza Palace in the mall — although she did not know it as love until later.

They became a couple, going steady. Walking along, hand in hand. They loved to walk. On the sidewalks of Burnside and Wickburg, along the banks of the Grange River, through the lanes of Jedson Park, but most of all at the mall. They were conscious of themselves as a couple, existing for themselves alone, wanting to be alone, yet aware of the people around them, wanting to be seen by others, glad to parade their love for all the world to observe.

She felt a pride of possession when she met fellows and girls she knew and managed to draw him closer to her. Once, they confronted Patti Amarelli and Leslie Cairns coming out of the Poster Store and Jane revelled in their envious glances, their undisguised awe as she and Buddy walked past. She could not keep herself from looking at him, stealing sly glances as they walked along. She loved the way he brushed back an errant lock of hair from his forehead or looked at her suddenly with a surprised expression on his face, as if he had just discovered her by his side and was delighted by the discovery. She could not stop touching him. Brushed against him, ran her hand along his arm, stroked that area at the base of his neck where his hairline stopped.

He became suddenly fastidious. Getting a haircut was now serious stuff, keeping his eye on the mirror as the barber snipped away, making certain every hair was in place. He had never used cologne, only simple Ivory soap, not even aftershave lotion. Now he used cologne after purchasing a bottle of Subtle at the perfume counter at Filene's. Sprayed the stuff on his cheeks and neck and arms. Wondering whether he had used too much or too little, he met Addy outside her room. She stopped, sniffed delicately, and shook her head.

"Buddy," she said, grinning, "you've got a girlfriend."

Stunned, he said: "How do you know?"

"That smell can only mean one thing." Seeing his frown of embarrassment, she smiled indulgently: "I think it's great, Buddy. You don't have to go into details about it. But let me give you a helpful hint . . ."

The hint involved the cologne. "Don't spray the cologne directly on yourself," she advised. "Spray it into the air and then walk into it." Which she did as a demonstration. "That way you won't knock her down with the smell, it will be subtle like its name and creep up on her."

Grateful for her advice, he decided to tell her a bit about Jane. Not too much, afraid this rare thing he and Jane shared might be jinxed if he went on at length. Cautiously, he told Addy the bare essentials: her name, how they met. Addy did not push for details, listening attentively, a strange expression on her face, which he later realized was tenderness. "I'm so happy for you, Buddy," she said, touching his shoulder lightly.

Maybe Addy and I will become friends, after all, he thought, astonished at what love could do.

He became aware of the beauties of the world around him. Colours more brilliant, sunsets breathtaking, neon signs dazzling. Laughed easily at jokes, laughed at stuff that was not really *that* funny, like the stupid jokes Randy Pierce told at lunchtime in the cafeteria. Caught his reflection in a mirror sometimes and saw the idiotic grin on his face and didn't care.

Certain nights or afternoons, he and Jane did not see each other. Need to do homework, Jane said. And Buddy found himself doing homework, too. Sometimes they met in the Burnside Public Library and did their homework in the reading room, sitting side by side, and he managed to do the lessons despite the distraction of her presence. He felt older, more responsible, knowing that someday, if he was lucky, he would marry Jane Jerome, become her husband, a father — the prospect enough to take his breath away.

Jane passed lovely weightless days, floating almost, as if her feet barely touched the earth, capable of drifting off into the sky like a balloon and never being seen again, which would be awful because life on earth was so incredibly sweet. Spring exploded in a cascade of bird songs and flowers and she felt like a flower herself, opening like the slow-motion flowers in a Disney movie. Ridiculous, of course, but not really. Walking along beside Buddy, she felt like a woman, yet irresistibly girlish at the same time. Wanted to flounce in dresses, feel silk next to her skin, nylon on her legs. Liked the sound of her clicking heels on the sidewalk or on the tile floor of the mall. Delighted with herself, hugged herself a lot. She had a million secret places in her body that had not existed before she met Buddy and wanted him to explore them all, find them all out because she sensed that, in the finding out, there would be some kind of bliss involved. She often found that her eyes were brimming with tears and yet she was not crying. Instead of showers, she took long baths, trailed her fingertips along her flesh, held her breasts in her hands and they seemed to ache.

They could not get enough of each other, which made it necessary for them to have rules. Unspoken rules but rules all the same, declaring boundaries, how far they could go, by some mutual instinct. How long kisses should be, how far touching and caressing could proceed. Cupping her breast drove him wild, thick juices in his mouth, the threat of a sudden embarrassing eruption. But never both breasts and never inside her sweater. They embraced lovingly in a sweet tumble of bodies. Buddy never pushed beyond those silent limits, although one night he stiffened in the middle of the longest kiss they ever had, their mouths meshed, tongues wrapped around each other, his hand kneading her breast, and he fell away from her, shuddering, then became still, silent. She reached out in the dark — they were in the back seat of his mother's car — and touched his cheek, felt moisture there, realized that tears had spilled from his eyes. And took him in her arms, tenderly, delicately, loving him for those tears as she had never loved him before.

Yet, there were mysteries about him that she could not solve. He grew silent on occasion, deep in thought, unreachable, which panicked her, afraid that he would somehow slip out of her grasp or her life. She wanted him to meet her parents but he always made some excuse for not doing so. He seldom picked her up at her home, but when he did he blew the horn and waited for her to come out of the house. Most often, they met downtown, at the library, at the mall. Although this meant that she had to bus it to downtown Wickburg, she didn't mind. He also had to bus it from the other side of Wickburg and needed a transfer to make the trip. She was vaguely disturbed but her accelerating heart, the small, sweet gasps of breath when he came into sight, obliterated her misgivings.

She pondered whether she should tell him about the trashing. Once or twice she brought up the subject. Subtly, she thought. Said: "Some terrible things happen these days, Buddy." She loved saying his name. "Like rape and trashing."

A startled look on his face, he turned away from her. Did not follow her lead. Changed the subject, in fact. Pointed out something or other in the park.

128

Another time, she said: "Some people have no respect for others."

"What do you mean?"

"Well, like other people's property. Wrecking it, trashing." That word again — *trashing*. Why couldn't she just come out and tell him about what had happened? About Karen in the hospital. Was she afraid that this would somehow alienate him, the way the trashing had come between her and Patti and Leslie? But what she and Buddy shared was different from those friendships, if they had been friendships at all.

Why, then, didn't she take a chance? Did that hidden part of him deter her? Or did it have to do with Harry Flowers?

There, she had said his name. Ever since she met Buddy, she had relegated Harry Flowers to the dim corners of her mind, refusing to think about him. Could not allow herself to think of him. She knew that Harry Flowers went to Wickburg Regional, where Buddy was also a student. Harry Flowers was a senior and Buddy a junior. Did Buddy know Harry Flowers? Did they nod to each other in the cafeteria? Buddy used to play basketball — had they been teammates? Stop it, stop it, she told herself. Stop asking those questions. Wickburg Regional was a huge high school, thousands of students, drawing them not only from that city but the surrounding towns as well. It was possible that they did not know each other, had not even *heard* of each other.

Revelling in the glow of Buddy's love, she managed, most of the time, to set aside her concerns about Harry Flowers. Except for her visits to Karen in the hospital, she could almost believe that the trashing had happened in another place, another time of her life, a time that was over and done with. Harry Flowers also belonged to that time.

She also realized that the foul odour was gone from her life along with the thought of Harry Flowers.

Thank God for Buddy Walker, she murmured one afternoon in the hospital chapel.

As if saying a prayer.

The first time Jane mentioned the word *trashing*, Buddy flinched, then turned away in self-defence, his thoughts racing wildly as he anticipated what her next words would be. He had to head her off, change the subject. Luckily, his eyes fastened on a funny-sad scene: A woman's shopping bag collapsed and all her groceries rolled haphazardly towards the gutter. He helped the woman retrieve the groceries and stood patiently with her, holding the soup cans, until her husband pulled up in his car.

Jane brought up the subject of trashing once or twice more and each time he was able to side-step or change the subject. He had the distinct feeling that she wanted to talk about the trashing at her house. Why did she hesitate? Why didn't she simply tell him? Terrible thought: Did she suspect that he had been involved? He shook his head in protest. How could she love him, let him hold her, kiss her, caress her, if she thought he had participated in the trashing, in hurting her sister? The possibility of having Jane find out that he was guilty after all, was an ominous shadow in their relationship. The shadow that kept him drinking, even though his desire for booze had lessened since he had met her. He had to be more devious now, of course. Had to keep Jane from the knowledge of his drinking. He worried about his breath, wished that he could buy a guaranteed breath-freshener. He chewed all kinds of gum, which he hated, the taste too sweet and cloying. Sometimes held his breath or breathed through his nose when he was close to her. Felt her stiffen on occasion when they kissed, and wondered if she could taste the gin on his tongue. The simple thing, of course, would be to stop drinking altogether. But drinking these days enhanced the happiness that Jane had brought to him. The marvel of liquor: changing with his desires, magnifying the good things of his life. Drinking gently, not gulping frantically any more but sipping slowly, bringing into focus the wonder of Jane and their love, allowing him visions of the two of them together through the coming years.

No more the intensity, the desperate quality of drinking but a different kind now, dream-like, gentle.

Stepping through the revolving doors of Filene's one afternoon, they emerged on the sidewalk and met his mother. Stunned glances, time suspended for the fraction of a minute as they stared at each other. He stumbled through the introductions: "Jane . . . my mother . . . Mom . . . Jane Jerome . . ." His mother, elegant as usual, every hair in place although a windy day, paused, eyebrows raised in curiosity, glancing at him enquiringly as if to ask: How long has this been going on? And he realized, sadly, the chasm between their lives, how they did not connect any more. She had not mentioned the retreat since that meeting in her bedroom. He had not asked her about it. Felt dismayed now.

"It's lovely to meet you," his mother said. He was proud of her stylish manner. Leaning confidentially towards Jane, she said: "Buddy has been so happy lately that I thought there must be something wonderful going on in his life. And now I see why . . ."

Which inflicted further guilt. He should have told her about Jane. Then thought: Why hadn't she enquired if she saw how much I had changed? He saw that life was never simple.

Walking along later, whipped by the winds, Jane's hand tucked in his and both their hands in his jacket pocket, he thought about his mother and father — and love. How they

*131*

had probably once been swept with the same kind of love he and Jane shared. Did love change over the years? Become diluted, pale? Or did it deepen? Or did it become less equal? His father had fallen in love with someone else. But not his mother. He knew how devastated his life would become if Jane were to leave him. Is that what had happened to his mother, abandoned by her husband, the man she loved, the man who was supposed to love her and keep on loving her through the years? Until death do us part. And his father: he was in love now with this woman, Fay, enough in love with her to leave his family. A terrible thing but — but did he feel towards that woman, Fay, the way Buddy felt about Jane? Suppose he had met Jane when he was involved with someone else and . . .

"What's the matter, Buddy?" Jane asked, pressing against him, warding off the wind, her hand still in his, warm and moist.

"Nothing," he said, confused by his thoughts, by the strange thing love could be.

"Your mother seems very nice," she said. "She's beautiful . . ."

Right. But my father still left her, he thought.

That night, he said to Jane: "I will love you for ever." Making a pledge, solemn, enduring.

He waited for her response, waited for her to say:

I will love you for ever, too.

But she didn't speak, her head inclined, her hair brushing his cheek, the scent of her shampoo radiant and fresh.

He waited. Then said: "Jane?"

"Yes?"

"I said: I will love you for ever."

She nestled closer to him.

"Will you love me for ever, too?" Sad, because he had to ask.

132

She drew back, puzzled, a frown creasing her forehead. "Don't you know that by now?"

He hugged her to him, trembling inside, having just seen, as if in a light-bulb flash, how empty and meaningless his life would be without her.

Shuddering, he drew her to him, kissed her passionately, unendingly, until they drew apart and she whispered tremulously: "Oh, Buddy."

The whole world in her voice as she spoke his name.

"When are we going to meet this mystery man of yours?" her father asked at the dinner table.

"He's not a mystery man, Dad," she replied. "He's just . . . shy." Fumbling for the word *shy*, unable to find another word for Buddy's reluctance to meet her parents.

"Maybe there's no Buddy at all," Artie said. "Maybe he's a figment of her imagination, Dad." At times, there were flashes of the brat who had been her brother before the trashing. Although he still did not play his video games, he did not have nightmares any more and had again joined the brat pack on the streets and sidewalks of the neighbourhood.

"He's real, all right," Jane said, remembering his touch, the way he had tremblingly cupped her breast the night before. "Give us time . . ."

"He may be a very nice boy, Jane," her father said, an edge to his voice, "but I think we should meet him. I don't like the idea of having you dash out of the house and into his car . . ."

"His mother's car," she amended.

"I'm not talking about whose car," her father said, voice sharp now. "I'm talking about a boy you're spending a lot of time with, that you're all dreamy-eyed about, and we've never met him. He's never set foot into this house . . ."

"We're just trying to show you that we care about you," her mother said, gently, placatingly.

"Don't you trust me?" Jane asked.

"Of course we trust you, hon," her mother said. "But is it so unreasonable to want to meet this boy you think is so wonderful? Don't you want to share it all with us?"

Brushing her hair later in her room, she knew that her relationship with Buddy would remain incomplete until two things happened: telling him about the trashing and introducing him to her parents.

Both happened unexpectedly that same night.

She and Buddy had just stepped off the bus that brought them back to Burnside from Wickburg when they encountered her mother and father strolling along Main Street after seeing a movie at the Downtown Cinema. Flustered, embarrassed, but delighted, she managed the introductions and then stood silently proud as Buddy, very politely, shook their hands, murmuring, "Pleased to meet you," a bit shyly, stammering endearingly. Looking at him through her parents' eyes, she was pleased at what she saw: a good-looking and polite young man, neat in his tan cords and brown sports shirt. Her pleasure increased when her father said: "Hope you'll drop around the house sometime," and Buddy answered: "Thank you, sir, I will."

Perhaps that meeting was the reason why, a few minutes later, Jane told him about the trashing as they sat on a park bench at the edge of Jedson Park, basking in the warmth and fragrance of the spring night. The words popped out of her mouth without plan or rehearsal.

"My house was trashed a while ago," she said. "These guys wrecked it. My sister is still in the hospital, in a coma. She fell down the cellar stairs. Or was pushed . . ." Could say no more, her throat constricting.

His arm went around her shoulder, gripped her tightly.

"I know," he said, voice hoarse as if his own throat were constricted.

"You knew all the time?" she asked, turning to him. "Why didn't you say something?"

"I didn't know how much it would hurt you to talk about it," he said. "I wanted you to do it in your own time."

"It was terrible, Buddy," she said, shuddering, relieved that the topic was out in the open and that he had not withdrawn from her. Her earlier reluctance to talk about the trashing was replaced now by a need to talk, to tell him what had happened from her point of view, not from what he had read in the newspaper or heard from other people. As she spoke he kept shaking his head, frowning, wincing sometimes as if her anguish was his own, as if he, too, had been damaged by the trashers. She had never loved him more than at this moment.

"Poor Buddy," she said, stroking his cheek. "Don't feel so bad. My family's fine now. The doctors are sure that Karen will come to soon. All the tests show that there is no brain damage." Actually, the doctors weren't sure at all — but she wanted to offer him consolation because he seemed so sad.

Later, when he left her at the steps of her house, he kissed her with a prolonged intensity that left her breathless, as if he would never kiss her again.

"I love you," she whispered as she slipped out of his arms. She had spoken those words to him a thousand times but never with such passion and fervour. "Thank you for being so wonderful . . ." Dashing into the house, she was exhilarated by the evening's events. But later, slipping on her pyjamas, she wondered if she should have asked him about Harry Flowers.

While Buddy, at home, desperately drank himself into a

stupor and then oblivion for the first time since he had met her.

They had just left the Pizza Palace at the mall two days later when he spotted Harry Flowers stepping off the escalator. Buddy stiffened, looked around wildly for a place to hide although he knew there was no way to escape. He turned towards Jane, trying to block Harry's view of her and she leaned against him, misinterpreting his movement, thinking he wanted to get closer to her body. She looked up at him, smiling that self-satisfied smile he loved to see on her face. Taking her elbow, he steered her away from the escalator and she allowed herself to be navigated. He could not resist looking back over his shoulder, however, risking a quick glance to assure himself that Harry had come and gone without seeing them. The pizza with pepperoni became lead in his stomach when he saw Harry standing twenty-five feet away, a weird and evil smile on his face as he waved to Buddy.

Buddy did not wave back, did not acknowledge Harry's presence but manoeuvred Jane around the corner, sick to his stomach suddenly.

That night, at home, he waited for the telephone to ring. He roamed restlessly around the house, looking out of the windows, turning the television on, watching it a while, then turning it off again. Harry Flowers: his nemesis, his downfall. After Jane had told him of the trashing on that park bench, he had been waiting for her to mention his name. His name had been in the newspaper. Jane had certainly read that story and seen it. Buddy waited, in fear that she would say: "Harry Flowers — he goes to Wickburg Regional, too. Do you know him?" She had not mentioned him, but ever since he had endured a special kind of torture when they were together. He felt trapped, helpless, sensing that he was on the verge of losing Jane Jerome.

The telephone rang as he went into the bathroom. He let it ring, standing motionless, hoped it would keep on ringing and nobody would answer. Which was impossible, of course. Phone rings, someone answers.

"Buddy, it's for you," Addy called.

He picked up the phone in the living room, out of earshot of Addy in her room and his mother going over household accounts in the den.

"Hey, Buddy, what's going on?" Harry asked. That sly insinuating voice.

"Nothing," Buddy said. Maybe he had not seen him and Jane together, after all.

"Saw you at the mall today, too bad we didn't have a chance to talk . . ." Voice casual now, almost too casual. But at least no phoney accent.

"Was that you? I thought it was you but wasn't sure . . ."

"Oh, it was me all right, Buddy, but you seemed in a hurry. Either that or you didn't want to talk to me right then . . ."

"Well, I *was* in sort of a hurry . . ." And let the sentence end, blowing air out of his mouth.

"You were with a girl, Buddy. You keeping secrets from Harry? Got a girlfriend and haven't told Harry about it?"

"She's not my girl," Buddy said. "Just a girl I know. We have a pizza together once in a while. I think we went to a movie once."

"You *think* you went to a movie? Aren't you sure, Buddy? Is your memory that bad? I mean, did you go to a movie with this girl or didn't you?"

"Yeah, that's right, we did go to a movie. I mean, it wasn't really a date . . ."

*How can I get out of this stupid conversation?*

137

"Who is she, Buddy? Anybody at school? Anybody I know?"

"No, you wouldn't know her."

"Why wouldn't I know her? I mean, I know a lot of people, Buddy, and you don't know everybody I know, do you? So how do you know I wouldn't know her?"

Jesus, Buddy thought, perspiration gathering in his armpits, his palms, his crotch, everywhere.

"Well, she's new in town. So I figured you wouldn't know her. I mean, she doesn't know many people here and she doesn't go to Wickburg Regional . . ."

"Where does she go then?"

Buddy's hand was so slippery with sweat that the telephone almost slid from his grasp.

"I don't know."

"You don't know? Let me get this straight. You're going out with this girl, right, you eat pizza with her, right, you go to the movies with her and you don't know where she goes to school?"

"She doesn't like to talk about it. About school, I mean. She's having problems transferring from out of town and would prefer not to discuss it."

Buddy's mind was racing so fast, to lie, to fabricate, that he felt dizzy.

"Poor kid," Harry said, and Buddy tried to pin down whether Harry's sympathy was real or synthetic. "Know what, Buddy? I just caught a glimpse of her. I mean, you were blocking my view of her, for crissakes. But she looked familiar. I don't know. I've been trying to place her ever since. Something about her. I've seen her before somewhere . . ."

"Is that right?" Could Harry hear the hollowness in his voice?

"Yes, it's one of those things. You know, like a name on the tip of your tongue and you can't quite remember . . ."

138

"Sure, I know what you mean." Was Harry toying with him, teasing him?

"Listen, what is her name, anyway? Maybe that will solve my memory problem . . ."

"Her name?"

"Yes, you know. What's on her birth certificate. What she signs on her theme papers at school, what she puts down at the end of her letters."

He knows, of course, he knew all along.

Reckless suddenly, figuring he had nothing whatever to lose, he said: "Guess, Harry."

"Guess what?"

"Guess her name. You're good at games. Go ahead, guess."

*Let him say her name, if he knows it. I'm not saying it.*

"Give me a clue, then."

"Like what?"

"Like her initials. The initial of her first name."

"Nope, you've got to guess the whole name."

Big pause. Buddy almost smiled. Harry liked cat-and-mouse stuff and he was being given a taste of it.

Harry sighed. "This is going to be hard. I mean, there are twenty-six letters in the alphabet and her name has to start with only one of them. I'll tell you what, Buddy. I'll have to think about it. I'll have to give it some time. Let me think about it tonight and I'll call tomorrow and give you my guesses. Okay?"

"Okay," Buddy said, trying to disguise the relief in his voice.

"But you know what might be even better?"

"What's that, Harry?"

"Maybe I should call up Jane Jerome and ask her about that fellow I saw her with this afternoon at the mall. Think she'd make me guess?"

139

Harry hung up almost before the word *guess* was out of his mouth and Buddy Walker stood there, the dialling tone like a small explosion in his ear.

Harry did not call back for two days and Buddy became anxious. Knowing Harry, familiar with his tricks and techniques, he wondered whether he was planning one of his exploits, as he playfully called them. On the third day, he decided to confront Harry and waited for him at the doorway to the school cafeteria before lunch break.

Harry was alone, for which Buddy was grateful. He stepped in front of him, planted himself in front of him in fact, barring his entry into the cafeteria.

"I want to talk to you," Buddy said.

"I'm really starved, Buddy," Harry said. "I hear they're having meat loaf. You know how I love meat loaf. And I hate to talk while I'm eating . . ."

The smirk on his face, the acne always there but always overlooked because of Harry's manner, the cool appraising eyes, the what-the-hell way he stood.

"This'll only take a minute," Buddy said. He had seen Harry talking a mile a minute many times while eating but knew that this was another pretence, another game he enjoyed playing.

Harry lifted his shoulders in surrender, indicating his patience with friends.

"Okay, Harry, so the girl is Jane Jerome."

Harry raised his nose to the air. "That meat loaf smells delicious." Buddy could detect no aroma at all in the air, only the stale smell of the corridor itself. "Why were you avoiding me at the mall, Buddy? Why didn't you at least wave? Maybe even introduce me?"

Aghast, Buddy said: "For crissakes, Harry, you were in court for wrecking her house. Your name was in the newspaper. And you wanted to be introduced?" Buddy bowed in exaggerated fashion. "Hey, there, Jane Jerome, let me introduce Harry Flowers. Name sound familiar? He's the guy who trashed your house . . ."

Harry smiled his lazy smile. "And then I would say: And how about Buddy Walker here? Has he mentioned that he was with me when we trashed the house and took special pains with your bedroom?" Frowning at Buddy: "Did you or didn't you piss on her wall? Or did you just vomit on the carpet?"

Speechless, Buddy turned away, all appetite gone, actually smelling the meat loaf wafting from the cafeteria but finding it repugnant. When he turned back to Harry, his face was only inches away, Harry leaning in to him.

"What the hell are you doing with her?" Harry asked. "You some kind of madman? Looking for trouble?" Then relenting a bit, withdrawing: "How did all this get started anyway?"

"I called her up. To tell her I was sorry."

"And she decided to go out with you?" Disbelief in his voice.

"No, she doesn't know it was me who called. But when I heard her voice on the telephone . . ." And he told Harry, who kept sniffing the air for aromas of meat loaf, about following her in the mall and falling down and the rest of it.

"I love her, Harry. And she loves me," he finished, lamely.

"But what happens when she finds out, Buddy? What happens then?" He seemed sincere now, as if he really cared.

"She won't find out," Buddy said, his words more convincing than his feelings.

"Of course she will," Harry said, "Wickburg's a small

place and Burnside is even smaller. Is her sister still in the hospital? Still in a coma?"

Buddy nodded, trapped, knowing what question Harry was going to ask before he asked it, because he had asked himself that question a thousand times. And Harry asked it:

"What happens when she comes out of the coma? When Jane Jerome says, 'Karen, I'd like you to meet my boyfriend, the guy I love.' And she looks at you and remembers that night?"

"I'm not sure if she saw me that night," he said. "I was upstairs when she came in the house."

"You're in a no-win situation, Buddy," he said. "Sooner or later, Jane Jerome's going to find out you were in the house that night, whether her sister remembers you or not. You picked the wrong girl to fall in love with. The wrong girl and the wrong time . . ."

"She's worth the chance, Harry," he said.

Harry stretched his arms, flexed his shoulders. "Ah, smell that meat loaf," he said, sniffing the air again. "Time to indulge the appetite."

"You go ahead, I'm not hungry," Buddy said. Even if he had been hungry, he would not have wanted Harry Flowers's company during lunch.

As Harry walked away, he shot Buddy a glance over his shoulder.

"Another thing you should worry about, Buddy," he said. "Suppose somebody decides to tell Jane Jerome all about you and what you did to her room?"

He left Buddy standing there, like a target on a shooting range with no place to hide.

The whiteness of the ceiling woke her up.

But that was silly.

Ceilings, not even white ones, didn't wake people up.

What did then?

She didn't know. Noise, alarm clocks, Mom calling from downstairs: "Get going, Karen, you'll be late for school." Those things woke you up.

But not ceilings.

Besides, she was looking down at the ceiling and ceilings should be *up*, not down.

She closed her eyes, demolishing the ceiling, but the darkness of her closed lids threatened to engulf her, eat her up, and she opened her eyes again.

The ceiling was still white but this time it was above her where it should be and she saw a crack in the ceiling, like a small streak of lightning caught for ever in white.

She blinked her eyes rapidly, testing them, to see if they worked, which was also silly but somehow necessary. She tried to move. Or rather she thought about moving, again testing, although she couldn't figure out why she should be testing herself like this. And why should she be here?

But where was *here*?

That's when the panic hit, like a wave engulfing her, swinging her up and over so that she felt her body lifting, straining at the sheet but more than the sheet, something pulling at her arm, her arm imprisoned, held fast, tied to a terrible something next to the bed, from which came a hum or a blip, she wasn't sure which.

She knew suddenly with the force of a door slamming in her face that she was in a hospital and she had an image of stairs tumbling around her, up and down, but the memory and the panic were like shivers now, even her blood seemed to be shivering like icy worms that had been disturbed under her flesh and she was about to scream when she plunged into darkness and everything was wiped away like crazy drawings on a blackboard.

         °

Jane found out about Buddy's drinking in the lobby of the Wickburg Cinema when a half-pint bottle of gin dropped out of his jacket pocket as he stooped to pick up one of her pearl earrings that had fallen to the floor.

Later, Buddy realized he had been stupid to have carried the bottle while on a date with Jane. Before leaving home, he had, on impulse, slipped the bottle into his jacket pocket. Just in case. In case of what? He didn't know. But he was jumpy. Had to be prepared. Prepared for what? For anything. In case. In case of what? In case Karen suddenly recovered and Jane wanted to take him to the hospital to meet her. In case Harry double-crossed him, made a phone call to Jane, for instance. In case, for crissakes.

Jane was stunned when she saw the bottle tumble out of his jacket and shatter on the lobby floor. She knew immediately that it was some kind of liquor even though it was as clear as water as it spread across the polished tile.

Still she asked:

"What's that?"

Buddy, speechless, on one knee, stared at the mess of broken glass and spreading gin.

"Bud . . . dee," she said, drawing out his name. "What were you doing with that bottle in your pocket?" Conscious now of the people streaming by, looking at them curiously, someone giggling, someone else snickering.

"I . . ." That was all Buddy could utter, not wanting to look at Jane, and not wanting to look at the mess either, and wondering what the hell he was supposed to do with it. He began to pick up the shards of glass, handling them gingerly to avoid cutting himself and then looked around for a waste container, couldn't see one through the legs of people passing by. He looked up, dreading to see the look on her face, the look that would match the horror of her voice. But she was gone.

Standing by his mother's car in the parking lot, Jane felt as though the pieces of a puzzle had come together to form a picture, not a really clear picture but a picture anyway. Of Buddy as a drinker, maybe an alcoholic. She wasn't sure about any of that. Yet there had been clues that she had ignored simply because they had not made any sense in relation to the Buddy she knew and loved. The smell on his breath sometimes, what she thought was some kind of medicine. His incessant chewing of gum or Life Savers after he had admitted once that he hated gum and Life Savers. His slurred speech on occasion. For a time, she actually thought he had a speech defect that he was trying to cover up. All unconnected in her mind, her suspicions coming and going so swiftly that she had barely acknowledged them. Waiting for him now, the crowd thinning out, thankful that he had parked under a floodlight, she winced as she thought of him kneeling on the floor of that lobby, his head hanging down, like the first time she had seen him at the mall. God, how she loved him. But that love was now a lonely aching that had found its way into every crevice of her body.

She saw him coming slowly across the parking lot, head down, like a little boy going home to be punished. Tenderness entered her aching and brought tears to her eyes.

"Oh, Buddy, poor Buddy," she murmured, a bit of pity mixed with the tenderness. Maybe she had leaped to wrong conclusions, maybe she had exaggerated those clues. All she wanted to do was to gather him into her arms and kiss away all the bad things in their lives.

The argument went on for more than an hour in the car in the parking lot, the theatre crowd long gone, the night turning chilly and the wind kicking stray bits of paper across the pavement.

"But it's not a problem," Buddy insisted. "I drink because

I like to drink. And if I stop drinking, then that's admitting that it was a problem. See what I mean?" He was amazed at his sharpness, how he could be so logical and persuasive, although doubt remained on Jane's face. And a distant look in her eyes, as if she were contemplating things she could not articulate.

"But it's not natural, Buddy," she said, trying to remain calm and keep her voice reasonable, disguising the panic that had her in its thrall. "You're in high school. You should not be drinking at all. All right, maybe at a party or something. But not as much as you do . . ."

He frowned, wondering what she would think if she knew how much he actually drank. He had told her that he liked a drink now and then while doing his homework and to relax after school. "Not very much," he had said.

"How much is not very much?"

His thoughts scurried. "Oh, maybe a pint every few days." Knowing he had to walk a delicate line here, not saying too much or too little. When he saw her face stiffen, he knew he had gone too far. And tried to amend it: "I never really count. I don't even think it's that much . . ."

Her questions were unending. Where do you buy the stuff? How can you buy it when you're not old enough? Who sells it to you?

He answered guardedly, telling her the truth but shading it. Did not tell her about the times he could not connect with Crumbs and lurked in the park with the bums, feeling like a bum himself. Did not tell her about the hangovers in the morning when he stumbled his way to school, waiting to get to his locker where he had stashed a bottle. Did not tell her that right now, this minute as they were talking, as he was insisting that he drank because he liked it and could give it up any time, he was desperate for a drink, he was dying for the sweet balm of the booze.

146

"Why did you take that bottle to the movies tonight?" she asked, honestly curious.

He lifted his shoulders in a weary shrug. Could not tell her the truth and could not think of a lie. He hated the word *lie. Excuse* was a better word. He could not think of an excuse that she would accept.

"When you went to the john once, was that so you could have a drink from the bottle?" She remembered how he had returned chewing Dentine furiously.

"No," he said. Lying. He was a liar.

"You're lying," she said, her voice flat with accusation and regret.

He turned to look at her and saw her as the enemy. The girl he loved but still an enemy. Her eyes flashing with anger and something else besides the anger. Sadness maybe.

"Okay, I lied because I didn't want you to feel bad," he said.

"But why did you have to go and have a drink of whisky during the movie?"

"It's not whisky. It's gin."

"It's liquor," she said.

"Because it makes me feel better," he said, blurting out the truth at last. "Because the world is sometimes a rotten place and it takes away the rotten things . . ." The rotten things he had done — like the trashing.

"How about me?" she said. "How about us? How can you say the world is rotten if we have each other?"

Tears flooded her eyes, more than tears. Sobs, her shoulders heaving, her body shuddering, uncontrolled. She had not cried like this since she was a baby, maybe never had cried like this. And then she was in his arms, encircled by him and he was murmuring against her cheek as she clutched him.

"I love you, Jane. You're not part of the rotten world

147

— you're the reason why I'm happy. You make the rotten things go away . . ."

Like the gin, she thought. I'm like liquor to him.

His love for her was a sudden rushing through his body and he saw what a wretched lonely thing his life would be without her. Worse than being without the booze. He thought of the emptiness of the days ahead if he should lose her. He started to cry, his tears joining hers as their cheeks met. "I love you, Jane," he said, his voice strangled, unrecognizable to himself. "I love you more than drinking."

Stifling her own sobs, moved beyond words at the sight of Buddy crying, his mouth crooked, his nose running, his hair dishevelled, she waited for him to say the words she longed so achingly to hear. And he said them:

"I'll stop drinking, Jane. I promise that I won't drink any more . . ."

He spent three drinkless days without any trouble at all, his desire for liquor obliterated by this second chance with Jane. Yet he admitted in a small part of his mind that there had to be a different solution. The prospect of living the remainder of his life without having another drink was impossible to contemplate. In his panic and desperation that night in the car, those words *I won't drink any more* were the final weapons he used to keep from losing her and he believed them utterly when he spoke them.

During those three days, wistfulness descended upon him like a sad mist, although he did not have any thirst for a drink or longing for its effects. However, a certain light seemed to have dimmed in his life, as if the sun were still shining but through dark clouds. Stop with the self-pity, he told himself. Jane is your sunshine, like that old song says.

Since he had started drinking seriously a few months before, he had become aware of articles on alcoholism and sometimes read them. Then he stopped reading them. He refused to take the tests the articles often contained, like on the seven or eight or nine signs of alcoholism. He had flunked too many tests in school, he didn't need to flunk any on liquor. But he became aware of the AA slogans, and in those first few days of his promise he made use of them, especially *One Day at a Time* and *Easy Does It*. He cut himself off from thoughts of the future. He concentrated instead on today, not tomorrow, or next week. The trick seemed to work, at least for the time being.

Another trick: the bottle of gin in the garage, which he had stashed away before the promise and was untouched. He had always tried to keep an extra bottle on hand, remembering the times of panic when he didn't have any liquor in the house or no money or Sunday when the stores were closed. (Once he raided his father's liquor cabinet but had been disappointed to find one lonely bottle of whisky, almost empty so that he could risk only a quick brief gulp.) As a result, he had tried to keep a spare on hand and that spare remained at this moment in the garage. Three days since he had had a drink, three days of bliss with Jane — she had never been so tender, so loving, allowing him the night before to remove her blouse and bra and kiss her breasts. Let the bottle stay untouched, he said to himself that afternoon of the third day as he plunged into his homework in his room, the volume on his CD turned up so high, the walls seeming to buckle with the assault of heavy metal.

But on the fourth day, depression set in. The blues. A rotten test in English Lit. simply because he hadn't read the chapter. Came face-to-face with Harry Flowers on three occasions and Harry's face had been like a stone wall, unreadable, cold. Diarrhoea this morning, upset stomach. Jane had remained at school this afternoon, trying out for the chorus. Rain slanted against the window. A perfect set-up, he thought, for the booze but I'm not buying. Despite the blues, the down feeling, the greyness of things. He wandered into his parents' bedroom. Saw the unmade bed. An unmade bed would have been impossible when his father was still here in the house. The sadness of the tousled blankets, the pillow rumpled and punched in, brought tears to his eyes. His mother did not seem to care any more. She had not mentioned going on retreat again and he had neglected to ask her if she had changed her mind. He should take more interest in his mother, Addy, and what was happening in all their lives. More reasons for the blues.

He wandered into the garage strictly out of curiosity, to see if the bottle was still there, knowing that he could not always trust his memory these days. He certainly would not take a drink from the bottle, not at this stage of events. Whistling softly, he reached under the usual pile of debris and found the bottle in its brown paper bag. Took it out and looked at it. Still sealed. *Think of Jane. And one day at a time.* He slipped the bottle back into the bag and returned it to the hiding place. Then stood there, feeling sad. More than sad. Down, depressed, the pits. Indecisive.

The telephone rang, far away, in the house. Let it ring. He thought of that bottle in the bag, so close. What if he only took a sip or two, enough to soothe the edges, smooth out the rough spots? The ringing continued. *First, answer the phone. Then we'll see.*

He went into the house, fearful now that he wouldn't reach the phone in time, that whoever was on the other end of the line would hang up before he reached it. But it still rang. When he picked up the receiver, he was astonished to hear his father's voice:

"Buddy, how are you?"

Without waiting for an answer, his father went on: "I'm calling to see if we might get together."

All thoughts of the bottle in the garage vanished as Buddy heard himself saying: "Great, Dad. Any time you say. Morning, noon, or night."

One minute not there.

The next minute there.

That was the way she reached consciousness the second time. She did not know precisely how or when, knew only that she was suddenly present and alive on the planet earth, staring up at the ceiling. The ceiling had a crack in it that was strangely familiar. She directed her attention away from the ceiling to the rest of the room and knew instantly she was in a hospital, and that she had been here for a long time. She did not know *how* she knew but was certain of her knowledge, as if she had absorbed it into her system the way she absorbed the liquid seeping into her arm from the bottle suspended above her at the side of the bed. She listened to the small beeping sound and the hum of a nearby machine and closed her eyes, content to lie dreamily, hazily in the bed.

Sounds leaped in her ears, magnified, as if her ears were actually speakers in some gigantic stereo system. Footsteps padded by, a door closed, then a muffled cry, all the sounds sweet, as if she had been deaf a long time and could suddenly hear. A small scratching sound — she listened intently, trying to drown out the other noises. More than a scratching sound, a kind of whistle — of course, a bird, a robin outside her window, louder than a robin, a blue jay, possibly.

Footsteps joined the small screeching of the blue jay and she looked towards the door as a nurse entered the room. Jolly face, apple cheeks, glasses perched on her nose, and a smile of happy surprise when she saw Karen awake.

Hello, Karen wanted to say. I'm Karen Jerome and I don't know where I've been but I'm back now.

When she tried to speak, the words would not form on her lips and her mouth worked futilely, as if it belonged to somebody else.

*Careening.* That was the word Jane used to describe the car as her father drove to the hospital. Ordinarily, her father was the safest of drivers to the point of making everyone crazy. He always slowed down, even as he approached a green traffic light, afraid it would turn to yellow if he continued into an intersection. He obeyed all the traffic rules and had never received a ticket, even for overtime parking.

But now he drove with what only could be called abandon through Burnside streets, taking a corner perilously, the engine protesting and the wheels squealing as if some demented teenager was at the wheel. To her father, every teenager at the wheel of a car was demented.

The speed with which they were driving was unnecessary because the hospital was only a few blocks away from their house. But her father seemed to enjoy speeding while her mother clamped her hand to her head as if she were holding an invisible hat, and Jane and Artie looked at each other with delight.

For the first time in his life, her father parked in a No Parking space directly in front of the hospital steps and almost leaped out of the door, running around the front of the car, waiting for the rest of the family to join him.

It was difficult to believe that in a few moments they would see Karen awake again, hear her speak, sit up in bed maybe or even leave it.

"Let's go," her father called impatiently over his shoulder, a lovely impatience as he led them up the steps to the hospital door.

❖

Karen studied her mother and father and Jane and Artie. Saw them clearly and sharply, no fuzz at all at the edges of her vision. The fuzz had been there earlier when she tried to focus on distant spots of the room. They were staring anxiously at her, which made her sad. But something else besides anxious. Expectant. The word was strange to Karen — but that was it. They looked as if they expected something to happen. And for a moment Karen was annoyed. Wasn't it enough that she was back, had returned from — she wasn't sure where but it had been far far away — anyway, what did they expect her to do? Jump up and sing and dance? She scolded herself. She should be happy to be back after all those weeks in the darkness.

She smiled at her family. Or at least she formed what she hoped was a smile, arranging her lips the way she would arrange flowers in a bouquet. Which was a crazy thought, of course. But everything was crazy. Being here in the hospital, all those weeks of nothing, not even sleep — it had not felt like sleep, although she could not express in words what being in a coma felt like.

They were still staring at her. Her father in his usual suit and striped tie, staring. Her mother, hair a bit askew and staring. Jane in a new blue sweater Karen had never seen before, staring. And Artie, video-mad Artie with his Nintendos, also staring. All of it weird.

She wanted to talk to them. Explain. Explain that she was fine, despite what the doctor had told her: She had fallen down the stairs at home. She could not remember falling down the stairs. She remembered something but wasn't sure what. She remembered shadows. She remembered being afraid like when she was a little girl and woke up in the middle of the night, resenting Jane who always fell asleep instantly and never woke up in the night afraid. She did not remember falling down the stairs. Do you remember anything else? the doctor had asked. She could not remember the doctor's name. He had told her his name but she could not remember it. She wanted to remember it because the doctor was very nice. He answered her questions before she asked him. Actually, she was unable to ask the questions. For some stupid reason, she could not speak. She had forgotten how to talk. Which was ridiculous, of course. But the doctor said that she had come a long way — *progressed* was the word he used — and that time would take care of things, don't worry. Then told her, without her having to ask, what had happened. How she fell down the stairs. But she knew that it was not that simple. There was something else, just beyond the horizon of her memory. A shadow, more than one shadow, and the shadows had faces. She did not know whose faces.

Please, she thought, looking at her family, don't look at me like that. Like I'm behind a glass wall and you can't touch me. When they first came into the room, they had gathered around the bed, hugging and kissing and saying sweet words and she had basked in those words, letting herself be carried in the caresses and the murmurs. Then tried to work her mouth but nothing came out. *Hey, everybody, look, I've forgotten how to speak.* Funny, but not funny at all.

She did not mind not being able to speak. Time will take care of it, the doctor whose name she could not remember had said. What made her feel sad was that she could not tell her mother and father not to worry. I'm all right. I feel fine. Later, when she was stronger, she would write them notes.

Then, for some reason, she began to cry.

Hated herself for crying.

For what her crying did to them.

Because they started crying, too. Her mother, her father, and Jane and Artie. Everybody crying.

154

Thank God the doctor entered the room at that moment. The doctor always looked tired. Long thin tired face. But then he smiled and didn't look tired any more. Made you feel good. And now he smiled at her family and this made her feel good, too.

She closed her eyes, afraid for just a moment that she might plunge into that coma again, but instead let herself drift into the sweet, sweet sweetness of sleep.

Buddy met his father for lunch at one of those brass-and-fern restaurants in downtown Wickburg. His father's eyes were bloodshot. His face drawn, as if he was not getting enough sleep.

"You look great," his father said, voice hearty but hoarse.

"You look great, too, Dad," Buddy lied, flooded with sudden affection for his father. He looked so . . . sad. Buddy was suddenly willing to forgive him here and now for whatever he had done to break up the family.

After the waiter brought the menu, his father ordered a martini, dry. Turning to Buddy: "Martinis have gone out of style these days. But I'm old-fashioned, I guess."

His father had two martinis before lunch and two glasses of white wine with the meal. Buddy drank three Cokes, Classic. Managed to eat the hamburger and french fries although his appetite was absent. Answered his father's questions about school, his marks, Addy. Waited for him to ask about his mother, his father's wife — they weren't yet divorced, for crying out loud — but waited in vain. He was tempted to tell him about Jane but held back for some reason, not certain why. He watched his father sipping the wine and sighing after each sip as if it were some rare vintage. He was surprised to find that he was not dying for a drink, as if through some kind of magic the booze his

155

father consumed was somehow being transfused into himself, taking away his own desire.

His father ate his small steak without enthusiasm, as if only marking time between sips of wine, smacking his lips a bit after each sip, holding the glass up once and looking at it appreciatively.

While Buddy waited. And wondered what he was waiting for. Then knew he was waiting for his father to get to the point, to divulge the purpose of the lunch. A wild hope rose. Was his father returning home? Was he building up to a big announcement?

The waiter removed their plates. Dessert menu? Both shook their heads and then his father said: "Wait, maybe another martini. Want another Coke?" his father asked.

As Buddy held up his half-filled glass, he studied his father more closely than ever before, trying to see him as a stranger would see him. The word that leaped into his mind was: *ruin*. As if his father's face, which he'd remembered as pink and lean and handsome, had fallen on hard times. Small veins were visible in his nose and cheeks, as if there had been tiny explosions under the surface of his flesh. More flesh had gathered under his eyes. His eyes were not only bloodshot but sore-looking, as if he'd been staring at the sun too long.

"You happy, Dad?" Buddy asked, the question startling him even as he spoke the words.

"What kind of question is that, Buddy?" he said, obviously taken by surprise.

"I just wondered." *You don't look happy*.

"I don't know whether we're meant to be happy or sad all the time," his father said. "I mean, it's like taking your temperature just to see if you have a fever when there's no need for it."

He's talking in circles, Buddy thought. Or maybe he's

156

right. Why do we always have to be either happy or sad? Why not just *be*?

"Don't you want to know how Mom is?" he asked, needing to lash out, say something, *do* something.

"I know how she is, Buddy," he answered, sighing wearily. "Miserable. And I'm the one who made her miserable. Guess I'm miserable, too, sometimes."

"Why, Dad? Why did all of this happen, to make everybody so miserable?"

His father glanced around the room, caught the waiter's eyes and signalled for his drink, mouthing the word *martini*. "Things happen," he said, settling back in his chair. "We don't go looking for things to happen but they do."

Buddy plunged: "Are you ever coming back home, Dad?" Not too big a plunge: if his father was miserable sometimes, maybe he wanted to come home.

Big silence. His father fingered the empty glass, looked around the room again. "Where's that waiter?" he asked, irritated, drumming the table.

With sudden clarity, Buddy saw that his father needed another martini more than he needed to answer Buddy's question. Or needed that drink before answering. He wondered about that old saying: like father, like son. Would he grow up to be like his father, still drinking, his face filled with the tiny flowers? Would he someday make Jane miserable and become miserable himself?

Giving up his search for the waiter, his father looked at him directly. "No, Buddy. I'm not coming back. I don't even think your mother wants me back or would take me back. It's like a broken window, Buddy, the glass shattered. You can't fix it. You get a new window . . ."

*These are not windows, Dad.*

That's what Buddy wanted to say but he remained silent as he saw his father still angling to see if the waiter was approaching with his drink, fingering the empty wineglass, glancing into it to see if there might be a drop or two left then actually, *actually* raised it to his lips to drain away whatever dregs might be left.

He could not wait for this terrible luncheon to end.

Jane called Buddy from the pay telephone in the lobby of the hospital, eager to share the good news of Karen's recovery. The telephone rang and rang.

Karen wasn't completely recovered, of course. She had regained consciousness, had suffered no loss of locomotion (the doctor's word) and was functioning normally (more doctor words) except for her inability to speak. Which was probably not physically originated (the psychiatrist's words now) but a temporary condition. Seven, eight rings. She hoped Buddy's lunch with his father went well. He had been excited about the invitation, like a little boy going to the circus with his daddy.

She was about to hang up when he answered. "Hello," his voice dim, subdued. Was something wrong?

"Buddy," she said. "How was lunch?" *Please say that lunch was fine, that you and your father had a good time.*

"Okay," he said, the word lacking in enthusiasm. Had the lunch gone wrong? She would have to deal with that later.

"Karen is out of her coma," she said, unable to suppress her excitement. "I'm calling from the hospital — she's going to be all right . . ."

Silence from Buddy. She was a bit angry that the lunch had not gone well and was spoiling her news about Karen.

"That's great," he said, the words booming with enthusiasm across the wires. Was he play-acting? He sounded *too* enthusiastic now, his voice, like, too loud, too high. "You must be happy. I mean, your parents must be walking on air."

His voice still sounded fake. It must have been a terrible lunch. "There's only one thing wrong," she said, "She can't speak. The doctor says it's psychological. Listen, can we get together somewhere? Can you come over to Burnside? We can get a Coke or something and you can tell me all about lunch with your father and I'll tell you all about Karen . . ."

"Sure, good," he said, and his voice was again normal, the voice of the Buddy she knew and loved.

"Give me fifteen minutes and I'll be there," he said.

After all this time, the sound of his voice still thrilled her.

The Avenger could not believe his eyes.

There she was, Jane Jerome, his Jane, with one of the trashers. Standing beside him on the sidewalk, holding his hand. Looking up at the trasher as if nobody else in the world existed. Looking up at him with — what? — a tender expression on her face. A look of love.

The Avenger stood still. Stood still on the outside, that is. Inside, he was all movement and turmoil, his blood surging through his veins, his temples throbbing, his face growing hot, hotter, until he was afraid his cheeks would explode and pieces of his flesh would fly through the air and splatter the sides of buildings. At the same time he needed to go to the bathroom, desperately, afraid he would have an accident right here on Main Street in front of Dupont's Drug Store. But the urge to go to the bathroom was replaced by the need to hide as they began crossing the street, heading in his direction. He had to get away, out of their sight. Spinning completely around, he searched for ways of escape, and saw the alley between Dupont's and Burnside Video. He hurried into the alley, and hugged the wall. Saw Jane and the trasher pass by, still holding hands. He waited a moment, surrounded by the smell of garbage from a nearby barrel. Did not breathe, did not want to inhale the smell of garbage, did not want to bring the smell inside his body.

After a while, he stepped out of the alley. Did not see them anywhere. He walked slowly towards the video store, looked in the window, using his hand as a visor. Saw them. Jane and the trasher. Was he really the trasher? He squinted, studying the boy. Yes, he was one of them, all right. No doubt at all. The images of the trashers were burned into his mind like with a branding iron. This trasher was not the one with the hammer and not the fat one who screamed loudest of all and not the thin ratty-looking one. But one of them. Good-looking, but evil just the same. You can't judge a book by its cover, his mother always said.

Did Jane know that he was one of the trashers? Maybe she didn't know. Maybe he was fooling her. Or maybe she knew and didn't care. He remembered something about a key, a rumour in the neighbourhood that Jane had given the trashers the key to her house. He had not believed that for a minute. Now he wasn't sure. Maybe she *had* given the key to one of the trashers, maybe to this boy in the store with her. At that moment, he saw the boy join her in one of the aisles. He saw Jane reach up and draw the boy into her arms. He saw her wrap her arms around him, saw her mashing her mouth against his, saw her tongue go into the trasher's mouth. Revolted, grimacing, he could not take his eyes from them. How could she do such a thing? She should have known when she touched him — with her tongue! her tongue! — that he was one of the trashers. Even if he wasn't a trasher, she should not be kissing him like that, like some animal.

It was at that moment that The Avenger began to hate Jane Jerome, hate her worse than even the trashers. She was not a nice person. No nice person would do what she was doing in that store with her mouth, her tongue. To a trasher.

Finally, he was able to tear his eyes away from that awful act, unable to look at her any longer, face twisted in agony as if his features would stay frozen like that for ever, caught in a storm of emotions he could not suppress or subdue. Flashes before his eyes now. Of Vaughn Masterson's exploding face when the bullet struck him. His grandfather's body twisting in the air as he fell.

He ran. Across the street, dodging the cars, knowing that cars would not hit him because he was on a mission. As he reached the other side of the street, he continued running, his mind filled with visions. Visions of what he would do to her. He pictured her sitting in a chair, all tied up — her arms and legs — but her chest free. He did not want to tie down her chest, although he wasn't sure why. He would not touch her after tying her down. He would play with her as if she were a toy. He would let something else touch her. Like a knife. He would let the knife do the touching like that old TV commercial, let your fingers do the walking. But the knife would do the walking, all over her body and her chest. She would be afraid. He would see in her eyes how she would be afraid. She deserved to be afraid. After what she had done with that trasher. She would be afraid of that knife and afraid of The Avenger.

After making her afraid, he would do to her what he had done to Vaughn Masterson and his grandfather.

First of all, of course, he would have to make his plans. Carefully and cleverly. Must draw her into his trap. Must strike at the right moment.

I am The Avenger, he cried silently, a cry of triumph that soared within him even as he stumbled along the street.

Eleven years old but smarter and wiser than ever before.

✻

Jane had just turned into the corner of Arbor Lane when she encountered Amos Dalton waving to her from across the street.

She waved back distractedly, eager to get home and report Karen's progress to her parents. In the week since Karen emerged from the coma, she had struggled to speak but had not uttered words that could be understood. Suddenly this afternoon, she managed to say, "Hello Jane," not clearly or distinctly and not without effort that bathed her face with perspiration. But saying the words clearly enough to be understood. *Hello Jane*. Wonderful. Buddy, too, would be impressed. He still had not met her. The doctor insisted that only family members visit her during this precarious time.

Amos Dalton had stopped waving and was running towards her now, crossing the street, running awkwardly with three books pressed to his chest.

"You've got to come with me, Jane," he said. "It's an emergency."

"What kind of an emergency?" she asked. Kids were always exaggerating, and Amos Dalton, middle-aged kid in his laced-up shoes, was probably no exception.

"I can't tell you — you've got to see for yourself." His chin trembled, his lips were bluish. "It's a matter of life and death."

She hesitated, in a hurry to be on her way but wanting to do the right thing if it *was* an emergency.

"Please," he begged. As he shifted his position the books spilled to the sidewalk. "You've got to come." Not moving to pick up the books. Amos Dalton: book lover, not picking up his books. He must be desperate. Turning away, he took a few tentative steps, calling over his shoulder: "Come on . . ."

"Hey, how about your books?"

"The heck with them," he said, hurrying away. "Please come . . ."

"God, this must really be important," she muttered, picking up the books as she began to follow him. Two paperbacks, Stephen King kind of books with gruesome covers, plus a copy of *The Adventures of Tom Sawyer*.

"Where are we going?" Jane called as Amos Dalton stretched the distance between them.

"Not far. But we've got to hurry."

At the corner of Arbor Lane and Vista Drive, Amos Dalton gave her another quick over-the-shoulder glance and plunged into the overgrown grass and shrubs of an empty lot. The tall grass almost hid a sign: LAND FOR SALE. She barely saw Amos Dalton's head above the wild growth.

Stopping at the edge of the lot, she called: "I'm not going in there unless you tell me what's going on . . ."

Amos Dalton paused, his face barely visible above the thick undergrowth. "It's Artie." His voice cracked a bit. "Something's the matter with him." Desperate suddenly.

"Why didn't you say that in the first place?" she said, alarmed, remembering Artie's night-time terrors. She threw aside all caution along with her fear of snakes which might be crawling around underfoot, and followed him into the abandoned lot. The grass, damp from a recent rain, brushed moistly against her legs, a slimy feeling that made her shudder with distaste.

Amos Dalton thrashed his way ahead; she almost lost sight of him. She dropped one of the books and said, "The hell with it," walking unsteadily through the growth, like trying to walk in a foot of water. At length, the growth dwindled into a crooked path that led to an abandoned part of the neighbourhood, woods where kids played their mysterious games. She saw a shed with sagging roof and boarded-up windows, set against a stand of pine trees. She had never explored this part of the neighbourhood. This was a kids' kind of spot, just the sort of place Artie and his brat pack would choose for their fun and games.

"I hope this isn't a trick," she called to Amos, a bit of anger diluting her fear for Artie's safety.

"It's not a trick," Amos said, halting now and facing her, perhaps ten feet away. Then pointing towards the shed: "He's in there . . ."

She, too, stopped. The area was still. No bird calls. No barking dogs. No wind rustling in the trees. "Artie," she called. "Are you okay?"

No answer. She took a few steps forwards.

"In here," a voice reached her from the shed. A muffled voice, full of anguish, pain maybe. Could be Artie's voice. "Hurry . . ." The word strangled, fading into a kind of gasp.

She ran instinctively towards the shed, knowing that if Artie was in trouble or some kind of danger, she simply could not turn away or abandon him. In her peripheral vision, she saw Amos Dalton scooting away, stumbling and tripping in his haste to leave, raising her suspicions but not compelling enough to make her change her course.

Out of breath, sweating now, aware of perspiration moistening her body, she arrived at the door. "Artie," she called. "Are you in there?"

The door swung open, revealing Mickey Looney, grinning at her, but a grin she had never seen before on his face: cunning, triumphant, his eyes wide and gaping.

He held a rag in his hand. A peculiar smell emanated either from Mickey or the rag or the hidden shadows of the shed itself. He stepped towards her as she stepped backwards, stumbled, almost fell. Mickey came closer, moving more swiftly than she had ever seen him move, menacing, grabbing her, the rag in her nostrils, the sweet, cloying smell overwhelming her. She flailed about, trying to escape Mickey's grasp and that sickening rag over her face. Just before she slipped into blankness, as if sliding down a long dark chute, she heard Mickey's gleeful voice saying:

"The Avenger strikes again."

She woke up suddenly, flashing into wakefulness, and found herself tied by clothesline rope to a chair, a foul-tasting rag stuffed in her mouth, her lips sealed with some kind of adhesive tape. Struggling to move, she realized she was helpless, wrists bound to the arms of a sturdy, throne-like chair, her ankles tied to its legs. The gag in her mouth threw her into a panic, threatening her with either suffocation or choking to death. Trying to calm herself, she squirmed to see how tightly she was secured. The rope chafed her wrists, dug into the flesh of her ankles. Breathing through her nostrils, she inhaled the smell of decay.

The sun slanting through a crack in the roof faintly illuminated the shed in which she was held captive. The shed was cluttered with debris, rusting tools, boxes stuffed with old rags, newspapers piled up in tottering stacks. She hated to look too closely at her surroundings, afraid to see rats scurrying around the floor or spiders crawling up the walls.

The door swung open and a slash of sunlight burst against her eyeballs. A dark bulk filled the doorway, blocking the sudden brightness. When the door closed, she saw Mickey Looney through the sunspots that danced in her eyes.

Instinctively, she tried to talk but emitted only strange animal-like sounds, the effort gagging her, making her retch. Afraid to choke, she fell silent.

As Mickey waddled towards her, she blinked with surprise, as if seeing him for the first time. He was fat but not

165

really fat. Bloated, really. Bulging stomach, bulging cheeks. No eyebrows, which made his eyes unusually large, as if they'd pop out of their sockets if somebody squeezed his head. He was bareheaded — and bald. She had never seen him without that old baseball cap. He grinned at her, coming closer, bending over and peering down, curiously, as if she were a specimen in a laboratory or a strange animal in a zoo. The grin was not the old Mickey Looney grin but a leering evil grin, not the Mickey who mowed lawns and fed the birds.

Then the grin was gone and he was like the old Mickey Looney she knew, who patted kids on the head and tipped his cap to everybody.

"Are you all right, Jane?" His eyes studied her, roaming across her body. She tried to twist away from him but was helpless to move.

Once again, she tried to talk. Tried to say: Why are you doing this? But could only make weird sounds. And was still afraid of choking.

Still regarding her curiously, he said: "I can take that rag out of your mouth if you promise not to scream." She nodded vigorously. "Even if you scream, nobody will hear you and it will make The Avenger mad."

She remembered that he had mentioned The Avenger when he had slapped that terrible rag across her mouth and nose. Who was The Avenger?

Still nodding vigorously, she tried to make her eyes say what her mouth could not.

He tenderly pulled the adhesive bandage from her mouth, tugging at it gently. His gentleness encouraged her. Her mouth was finally free. She tried to spit out the taste of foulness. Her teeth ached.

"Why are you doing this, Mickey?" she sputtered at last. "What's the matter with you?"

166

"Nothing's the matter with me, Jane," he said, stepping backwards, hands on his hips, eyes still popped open. "It's you. Something's the matter with you."

"What are you talking about?" Her voice rising, anger overcoming her fear of this crazy situation.

"Don't yell — don't scream. If you scream, I'll have to do to you what I did to Vaughn Masterson and my grand-father." He put his hand to his mouth, and giggled. "Of course, I'm going to do that to you anyway but not right away . . ."

She did not have to ask him what he had done to Vaughn Somebody-or-other or his grandfather. She could easily guess from the look on his face, the matter-of-fact way he spoke. More chilling than ghoulish laughter.

"Why, Mickey? Why?" she asked again. No other ques-tion mattered at the moment. If he answered that question, she would know the answer to all questions.

"Because you were with him," he said, petulant, a child suddenly.

"With who?"

"With your boyfriend."

"Buddy? Buddy Walker?"

"Is that his name? I don't know his name but you were with him. You were holding hands with him. And . . ." Now he frowned, a strand of spittle at the corner of his mouth. "You kissed him. You put your tongue in his mouth . . ." Spitting on the floor now, as if to rid himself of something vile and foul-tasting.

"You're angry with me because I have a boyfriend and kissed him?" she asked, astonished.

"No, no," he said, shaking his head. "You're pretty and you should have a boyfriend."

"Because I kissed him?" Trying to recall his exact words. "Because I touched his tongue with my tongue . . ."

167

"That wasn't nice," he said. "But if you wanted to do it, you could do it . . ."

"Then why are you so angry?"

"Because it's him!" Loud, shouting, stamping his foot, his jowls moving like jelly in a bowl.

Struggling against the ropes, ignoring the painful chafing her struggle caused, she raised her own voice. "I don't know what you're talking about." Her anger buoyed her, gave her hope and confidence. "What the hell are you talking about?"

"You shouldn't swear, Jane," he said. "Nice girls don't swear." Shaking his head sadly. "But you're not a nice girl any more, are you? You were with him so you can't be nice . . ."

She sagged in the chair, as much as the ropes allowed. She could smell her own perspiration, her hair was damp, a lock fallen across one eye. She blew air out of the corner of her mouth.

Mickey reached out, pushed the lock of hair away.

"Him," he whispered, face close to hers now. The word imbued with all the hate one small syllable could convey. "Him, Jane. Your boyfriend. One of *them*. One of them in your house that night. I saw them, saw *him*, wrecking your house. I was at the window and watched them. They didn't see me but I saw them, all right. And he was one of them."

Buddy? In her house?

"They were like animals," he said, drawing away, speaking quickly now, his eyes bulging even wider. "Breaking everything. Running through your house, screaming and laughing. Like animals."

Shaking her head, she heard herself saying: "No, no, no." Denying what this crazy person was saying.

"I saw Karen come in and they grabbed her." Then whispering: "The lights went out . . ."

A final gasping "No," a harrowing scream of a word torn from her throat in a spasm of denial.

"Yes, yes, yes, yes," he said, leaping in the air, dancing, his lumbering body shaking the floorboards. "And the other day you held his hand and I saw you. You looked at him like you loved him. In that video store, you put your lips on his lips and put your tongue in his mouth." The dance over, breathing heavily, standing before her, rivulets of sweat pouring down his cheeks. "That's why I have to do what I have to do, Jane. I am The Avenger and I must avenge your house . . ."

The nausea engulfed her stomach so suddenly that she gasped in surprise as the vomit erupted from her mouth, burning her throat with acid, gushing through her lips in a sickening torrent. Her body responded painfully, her stomach stretched beyond its limits because she could not move, could not bend forward to ease the flow of vomit, and for an eternal moment the vomit blocked her throat and she coughed, choking, panic rushing through her, until it gushed forth again, spewing out of her mouth, spilling on her blouse, her skirt, splashing to the floor.

Mickey Looney leaped out of the way but flecks of vomit, pink and orange, splashed on his trousers and he cried out, "Oh, Oh," again and again, "Oh, Oh." Then stood fascinated, watching her retch.

Wrists and ankles stinging with rope burns, stomach heaving, the taste of foulness in her mouth, the smell of her own vomit filling her nostrils, Jane sank into an abysmal despair that made the nausea and the stench of vomit pale by comparison. Buddy a trasher? One of them? Her Buddy? Whom she'd loved with a love that was bigger than her own life. Buddy who had kissed her and caressed her, held her breasts so tenderly.

Mickey was dancing around again, a dance of desperation

now. "I'm sorry, I'm sorry," he said. He found another rag and began to wipe her face, her chin, dabbing at her chest, his hand lingering on her breast.

"Now can you see what I have to do?" he said, leaping away from her, his face flushed, avoiding her eyes.

She did not ask what he had to do, still stunned by what he had said about Buddy, trying to deny the truth of his accusation. Mickey gazed at her breasts and looked away again. Would he rape her?

"I have to remove you from the world, Jane."

The thought of Buddy fled as she realized what he was saying. "You mean — kill me?" she said, aghast, the terrible words blazing in the air. She was immediately sorry that she had said the words, as if speaking them made them real.

"That's the only way, Jane. I have to do it . . ."

Her mind raced, seeking arguments, *anything* to stave him off. "Why me, Mickey?" Needing to stall, play for time. Had to use everything at her disposal. Including Buddy, guilty or not. "Why not my boyfriend? He was one of the trashers, you said. I didn't trash my house — he did." Felt like a traitor to Buddy now, even if he *did* trash her house. Yet, a small part of her denying that Mickey would actually kill her or Buddy.

"Oh, I'm going to do it to him, too," he said. "To all of them. The Avenger must seek his revenge. I am eleven years old and must avenge your house."

Had she heard correctly? Had she missed a beat?

"What did you say?"

Speaking distinctly, emphasizing every syllable, he said: "I am eleven years old and I am The Avenger and I must avenge your house . . ."

"But you're not eleven years old. You're Mickey Stallings and you're not The Avenger." Whoever The Avenger was. Some comic-book hero he was confused about?

170

"Oh, I'm eleven all right," he said, smiling, docile, child-like now. "Whenever I'm on the job as The Avenger, I'm always eleven years old."

*Keep him talking, and don't think about Buddy.*

"Why are you eleven, Mickey?" she asked, wanting to spit the residue of foulness out of her mouth but forcing herself to swallow. "What happened to you that makes you eleven again?" Shots in the dark, shooting out words without knowing the target of those words.

"Vaughn Masterson," he declared, triumph in his voice. "That was my best time. The best time of my life. Know what it feels like to remove someone like Vaughn Masterson from the world, Jane? A bully who was mean to other kids? It was beautiful, Jane. But then my gramps got suspicious of me. He began to ask me questions and I became eleven again so that I could remove *him* from the world. Became eleven like with Vaughn Masterson." He smiled at her, pride in the smile, as if he had revealed to her the pride of his life, the sum of his accomplishments. "Poor Mickey Stallings had to grow up and get big and his mother died and he remembers all the things his mother told him and the songs she sang. But Mickey Stallings can still be eleven." He raised his eyes to the sagging wooden ceiling. "Eleven and The Avenger." He looked down at her and Mickey Stallings was gone. The old Mickey who had repaired broken faucets and planted tomatoes and who tipped his hat to everyone.

From somewhere in the folds of his flesh around his waist, he drew a knife. A kitchen knife but a big one. The kind turkeys are sliced with. A blade that gleamed even in the dimness of this godforsaken shed.

Stall, she commanded herself. She was dealing with a madman and had to stall him off. She also knew she had nothing to lose. Her world had already ended, in a way.

With the knowledge that Buddy had trashed her house. All doubts gone. He had sought her out and trashed her. With his kisses and his caresses. She saw clearly now why he had avoided her house and the hospital. Why he drank. Buddy, Buddy, she thought, and he was part of the stench of vomit that surrounded her, part of Mickey Looney and what he was doing to her, what he planned to do to her. But stall. Forget everything else, forget Buddy and Karen and everything else. She had to survive, get away, escape.

"The only person I ever loved was my mother," Mickey said, holding the knife in both hands as if it was an offering to Jane. "I loved my mother but I liked you, Jane."

Chilled at the past tense of *like*, she said: "I always liked you, too, Mickey. You were always kind and gentle to everyone." Noticing her own use of the past tense, which seemed more chilling than his.

"I used to watch you undress in your room. Until you started pulling down the shades. That made me sad . . ."

"I'm sorry it made you sad," she said, shivering with the knowledge he had watched her taking off her clothes.

Although he still held the knife balanced in the palms of his hands, he had become gentle again, his voice normal, like the Mickey she had known.

Think, she urged herself. Out-think him.

"How about Amos Dalton?" she asked.

"What about him?" Suspicious, eyes narrowing.

"He looked scared when he led me here. How did you get him to do that?" Keep him talking.

"He likes books. I gave him ten dollars to buy books." Brightening, eyes popping again.

"I don't think he's out buying books," she said. "I think he might be calling the police."

Mickey shook his head. "He won't call the police. I gave him ten dollars . . ."

172

She was surprised at how sharp and clear her mind was, rising above the stench that surrounded her, that *came* from her. Shaking her head, she said: "He told me to be careful in here. I think he was suspicious, Mickey. He said if I didn't come out in ten minutes, he was going to call the cops . . ."

Mickey tilted his head, appraising her differently now, not like a denizen of a zoo.

Mickey smiled, a wide smile that revealed his teeth. "You think The Avenger isn't smart," he said. "You think you can fool him . . ."

"I'm not trying to fool you. I'm only telling you what Amos Dalton said."

Mickey took the knife in his right hand, brandishing it, slashing at the air with the long blade. "Well, if the cops are on the way, then The Avenger has to work fast." He giggled, coming closer. "Won't he? It's better to work fast, anyway. That way it won't hurt you so much."

He stood looking at her, face still with sadness, eyes full of regret. In that instant, she knew that he was really going to kill her. If he had continued to rant and rave, jump up and down, giggle or scream, she would have held out hope for herself.

*Give me time to say a prayer.* That was what she was about to say. One last request, beyond panic now, accepting the situation. "No," she cried out, denying her panic, her acceptance. It wasn't supposed to happen this way. *I am sixteen years old and I am not going to die this way.* This was Mickey Stallings in front of her. Not The Avenger, not some monstrous eleven-year-old. She had to make him see who he really was.

"Know how old you are, Mickey?" she asked, trying to keep the desperation out of her voice.

"I am not Mickey. I am The Avenger."

"You can't be The Avenger. The Avenger is eleven years old."

"I *am* eleven," he said, the knife dangling from his hand, his voice petulant.

"No, you're not."

"Yes, I am."

Like children arguing in the schoolyard.

"Know why you're not eleven?"

Curious, he tilted his head. "Why?"

"Because if you were really eleven years old, you wouldn't be looking at me all the time. At my blouse, my breasts." As if hypnotized by her words, he looked at her chest. Remembering how he had touched her breast with the rag in his hand, she said, "Eleven-year-old boys don't do that. But you do. You're doing it now. You're looking at my chest now."

He took his eyes away. She saw the guilt in those big eyes.

"Did you touch me when you tied me up? Feel my chest? Eleven-year-old boys don't do that, either. If you did that, then you're not The Avenger, not eleven . . ."

"I am The Avenger," he said, appalled, eyes bulging again. "I'm The Avenger and I avenge the bad things in the world and I'm eleven years old."

"You were eleven a long time ago, Mickey. When you killed that bully. That was bad. But you are not eleven any more. And I'm not a bully. I'm Jane Jerome and you're Mickey Stallings . . ."

"I'm . . ." He was at a loss now for words, frowning, his mouth open, pink tongue fluttering against his lips, his eyes flickering to her chest and away.

"*You* killed your grandfather," she said. "The Avenger didn't do it. You did. Mickey Stallings. What would your mother say if she knew? Your mother would be mad at you, would punish you."

"No," he cried. "No."

"Yes." Straining against the ropes that held her, cheeks stiff with caked vomit, hair falling across her eyes, wrists chafed, eyes searing. "Yes, yes, yes." Each syllable erupting out of her fear and her determination and her desperation. "You killed your grandfather . . . your grandfather who loved you."

"No," he cried again. Anguished, the word like a howling in the air . . . nooooooooooo . . . drawn out . . . nooooooo . . . echoing in the dusty shed . . . terror and tears in the word . . . nooooooo . . . and pain and futility . . . nooooooooo . . .

He sank down on the floor, looked at the knife as if seeing it for the first time. He lifted his hand, and turned his wrist and slashed it with the knife. "I loved my gramps," he said. "He took me to the movies and bought me M&Ms and then we grabbed some grub." He looked at the blood oozing out of his wrist. "The Avenger made me do it." Looking at Jane, huge tears in the huge eyes. "I didn't want to do it." Then looking back at his wrist, the blood dripping now, onto the floor. He switched the knife into his other hand, the action slow and deliberate, watching his hand doing it, and Jane, astonished, felt that she was seeing two people before her, poor old gentle and kindly Mickey Stallings and the eleven-year-old Avenger who was killing him. Now he slashed the other wrist and watched calmly, curiously, as the blood gushed forth, the incision deeper than the first cut, the blood spurting in the air as if from a miniature fountain in his flesh. He took the knife and plunged it into his stomach, groaning and turning to look at her. "Mommy," he said, looking up at Jane. "Mommy . . ." Voice fading, blood spreading now across his shirt, the smell of blood — did blood actually have a smell? — mingling with the smell of vomit in her nostrils.

Watching his life ebbing away, she felt part of herself

ebbing away, too, as her thoughts returned to Buddy. Buddy, her betrayer.

"Jane," Mickey murmured, raising his head, trying to say more, mouth moving, a pleading in his eyes, tiny bubbles forming on his lips, uttering sounds she could not recognize, dying sounds. Poor Mickey Looney.

As he closed his eyes the door swung open and two police officers were suddenly stomping into the shed while sirens howled outside. Dazed by the sudden activity, she saw Amos Dalton, still clutching his books, standing in the doorway in his laced-up, middle-aged shoes. "Sorry it took so long," he said, and burst into tears.

Poor all of us, Jane thought, as her own tears finally came.

Buddy did not learn of Jane's ordeal until eleven o'clock that night. He and Jane had not planned to see each other that evening: she and her mother were off on a shopping spree at the mall for summer clothes. Buddy had decided to stay home and catch up on homework even though it was a Friday night. The house was eerily quiet. His mother had finally chosen that weekend to go off on her retreat after a lot of table talk, which was a relief from the usual dinnertime conversations. "If I go, will I be giving up control over my life?" That was her big question. "No worse than going to a therapist" was Addy's usual answer, which Buddy supported. Despite pangs of conscience Addy was spending the night at a friend's house, going over last-minute production problems with her school play. As she was about to leave she paused at the door, a look of concern on her face. "I'll be fine by myself — I'm not going to drink," he said. "I wasn't thinking about that," she said. "I just didn't want you to be lonesome." He nodded, didn't know what to say, touched by her concern.

He pondered going to the mall and surprising Jane and

her mother, probably buy them coffee at Friendly's. But he still did not feel comfortable with either of Jane's parents and decided to stay home. Did most of the homework. Heated a casserole of scalloped potatoes and ham slices that his mother had prepared beforehand. Fell asleep on the couch reading *Time* magazine. Woke up at ten-twenty, astonished that he had slept that long.

He went to his bedroom, removed the bottle of gin from his hiding place in the closet, looked at it, thanked God for the presence of Jane Jerome in his life, and put it back. Someday he would really have to thank God but did not know exactly how. He conducted this ritual with the bottle every night, usually before he went to bed.

Downstairs again, bored, restless, he checked his watch. A bit before eleven. He turned on the television set, stared dully at the final scenes of a stupid comedy, the laugh track annoyingly loud. He had read somewhere that laugh tracks were recordings of audiences long ago, that most of the laughing people were probably dead by now.

Half dozing, he barely reacted to the newscaster who announced that among tonight's headlines was the abduction of a Burnside girl by a man who later committed suicide. Had the newscaster actually said Burnside? Burnside seldom figured in nightly newscasts on the Wickburg channel except for city council meetings and other dull stuff.

A moment later, his attention was drilled on the TV as the announcer said: "Drama in Burnside today as sixteen-year-old Jane Jerome escaped capture and possible death at the hands of her abductor, who committed suicide moments before her rescue." Flashes of a shed, woods, police milling about.

"Her abductor, forty-one-year-old Michael Stallings, stabbed himself several times and died as police broke into the shed, led by ten-year-old Amos Dalton, who had reported the abduction to them. The Jerome girl had been bound hand and foot to a chair in the shed. After a checkup at Burnside Hospital, she was reported unharmed."

Shots now of Arbor Lane, Jane's house, other houses, twilight shots, stark in floodlights, almost colourless, and then a swift glimpse of Jane, huddled between her parents and police, being hurried up the front steps.

"The Jerome family is now in seclusion elsewhere at this hour and their whereabouts are unknown. The family of young Amos Dalton has not allowed the boy to speak to the news media." Shot of a different house, the boy's evidently. "Police Chief Darrell Teague said that the investigation is continuing."

Buddy watched the images on the screen and listened to the voices without moving, although aware of the thudding of his heart. He thought: Did I really wake up a few minutes ago or am I still dreaming? He shook his head, to rouse himself, and the room went out of focus. His hand reached out to prevent him from plunging off the sofa in a swirl of dizziness. He remembered something from a long-ago first-aid lesson. Put your head between your legs to keep yourself from fainting. But he still did not move.

The telephone rang.

Like an alarm clock waking him up.

Suddenly, the details on the television screen achieved a stark reality — Jane had been kidnapped and then rescued — and he reached for the phone, knowing that she was calling him to tell him that she was fine, not to worry, everything was all right.

But Jane was not on the phone.

"I just saw on TV what happened to Jane," Addy said. "Are you okay?"

"Sure," he said. But was he okay? "I just saw it, too. On television . . ."

"You mean you didn't know about it?" Addy asked. "She didn't call? I mean, this happened, like, hours ago . . ."

He shook his head as if to deny Addy's remarks, groped for a response. "Everything looked so hectic," he said. "The announcer said she's in seclusion with her family. She'll call, Addy. When she gets a chance . . ."

"Of course, she will. Poor kid . . . this must be like a nightmare for her," Addy said. "Do you want me to come home, Buddy?"

"No, no," he said. "I'm fine. I know she'll call as soon as she can. I'd better hang up. She's probably trying to reach me right this minute . . ."

He hung up. Then looked down at the phone, actually expecting it to ring. Waited. The house silent. *I need a drink.* But couldn't drink now. Had to keep sharp and alert in case she called and needed him at her side: *Please hurry, Buddy, please come . . .*

He glanced at the clock on the mantel. Twenty past eleven. Getting late. She should have called. Why hadn't she?

He picked up the phone, punched her number. He didn't count the rings, merely listened, long lonely sounds. No answer. Maybe he had touched the wrong number. Tried again, knowing it was useless, the words of the newscaster echoed in his mind: *The family has gone into seclusion elsewhere.* Where was elsewhere?

Torn with the need to take some kind of action, he considered driving to her street. Perhaps she had left a message with neighbours. He cursed himself now for not making friends with her friends, her neighbours. He was a stranger to them. Anyway, why should she leave a message with neighbours when she could have called him? Or sent someone with a message? He had been home the entire evening. Slept a while, yes, but the ringing of the phone or the doorbell would have awakened him.

Why hadn't she called?

He did not try to answer that question.

He awoke with a start, grubby in his clothes, which he had not removed before falling to sleep finally about four o'clock in the morning. He had dozed fitfully during the long hours of the night. Tossing and turning on the couch which allowed no room for tossing and turning, he had decided at three-thirty or so that she was never going to call. What would he do if she didn't? The solution came to him in a flash out of his desperation. And this decision allowed him finally to drift into a deep sleep but not deep enough or long enough.

Awake, the sun streaming in, he sat up on the couch. Stale taste in his mouth, head aching a bit, he remembered that he had not taken a drink, the only good thing about a bad night.

He reached for the phone, the movement automatic, punched her number. He did not expect an answer and did not get one. The clock said eight-ten. Time for the only action he could take, the plan he had devised during the night.

Twenty minutes later, he took up his vigil in the parking lot in the space that was nearest to the front entrance of the hospital. Weary, despondent, he watched the entrance. Tried not to blink. Tried not to think. Blink, think. Felt clever for thinking of the hospital, how sooner or later someone in Jane's family was certain to visit Karen. They would not abandon her despite what had happened to Jane. Slouching in his seat behind the wheel, he prepared himself for a long wait, a long day. Why hadn't she called? Let's not think about that. Don't blink and don't think. She has her reasons. But what reasons? What if . . . don't answer that question. No blinking and no thinking.

For an hour or so, he watched visitors come and go, heard a siren as an ambulance pulled up to the emergency entrance. Jane had told him that Karen's room was on the fourth floor, front, third window from the right, and he watched the window for signs of movement, someone pulling the curtain aside, thinking that perhaps a visitor to Karen had somehow eluded him. No movement. He yawned, bored. Wished he had brought something to eat, wondered if there was a vending machine in the hospital lobby. Then decided he had better not leave the car or his vigil.

He woke up with a start, a horn blowing somewhere, and struck his chest on the steering wheel, eyes dazzled by the sun flashing on the windshield, limbs aching. Cripes, he had fallen asleep, couldn't believe it. Checked his watch — eleven-thirty. The parking lot had filled up. He looked up at Karen's room. The curtain was undisturbed.

A sudden rap on the window next to him made him jump, this time striking his elbow on the shift stick. He turned to find himself confronting the beefy face of a police officer, who motioned him to open the window. Buddy fumbled for the key. The windows were automatic, would not go up or down unless the motor was on. Turning the key, he listened to the engine leap with life and then hit the window button.

"Hello, Officer," Buddy said, still half asleep, trying to speak brightly, alertly.

"You been here quite a while, fella," the officer said. The badge on his chest read *Security No. 15*.

"I've been waiting for someone." Speaking lamely, face flushed with guilt as if he were a criminal, for crissakes.

"Who might that be?" the officer asked, a hard edge to his voice.

"My mother," he said. "She said she'd meet me here but

I think I missed her. I fell asleep . . ." Easy to lie when you are desperate.

The police officer obviously did not believe him, seemed to be pondering his next step. Then his face softened: "Look, kid, I don't know what this is all about but you'd better move on, okay?"

He drove out of the parking lot, roamed aimlessly for a while and then headed for Arbor Lane, where he cruised slowly down the street. Quick glances at Jane's house. Shades down, no signs of life. No car in the driveway. An empty house sends a lonely message: nobody home.

I'd better get home, maybe right this minute she's trying to reach me, he thought. Angry at himself for spending all that useless time at the hospital, he gunned the motor in a fury. The phone could be ringing right this minute at his house, echoing through the empty rooms.

At home, the house gathered him into its silence.

Why doesn't she call?

Why *hadn't* she called?

The beginning of an answer like a quivering worm crept into his mind.

He could no longer deny himself a drink and made his way upstairs to his bedroom where the bottle waited.


Blood suffused Jane's dreams during the two nights she and her family spent at the Monument Motel. Blood dripped from trees, gushed from springs, streamed from faucets, flowed through streets. Blood everywhere, on everything, swirling across the floor, seeping between her toes when she realized, to her horror, that she was barefoot. She could not run, the blood having turned to a crimson clinging ooze through which she waded helplessly.

She woke up, trembling in the unfamiliar room. Searched for signs of identity. Her body was sticky with perspiration which she feared was blood. She sat up on the edge of the bed, fumbled for the switch to the lamp, pressed it, the room blindingly bright, stinging her eyes. No blood on her body, her pyjamas limp only with dampness. Artie slept in the twin bed next to hers. Her father and mother slept in the adjoining room, the door between left open. She sat there miserably, her feet touching the carpet, shivering slightly yet savouring these moments alone. She had not been alone since her departure from the cabin, the last signs of life pulsing out of Mickey Looney. A frenzy of activity, police, ambulance, television cameras, reporters, all of it a mad swirl. Her father became her protector, her salvation and strength. Even the police abided by his rules as he limited questions at police headquarters, his arm around her shoulder in the cruiser on the way home. Her street was hectic with people, cars, bicycles, faces she did not recognize, everyone trying to peek at her as if she were some rare specimen brought home from Mars by explorers.

Her father decreed: no interviews with the news media and kept his word despite the battering questions, the angry reactions of reporters and newscasters clustered on the sidewalk in front of her house. Peering out once, she recognized a newscaster from the Wickburg TV station. Nothing, however, impinged on her. She was numb inside, even her thought processes in limbo.

Everyone seemed to be whispering and in the whispers she heard words like *courageous* and *heroic* but did not feel courageous or heroic. Chief Reardon from Monument, her father's old golfing buddy, arrived along with her favourite relatives, her aunt Josie and uncle Rod. Her family rallying around. She heard her mother say: *this place*, anger in her voice. We'll be moving, she thought, but the words were meaningless. She had not had time to think, while being driven to the hospital for a checkup, then to the police station, answering the questions, signing reports, coming home, into her mother's arms. "Better rest, lie down a while," her mother had said. But she did not want to rest, did not want to lie down even for a while, did not want to be alone. Because once she was alone she would begin to think. And she would think of Buddy. Everyone thought she was stricken with the events of her ordeal, everyone thought she was stunned and shocked because of poor Mickey Looney. But it was Buddy all the time. Buddy who had betrayed her. Buddy who had trashed her house and later trashed her, desecrated her. She had loved him, built her world around him and their future together.

They were like prisoners in the house, the crowds lingering outside. Chief Reardon came up with the solution. "Let's get her away from here for a couple of days till the heat dies down." He talked like an old movie tough guy. "Come on back to Monument, the wife and I'll put you up." In the end, they drove away, back to Monument, eluding reporters' cars. At the motel, she swallowed the pill Dr Allison had given her. Sleep came in a wave of blood.

Now she sat on the edge of the bed, listening to the sleep sounds of Artie, the familiar snoring of her father from the next room. She was finally, truly alone. With her thoughts. Her thoughts of Buddy. She had not mentioned to anyone what Mickey Looney had revealed about Buddy, pretended innocence about Mickey's motives for abducting her. No one pressed her or seemed suspicious, took it for granted that Mickey had simply picked her at random. Buddy's part in the nightmare was her secret, which she would never divulge to anyone.

At one point before leaving the house in Burnside, her mother said: "What about Buddy?"

She shook her head. Did not trust herself to speak. Then spoke anyway. "I'll call him later," she said, turning away from her mother's puzzled expression. Her mother said no more, kept her suspicions, if she had any, to herself.

Alone now at three o'clock in the morning, she thought of what F. Scott Fitzgerald had written — *In a real dark night of the soul it is always three o'clock in the morning.* Spoken by her teacher in the classroom, those words had left her unmoved, probably because she had seldom been awake at three o'clock in the morning. Now she knew the desolation of the words and how it felt to be so alone, abandoned, and betrayed. Oh, Buddy, she thought. You've done this to us. Everything could have been so wonderful.

She climbed back into bed, reached for the light switch, and was grateful for the darkness. She thought of Buddy at home, waiting for her call, wondering why she hadn't called. She took consolation, imagining his misery. Let him be miserable, too. She clung to the thought although tears formed in her eyes. Damn him, damn him. Why did he have to spoil everything? But realized that he had already spoiled everything even before they met and fell in love, hadn't he? Had trashed their love before it had even happened.

Sleep, dark and ugly, came at last as the first fingernails of dawn pried at the motel room's draperies.

"Buddy?"

Her voice saying his name trembled in his ear and he pressed the receiver closer, afraid that he might miss every nuance and tone.

"Yes," he said. Then, needlessly: "Jane?" Because he knew it was Jane, of course, would know that voice anywhere. And without waiting for an answer said: "Are you okay?" Relief sweeping the words out of him: "Jane, I was so worried. I didn't know what to think." Unable to stop talking, "Where are you? I've been trying to reach you.

Your phone doesn't answer . . . I drove by your house a thousand times . . ." *Why don't you please shut up and let her speak?*

"I'm okay," she said, almost a whisper, the ghost of a voice. "I'm home. Can you come over?"

"Of course. Sure, anytime. When?" *Stupid, stop talking* but soaring inside. She had called. The long agony ended. But a warning bell going off inside him. Her voice so subdued. Yes, but she's been through such an ordeal. She wouldn't be telling jokes, making wisecracks. He wanted to ask her a thousand questions.

"Right now. Can you come over right now?" she asked.

"I'll be there before you know it," he said, but lingering on the phone a minute.

"Okay," she said and hung up. Gone. Her voice a still soft echo in his mind.

As soon as he saw her face, he knew that it was over. That she had found out about him and did not love him any more. He saw the knowledge in her eyes, flat and wounded, in her features as if set in stone, a hard flint face. He would never have thought it possible for her to look at him like this. Distant and cold, as if looking at him from a great distance, even though she stood only a few feet in front of him.

She knows, he thought. About me and this house.

"Come in," she said, stepping back.

"What's the matter?" he asked. "Are you okay?" His words hollow and meaningless, going-through-the-motion words. What killed him was this: She was so beautiful even in her coldness.

"Come in, Buddy," she said. "I want you to come in." Her voice giving orders.

Obeying the command, he stepped inside, dreading the

moment he would enter this hallway where her sister had been pinned against the wall. He kept his eyes fastened on Jane's eyes, did not want to see the cellar door through which her sister had plunged. Did not want to look towards the stairway where he had stood with a bottle of vodka. Did not want to *think* about her room upstairs.

"I know why you never wanted to come into this house," she said. "My house."

Buddy said nothing, could say nothing, the mechanisms of his body not working.

"Because of what you did here."

And now the impact of her knowledge struck him, like a giant mallet hitting a gong inside him, the vibrations echoing throughout his body. For one impossible moment, he went blind, blacked out, and then came back again, her face and eyes piercing him.

"I didn't mean . . ." he began, then stopped, realizing that he could never explain to her what had happened, or why it had happened. He could not explain, even to himself.

"You trashed my house," she said. "Did you trash my bedroom, too? Tear my bed apart? Vomit on the carpet? Piss on the wall?"

The word *piss* shocked him. She never swore. That one word, *piss*, spelled his doom. He knew that as soon as she said it. He was linked in her mind with pissing.

"To think I loved you," she said. And now there was sadness in her voice and in this sadness hope renewed itself in him. Maybe there was a chance. "To think that I let you kiss me and touch me. And I kissed you back." Her arms had been hanging loose at her sides but now she wrapped them around her chest.

"Jane . . ." he said. But could say no more. He had heard of people being speechless and knew now exactly what that meant. He wanted to say so much, defend himself even

187

when there was no defence, but could not speak, could not find the words and even if he could find them did not know how he would express them, where to begin even.

"You make me sick," she said, shivering, as if the fury of her words alone truly sickened her. "I don't want you here in this house, don't want you in my life. I only wanted you to come in here one more time. Now, get out. Out of my house. Out of my life . . ."

Did her voice break on that final word?

He didn't know. All he knew was that he said *Jane* and wasn't sure later whether he had said it out loud or tried to speak. Could not remember afterwards. Remembered only the pale fury of her face, her eyes blazing not like fire but like ice, remembered standing there mute, absolutely numbed, and then turning, almost running into the door which was still open, turning away from her whom he loved with such desperation and desire, and running, running down the sidewalk, running to the car, knowing that he was guilty of what she had said, knowing that he was one of the bad guys, after all.

She had just returned from visiting Karen in the hospital when Harry Flowers called.

Her visits to Karen were the only moments of light and gladness — not gladness exactly but absence of sadness, perhaps — in the greyness that her life had become. Able to speak again, Karen was a nonstop talker, filled with plans for resuming her life, shopping for new clothes, seeing all her friends. Her hospital room was filled with gifts from her classmates, crazy get-well cards on the bulletin board, balloons floating above her bed, flowers everywhere. Although Karen delighted in all the attention, a shadow sometimes crossed her features. She still could not remember what had happened on the night of the trashing. Her memory was a blank beyond the point where she opened the door and stepped into the house. For which Jane was grateful.

Jane was also grateful that her abduction and subsequent escape had disappeared quickly from the newspapers and television. The fact that Mickey Stallings left no survivors and his earlier crimes happened thirty years ago in a small town in Maine five hundred miles away contributed to the swift neglect of the story. The media lost interest in Jane and Amos Dalton when interviews were refused and Amos was packed away to relatives in Indiana. Poor Amos, who had done the brave thing in the end. Someday, when he returned, she would tell him how courageous he had been, after all.

No one in the family spoke of the future, whether they would remain in Burnside or move away. Jane was certain they would stay. One afternoon, she went by Artie's room and heard again the weird blips and bleeps from his video game and found herself smiling. Artie himself brought up the subject at the dinner table that night. "Are we going to move, Dad?" he asked, frowning, making one of his grotesque bratty faces.

"We'll make a decision later," her father said. "When Karen is back from the hospital." Glancing tenderly at Jane: "And Jane has sorted out her feelings . . ."

Jane had no feelings to sort out. That was the problem. Her ordeal with Mickey had taken on an aspect of unreality, as if it had happened in a dream long ago. She had refused efforts to have her consult a psychiatrist. She did not have nightmares. The episode had been so brief, so fast-moving, that she could not remember all the details. She pitied Mickey Looney, would never forget his pain and anguish as she sat helplessly bound to the chair. She was not convinced that he would have actually killed her. She was surprised at her ability to relegate Mickey and the events in that shed to a distant corner of her mind.

Buddy was different. For the first few days, he was a pain in her heart. Knew that sounded dramatic but she actually felt that her heart was fiery with pain, like a knife blade twisting and turning in it. She knew vaguely that she still loved him. But also knew it was an impossible love. The damage was too great — the damage to her house, her life, her heart. If he had confessed earlier . . . if he had told her what he did and explained why . . . she might have felt differently. But she would never know. The worst thing was that she could not talk to anyone about Buddy. Merely told her family that the relationship was over.

"Did something happen in that shed to affect how you feel about him?" her mother asked, and Jane looked up sharply, amazed at her mother's astuteness.

"No," she said, conscious of lying but finding no other way to answer. "We were beginning to drift apart any-way . . ."

Doubtful glances from her mother in the next few hours did not change Jane's decision to remain with the lie.

Often at night, before sleep came, his image formed itself in her mind. She would think of him in this room, on a rampage, the pee stains on the wall. She imagined the stains still there under the paint. Is that what he had become: pee stains on the wall? She sometimes cried just before falling off to sleep. Strange crying, without tears.

One morning, she opened her eyes and saw only the bare walls without posters or pictures. Something was different. But what? The sun edged into the room along the borders of the window shades. She threw off the blankets and sat up, glanced as always at that certain spot on the wall, trying to see under the paint. *She* was different. Not the room. The ache of Buddy's loss was absent. No pain at all, no anger. No odour under the surface, either. Just this hole inside of her now, like that black hole in space, and all her emotions, anger, regret, sorrow, had been pulled into that hole. She slipped out of bed, raised the shades, closing her eyes against the invasion of the sun. Then drew back, testing herself. How she felt. She felt — nothing. Numb. Vacant. Half believed that if she cut herself at this instant, no blood would flow from her veins. As if her veins were as empty as her body. Buddy was really gone now, not only from her life and her days and nights, but from herself or whatever she was deep inside. Had it really been love, then, if it could abandon her like this? What would take its place? Could you go through your life without feeling anything? She had read somewhere that nature hated a vacuum. This vacuum inside her now — what would move into it?

Harry Flowers called that day.

A pleasant aroma filled the house as she picked up the phone: her mother was boiling carrots spiced with cinnamon in the kitchen.

"Hello, Jane Jerome?"

"Yes," she said, hesitant. She did not recognize the caller's voice.

"Listen, you don't know me. But you know my name. My name is Harry Flowers." Then quickly, at her intake of breath: "Wait, don't hang up, please don't do anything. Just listen, that's all, a minute, two minutes. Just let me say what I have to say . . ."

Her mother came to the door, peered in questioningly. Jane shook her head, gave her an it's-not-important look and her mother returned to the kitchen.

"What I have to say is this: You've got Buddy Walker all wrong. Sure, he was with me and the others that night at your house. But he was drunk, didn't really know what he was doing. He didn't touch your sister. What happened to your sister was an accident whether you believe it or not, but Buddy had no part in it . . ."

"Why are you telling me this?" she asked, surprised at how calm and reasonable she sounded. How cool.

"I owe him this call. Look, I don't even like him. He's the kind of guy that I can't stand. Thinks he's better than other people, including yours truly. But he's sorry about what he did that night. His father and mother were getting divorced and I took advantage of his crappy life. That's why he got drunk and came with us to your house."

I should hang up, she thought. But didn't. She was curious. She wondered what Harry Flowers looked like. Wondered if she had already seen him on the street or at the mall without realizing it. She tried to imagine his face, his features. But saw only Buddy in her mind.

"Buddy's in trouble. He's drinking again. He stopped for a while but now he's drinking more than ever."

She heard him take a deep breath.

"I was thinking," he said, his voice becoming intimate, like a caress in her ear. "Maybe we could get together sometime." Smooth, sly. "You know, to talk about all this. Just you and me . . ."

The telephone was suddenly like a snake in her hand. She dropped it to the floor and let it lie there for a moment before slamming it down on the receiver.

Jane and Buddy met by accident at the mall on a Saturday afternoon in November, five months later.

She had been purposely avoiding the mall, shopping instead at the small speciality stores on Main Street in Wickburg or a new mall that had opened a few miles away, near Monument.

He haunted the mall, hoping to see her. Went out of his way to roam the stores, lurking near the entrances, sitting on the edge of the plastic bench in the lobby. The fountain still was not working, peeling even more than ever these days.

He sometimes drove to Burnside High in the afternoon and parked near the entrance — but not too near — hoping to catch glimpses of her. The sight of her walking along, her book bag slung over her shoulder, caused him such anguish and longing that tears sprang to his eyes and his chest hurt. He vowed not to return but always did.

On that November afternoon, they met face-to-face as he stepped off the down escalator and she approached the up.

Caught by surprise, she frowned, annoyed at herself for agreeing to meet her mother at Filene's, having forgotten her intention to avoid places where she might run into him.

"Hello, Jane," he said.

Although the Pizza Palace was several doors away, the smell of tomato sauce and pepperoni spiced the air with reminders.

He was pale. He had lost weight. She had once thought his blue eyes were beautiful. Now they were more grey than blue. The whites of his eyes laced with red.

"How have you been?" he asked.

She had wondered how she would react when they met again. "Good," she said. She had no reaction. He might have been a stranger. Not to be needlessly cruel, she asked: "How are you?"

Her question energized him, the fact that she had enquired about him. "Fine," he said. "I'm doing real good in school this year. All A's and B's so far." Had to keep talking, had to keep her here. Silence would take her away. "Things are fine at home. I mean, my mother and father are definitely getting divorced but it's a friendly divorce. Addy is doing fine, and my mother's doing fine, too."

*How many times have I said* fine? "I don't drink any more. I'm concentrating on my studies . . ."

"Good," she said. He was obviously lying. She was amazed that he had once been able to deceive her so easily.

He realized that she had said *good* twice but had made no other comment except for that one question. He wanted to ask about her sister, Karen, but couldn't do that because it would bring up the subject of what had happened at her house. His mind skittered, went askew — how many times he had dreamed of meeting her like this, arranging conversations in his mind, what he would say and what she would say, and was now speechless. More than that: without thought, the way it happened sometimes in class when he gave an oral talk and everything went blank.

"Well, I have to go," she said. "My mother's waiting for me — I'm already late."

"Jane," he said, unable to let her go.

She paused, half-turned towards him, not saying anything, waiting.

His mind cleared and he found himself speaking words he had rehearsed countless times in his head, words to make her remember the good times.

"It was beautiful there for a while, wasn't it, Jane?"

He looked as if he was about to cry.

She thought of the trashing and Karen in the coma all that time and Mickey Looney dead and her father and mother and Artie. And those yellow stains under the paint in her bedroom.

"Was it?" she said, suddenly sorry for him, so sorry. As pity moved into that hole inside her, she discovered how distant pity was from hate, how very far it was from love.

She stepped on the escalator and slowly ascended, not looking back, leaving him down below.

www.puffin.co.uk.www.puffin.co.uk.www.puffin.co.uk

bookinfo.competitions.news.games.sneakpreviews

www.puffin.co.uk.www.puffin.co.uk.www.puffin.co.uk

adventure.bestsellers.fun.coollinks.freestuff

www.puffin.co.uk.www.puffin.co.uk.www.puffin.co.uk

explore.yourshout.awards.toptips.authorinfo

www.puffin.co.uk.www.puffin.co.uk.www.puffin.co.uk

greatbooks.greatbooks.greatbooks.greatbooks

www.puffin.co.uk.www.puffin.co.uk.www.puffin.co.uk

reviews.poems.jokes.authorevents.audioclips

www.puffin.co.uk.www.p   co.uk.www.puffin.co.uk

interviews.e-mailupdates.bookinfo.competitions.news

# www.puffin.co.uk

games.sneakpreviews.adventure.bestsellers.fun

www.puffin.co.uk.www.puffin.co.uk.www.puffin.co.uk

bookinfo.competitions.news.games.sneakpreviews

www.puffin.co.uk.www.puffin.co.uk.www.puffin.co.uk

adventure.bestsellers.fun.coollinks.freestuff

www.puffin.co.uk.www.puffin.co.uk.www.puffin.co.uk

explore.yourshout.awards.toptips.authorinfo

www.puffin.co.uk.www.puffin.co.uk.www.puffin.co.uk

greatbooks.greatbooks.greatbooks.greatbooks

www.puffin.co.uk.www.puffin.co.uk.www.puffin.co.uk

reviews.poems.jokes.authorevents.audioclips

www.puffin.co.uk.www.puffin.co.uk.www.puffin.co.uk

www.puffin.co.uk.www.puffin.co.uk.www.puffin.co.uk
bookinfo.competitions.news.games.sneakpreviews
www.puffin.co.uk.www.puffin.co.uk.www.puffin.co.uk
adventure.bestsellers.fun.coollinks.freestuff
www.puffin.co.uk.www.puffin.co.uk.www.puffin.co.uk
explore.yourshout.awards.toptips.authorinfo
www.puffin.co.uk.www.puffin.co.uk.www.puffin.co.uk
greatbooks.greatbooks.greatbooks.greatbooks
www.puffin.co.uk.www.puffin.co.uk.www.puffin.co.uk
reviews.poems.jokes.authorevents.audioclips
www.puffin.co.uk.www.p    co.uk.www.puffin.co.uk
interviews.e-mailupdates.bookinfo.competitions.news

# www.puffin.co.uk

games.sneakpreviews.adventure.bestsellers.fun
www.puffin.co.uk.www.puffin.co.uk.www.puffin.co.uk
bookinfo.competitions.news.games.sneakpreviews
www.puffin.co.uk.www.puffin.co.uk.www.puffin.co.uk
adventure.bestsellers.fun.coollinks.freestuff
www.puffin.co.uk.www.puffin.co.uk.www.puffin.co.uk
explore.yourshout.awards.toptips.authorinfo
www.puffin.co.uk.www.puffin.co.uk.www.puffin.co.uk
greatbooks.greatbooks.greatbooks.greatbooks
www.puffin.co.uk.www.puffin.co.uk.www.puffin.co.uk
reviews.poems.jokes.authorevents.audioclips
www.puffin.co.uk.www.puffin.co.uk.www.puffin.co.uk

www.puffin.co.uk.www.puffin.co.uk.www.puffin.co.uk

bookinfo.competitions.news.games.sneakpreviews

www.puffin.co.uk.www.puffin.co.uk.www.puffin.co.uk

adventure.bestsellers.fun.coollinks.freestuff

www.puffin.co.uk.www.puffin.co.uk.www.puffin.co.uk

explore.yourshout.awards.toptips.authorinfo

www.puffin.co.uk.www.puffin.co.uk.www.puffin.co.uk

greatbooks.greatbooks.greatbooks.greatbooks

www.puffin.co.uk.www.puffin.co.uk.www.puffin.co.uk

reviews.poems.jokes.authorevents.audioclips

www.puffin.co.uk.www.puffin.co.uk.www.puffin.co.uk

interviews.e-mailupdates.bookinfo.competitions.news

# www.puffin.co.uk

games.sneakpreviews.adventure.bestsellers.fun

www.puffin.co.uk.www.puffin.co.uk.www.puffin.co.uk

bookinfo.competitions.news.games.sneakpreviews

www.puffin.co.uk.www.puffin.co.uk.www.puffin.co.uk

adventure.bestsellers.fun.coollinks.freestuff

www.puffin.co.uk.www.puffin.co.uk.www.puffin.co.uk

explore.yourshout.awards.toptips.authorinfo

www.puffin.co.uk.www.puffin.co.uk.www.puffin.co.uk

greatbooks.greatbooks.greatbooks.greatbooks

www.puffin.co.uk.www.puffin.co.uk.www.puffin.co.uk

reviews.poems.jokes.authorevents.audioclips

www.puffin.co.uk.www.puffin.co.uk.www.puffin.co.uk

# Read more in Puffin

For complete information about books available from Puffin – and Penguin – and how to order them, contact us at the appropriate address below. Please note that for copyright reasons the selection of books varies from country to country.

# www.puffin.co.uk

In the United Kingdom: Please write to Dept EP, Penguin Books Ltd,
Bath Road, Harmondsworth, West Drayton, Middlesex UB7 0DA

In the United States: Please write to Penguin Putnam Inc., P.O. Box 12289,
Dept B, Newark, New Jersey 07101–5289 or call 1–800–788–6262

In Canada: Please write to Penguin Books Canada Ltd,
10 Alcorn Avenue, Suite 300, Toronto, Ontario M4V 3B2

In Australia: Please write to Penguin Books Australia Ltd,
P.O. Box 257, Ringwood, Victoria 3134

In New Zealand: Please write to Penguin Books (NZ) Ltd,
Private Bag 102902, North Shore Mail Centre, Auckland 10

In India: Please write to Penguin Books India Pvt Ltd,
11 Panscheel Shopping Centre, Panscheel Park, New Delhi 110 017

In the Netherlands: Please write to Penguin Books Netherlands bv,
Postbus 3507, NL–1001 AH Amsterdam

In Germany: Please write to Penguin Books Deutschland GmbH,
Metzlerstrasse 26, 60594 Frankfurt am Main

In Spain: Please write to Penguin Books S. A., Bravo Murillo 19,
1° B, 28015 Madrid

In Italy: Please write to Penguin Italia s.r.l.,
Via Felice Casati 20, I–20124 Milano

In France: Please write to Penguin France S. A.,
17 rue Lejeune, F–31000 Toulouse

In Japan: Please write to Penguin Books Japan, Ishikiribashi Building,
2–5–4, Suido, Bunkyo-ku, Tokyo 112

In South Africa: Please write to Longman Penguin Southern Africa (Pty) Ltd,
Private Bag X08, Bertsham 2013